EDUCATIONAL LEADERSHIP OF IMMIGRANTS

This book prepares current and future educational leaders to adapt to the changing terrain of U.S. demographics, education, and immigration policy. *Educational Leadership of Immigrants* highlights the educational practices and discourses around immigration that intersect with policies and laws, in order to support K–12 students' educational access and families' participation in schooling. Drawing primarily on research from the fields of educational leadership and educational policy, this book employs a case study approach to address immigration in public schools and communities; school leaders' responses to ethical dilemmas; the impact of immigration policy on undocumented students; and the varying cultural, sociopolitical, legal and economic contexts affecting students' educational circumstances. Special features include:

- case narratives drawn from real-life experiences to support the educational needs of immigrant students;
- teaching activities and reflective discussion questions pertaining to each case study to crystallize leaders' knowledge and facilitate their comfort levels in practice;
- discussions of current challenges in education facing immigrant students, their families, educators, and school leaders, especially with changing immigration law.

Emily R. Crawford is Associate Professor of Educational Leadership and Policy Analysis at the University of Missouri-Columbia, USA.

Lisa M. Dorner is Associate Professor of Educational Policy and a Faculty Fellow of the Cambio Center at the University of Missouri-Columbia, USA.

EDUCATIONAL LEADERSHIP OF IMMIGRANTS

CASE STUDIES IN TIMES OF CHANGE

Edited by

Emily R. Crawford and Lisa M. Dorner

Routledge
Taylor & Francis Group
NEW YORK AND LONDON

First published 2020
by Routledge
52 Vanderbilt Avenue, New York, NY 10017

and by Routledge
2 Park Square, Milton Park, Abingdon, Oxon, OX14 4RN

Routledge is an imprint of the Taylor & Francis Group, an informa business

Library of Congress Cataloging-in-Publication Data
A catalog record for this title has been requested

ISBN: 978-0-367-18625-8 (hbk)
ISBN: 978-0-367-18627-2 (pbk)
ISBN: 978-0-429-19727-7 (ebk)

Typeset in Sabon
by Newgen Publishing UK

Visit the eResources: www.routledge.com/9780367186272

We dedicate this work to our families. Todd, Chip, Locke, and Amalia—your love and support mean more than you may ever know. We appreciate your patience, listening ears, and good humor as we strove to bring this project to fruition. We also dedicate this work especially to our family members who were or are the children of immigrants.

Contents

Contributors

St. Claire Adriaan is Middle School Principal at Academia Avance Charter School in Los Angeles, California. He grew up in Apartheid South Africa, and at a young age realized that education was his only weapon against injustice, inequality, and oppression. As a student activist, he fought for democracy and the release of Nelson Mandela. He is continuing that passion for justice, equality, and freedom here in the U.S.A. by advocating for minority students and immigrant students and working relentlessly to redirect the school-to-prison pipeline.

Eulogio Alejandre is pursuing his PhD from the University of Utah in the College of Education. He received his bachelor's degree from Weber State University in 1986 and master's in language acquisition from Weber State University in 1989. Additionally, Eulogio earned his school administration certification from Utah State University in 1992.

Chris Belcher currently serves as Assistant Teaching Professor in Educational Leadership and Policy at the University of Missouri. He has worked in education for 37 years as a teacher, principal, superintendent, and college professor. Chris is engaged in equity work with high schools across the United States to increase access and opportunity for underrepresented students in rigorous academic courses.

Catharine Biddle is an Assistant Professor of Educational Leadership at the University of Maine. Her research focuses on ways in which rural schools and communities respond to social and economic change in the 21st century. She is particularly interested in how schools can more effectively leverage partnerships with external organizations or groups to address issues of social inequality and how non-traditional leaders—such as youth, parents, and other community members—may lead or serve as partners in these efforts.

Edwin Nii Bonney is a doctoral student in Educational Leadership and Policy Analysis at the University of Missouri-Columbia. His research interests include recognizing and valuing the language, cultures, and experiences of immigrant groups as a way to improve equity in education. He is currently a researcher as part of a U.S. Department of Education National Professional Development grant in Missouri called *Strengthening Equity and Effectiveness for Teachers of English* (www.see-tel.org).

Kristina Brezicha is an Assistant Professor of Educational Policy Studies at Georgia State University. Her research interests focus on how education supports individuals' abilities to equitably participate in the democratic processes at both the local and national levels. Her research has been published in *Peabody Journal of Education*, *Educational Administration Quarterly*, and *Journal of School Leadership*, among others.

Jeffrey S. Brooks is Associate Dean for Research and Innovation and Professor of Educational Leadership in the School of Education at RMIT University. He is a two-time J. William Fulbright Senior Scholar alumnus who has conducted studies in the United States, Australia, Thailand, Indonesia, the Philippines, and other cross-national contexts. His research focuses broadly on educational leadership, examining the way leaders influence (and are influenced by) dynamics such as racism, globalization, social justice, student learning, and school reform.

Germán Cadenas is an Assistant Professor in the Counseling Psychology program at the College of Education, Lehigh University. His research focuses on immigrant psychology and educational equity. He specifically studies the role that critical consciousness developed in activism/advocacy plays in undocumented students' educational outcomes, how to create welcoming communities where immigrants can thrive, and how to heal trauma experienced by immigrants due to sociopolitical hostility.

Liliana E. Castrellón is a doctoral candidate in the Department of Educational Leadership and Policy at the University of Utah. Her research highlights how institutional agents, across the P-20 pipeline, enact education policies that affect immigrant populations. Liliana's research posits that even when policy is intended to create equity and/or access, it can reinforce systemic inequities. In this way, her research uncovers how the practices of well-intentioned institutional agents can often continue to exclude undocumented/DACAmented students from educational access.

Andrea Chevalier is a doctoral student in the Education Policy and Planning program at the University of Texas at Austin. Prior to graduate school, she was a teacher for four years in the Texas public school system. Her research interests focus on how political educational ideologies are formed and how these ideologies influence education policy.

Jesus Cisneros is an Assistant Professor of Educational Leadership and Foundations at the University of Texas at El Paso. His research moves gender, sexuality, and immigration status, and their conceptual margins, to the center of analysis in an effort to explore and understand the way politics and identity interact with various axes of inequality.

Michael D. Corral completed his PhD in Educational Leadership with a focus in Learning, Leadership, and Education Policy from the University of Connecticut. Broadly speaking, Michael's work and research focus on historically marginalized communities of color, their schooling systems/experiences, teachers of color in those systems, and the infrastructures that continue to marginalize and oppress certain populations. Further, based on his lived experiences as a first-generation Mexican-American from the Pacific Northwest, much of his work is anchored in the experiences and challenges that Latinx communities face throughout the western United States. Michael is currently a research associate and program director for Inflexion, an education non-profit based out of Eugene, OR.

Emily R. Crawford is an Associate Professor in the Educational Leadership and Policy Analysis department at the University of Missouri. In addition to teaching doctoral students, she enjoys teaching courses on PK-12 politics and policymaking and ethics for pre-service educational leaders. Her research explores the intersections among immigration policy, educational policy, leadership, and ethics in rural and urban schooling contexts. Her projects seek to understand the ways PK-12 educators—particularly school leaders—perceive and provide educational and schooling access for immigrant students and families of mixed legal status.

Jason DelPorto, the Assistant Principal at Watertown Middle School, has been an educational leader for the last 20 years in both the public and private sector. With a primary focus on serving at-risk students, Jason's relational, collaborative approach and focus on connected communities has generated success over his tenure.

David DeMatthews is an Associate Professor in the Department of Educational Leadership and Policy at the University of Texas at Austin. David has worked with urban districts as a high school teacher, middle school administrator, and district administrator. He studies issues related to school leadership, bilingual and special education, and social justice.

Lisa M. Dorner is an Associate Professor of Educational Policy and a Faculty Fellow of the Cambio Center at the University of Missouri-Columbia. Her research centers on language policy and planning, educational policy implementation, and immigrant childhoods (see www.lisamdorner.com). As co-founder of the Missouri Dual Language Network, she enjoys connecting people and resources for language learning and policy development (www.modlan.org) and, most recently, co-leading a U.S. Department of Education National Professional Development grant in Missouri (www.see-tel.org).

Yvonne Endara is an English as a Second Language Program Coordinator in the Public School district of Watertown. Previously, she taught English Learners at the high school level for over a decade. Ms. Endara is a native of Puerto Rico and has focused most of her professional career on advocating for English Learners.

Erica Fernández is an Associate Professor in the Department of Educational Leadership at Miami University – Oxford. Her research is focused on centering, listening to and sharing the educational engagement experiences of Parents of Color, particularly the experiences of Spanish-speaking Latinx immigrant parents living amid threatening and hostile anti-immigrant environments. She hopes that the narratives of Latinx immigrant parents will help highlight how oppressive institutional policies create barriers for authentic engagement within schools. Other research interests include family and community partnerships as well as family engagement policy initiatives (at the local, state, and federal level).

Maria Frankland is a doctoral student in Educational Leadership at the University of Maine and a practicing school counselor at a remote rural junior/senior high school. Her research interests center around the impact of trauma on rural students and teachers, and ways in which trauma-informed approaches may support the academic, career, and personal/social development of rural students.

Ofelia García is Professor in the PhD programs in Urban Education and Latin American, Iberian and Latino Cultures at The Graduate Center of the

City University of New York. García has published widely in the areas of bilingualism and bilingual education, the education of emergent bilinguals, sociology of language, and language policy. She is the General Editor of the *International Journal of the Sociology of Language* and the co-editor of *Language Policy*. Among her best-known books are *Bilingual Education in the 21st Century: A Global Perspective* and *Translanguaging: Language, Bilingualism and Education* (with Li Wei).

Elizabeth Gil is an Assistant Professor in the Department of Administrative and Instructional Leadership at St. John's University. Her community engaged perspective and research interests stem from her experiences teaching in New York City public schools for over ten years. Gil's research interests include understanding the experiences of diverse families in schools, leadership and teaching for culturally and linguistically diverse student populations, and the application of experiential intercultural education abroad to domestic contexts.

Shu-Sha Angie Guan is an Assistant Professor in the Department of Child and Adolescent Development at California State University, Northridge. She earned her BA in Psychology at the University of California-Berkeley and PhD in Developmental Psychology from the University of California-Los Angeles. Her research focuses on the role of immigrant and acculturative experiences in the socioemotional, mental, and physical development of ethnic-minority adolescents and young adults.

Khristina H. Haddad, Associate Professor of Political Science at Moravian College, teaches political theory and gender studies. Challenging conventional approaches to teaching political theory, her pedagogy integrates the textual study of political concepts with classroom enactments. Closely following efforts to resettle refugees in Germany, where Dr. Haddad was raised, she developed a Moravian course on humanitarian responses to the ongoing displacement and movement of refugees. She also holds affiliated faculty status in German Studies and Women's, Gender, and Sexuality Studies at Moravian College.

Sarah L. Hairston is pursuing her PhD in Educational Leadership and Policy Analysis at the University of Missouri-Columbia. She holds a specialist degree in Educational Leadership and Administration and a master's in education with an emphasis in Curriculum and Instruction. Sarah taught performance art and communications for 16 years to diverse populations, ages five to adult, at various institutions including public and private schools, an arts academy, and at the collegiate level. Her research focuses on institutional violence and power structures within education, student agency, democratic education, and educational activism.

Edmund T. Hamann is a Professor in the College of Education and Human Sciences at the University of Nebraska-Lincoln. An anthropologist of education, he studies how transnational movement of students and families shapes the development of education policy locally and more broadly. This includes an interest in how school reform and teacher professional development efforts do or do not make provision for students' and families' language heritages and abilities. Author of ten books and more than 60 articles and book chapters, as part of a team with two Mexican colleagues, he was recognized by AERA with the 2018 Henry T. Trueba Award for research that transforms educational contexts.

Megan Hopkins is Associate Professor in the Department of Education Studies at the University of California-San Diego. Having begun her career as a bilingual teacher in an English-only state context, her research examines how policy implementation and organizational change efforts foster equitable learning opportunities for English Learners and systems of support for their teachers. She is author of numerous journal articles and book chapters and co-editor of *Forbidden Language: English Learners and Restrictive Language Policies* and *School Integration Matters: Research-Based Strategies to Advance Equity*. In 2016–2017, she was awarded a postdoctoral fellowship from the National Academy of Education/Spencer Foundation.

Sujin Kim is an Assistant Professor at George Mason University. Her research interests include immigrant students' academic content and language learning, identity construction, teacher training in TESOL, digital translanguaging, and qualitative research methodology.

Stephen Kotok is an Assistant Professor in the Department of Administrative and Instructional Leadership at St. John's University. His research focuses on the extent that school contexts contribute to opportunity gaps for low-income and minority students. Specifically, Kotok examines issues of school-level leadership such as school climate and tracking as well as policy-level equity issues including school choice, resource allocation, and segregation.

Jill Koyama, a cultural anthropologist, is Associate Professor in Educational Policy Studies and Practice and Program Coordinator of Educational Leadership at the University of Arizona (UA). She also serves as the Director of UA's Institute for LGBT Studies. Her research focuses on the impact of social and education policy on the lives of refugees and other newcomers. She applies critical ethnography to the study of policy and politics associated with civil and human rights and the persistent segregation and marginalization of racial and linguistic minority children.

Van T. Lac is an Assistant Professor at the University of Texas-San Antonio in the Department of Educational Leadership and Policy Studies. Prior to this position, she taught high school English and coached beginning teachers in Richmond, California. Her research focuses on the intersection of critical youth research and leadership for social justice. She is the daughter of Southeast Asian refugees.

Sandra Leu Bonanno is a doctoral student at the University of Utah, pursuing her PhD in Educational Leadership and Policy. Her research examines culturally sustaining school leadership and this framework's potential to create more equitable environments and practices in dual-language spaces.

Dina López is an Assistant Professor in the Bilingual Education and TESOL Programs in the Department of Teaching, Learning, and Culture at the City College of New York. Professor López has written extensively about bilingual education, immigration, language, and literacy both in Latin America and the United States. Through her work, she examines the situated nature of educational practices, particularly as they relate to processes of social identification and student agency.

Gerardo R. López is Professor in the Department of Educational Leadership and Policy at the University of Utah. His research interests focus on issues of (im)migration, parental involvement/engagement, racism, and social justice for marginalized communities. His current research focuses on creating pathways for effective Latina/o/x parental engagement through community organizing and empowerment.

Rebecca Lowenhaupt is an Associate Professor of Educational Leadership in the Lynch School of Education at Boston College. Drawing on multiple methods of empirical research, her work investigates educational leadership and policy in the context of immigration, with a focus on new immigrant destinations.

Warapark Maitreephun received his doctorate in Educational Leadership and Policy Analysis at the University of Missouri-Columbia, and holds a master's in Educational Supervision and Curriculum Development from Chulalongkorn University, Thailand. He previously taught mathematics in grades 10 to 12, and is currently affiliated with Prince of Songkla University's Department of Educational Administration, Thailand. His research focuses on culturally, linguistically, and religiously responsive school leadership, particularly how prospective school leaders are prepared for diverse communities.

Dea Marx is Coordinator of Field Experiences, University of Missouri-Kansas City. She is a former elementary teacher, charter school principal, and Kansas City native. Her research interests include multicultural education, culturally responsive teaching, and mentorship for Latino/a undergraduates.

Kate Menken is a Professor of Linguistics at Queens College of the City University of New York (CUNY), and a Research Fellow at the Research Institute for the Study of Language in Urban Society at the CUNY Graduate Center. Her research interests include language education policy, bilingual education, and the education of emergent bilinguals in U.S. public schools. Further information can be found on her website: http://katemenken.org

Andrea Mercado is a PhD student in Educational Leadership and a career educator with over 20 years of experience working with English Learners in varied contexts. Advocating for immigrant families and their children drives her interest in researching the impacts of school leadership on English Learners in rural contexts.

Jessica Mitchell-McCollough is a doctoral candidate and graduate assistant in the College of Education and Human Sciences at the University of Nebraska-Lincoln. Previously a secondary teacher of Spanish as both a foreign and a heritage language, she now studies how different educational contexts and programs support the sustainability of heritage languages of students and their communities, both local and global. This includes how social reform and education policy interact with student and community agency to inform education theory and classroom practices.

Trish Morita-Mullaney is an Assistant Professor of Language and Literacy at Purdue University where she teaches pre- and in-service teachers in English Learner and bilingual education. Her current research focuses on the agnostic conditions of recent educational reforms that focus on outcomes, creating language and colorblind approaches within classrooms that cumulatively diminish equitable access for minoritized youth.

Marco A. Murillo is a Senior Research Associate at the Center for Equity for English Learners at Loyola Marymount University. Previously he served as Postdoctoral Scholar in the University of California-Berkeley Graduate School of Education, where he conducted comprehensive evaluations of UC Berkeley's Academic Talent Development Program and the UC Network Schools, which were developed as part of university–school district partnerships to serve low-income students. His research focuses on the secondary school experience of immigrant youth as well as issues relating to college access for low-income students of color.

Anthony H. Normore is a Professor of Educational Leadership and Department Chair of Graduate Education at California State University-Dominguez Hills in greater metropolitan Los Angeles. His research focuses on socialization, preparation, and development of educational leaders in the context of ethics and social justice. He is the 2012 recipient of the AERA Leadership for Social Justice Bridge People Award, and the 2015 recipient of Excellence in Research Award for the International Consortium for the Study of Leadership and Ethics in Education.

Nathern S. Okilwa is an Assistant Professor in the Department of Educational Leadership and Policy Studies in the College of Education and Human Development at the University of Texas-San Antonio. His research interests include educational and life outcomes of disadvantaged, underserved, or marginalized students; preparing school leaders that serve diverse learners; sociocultural contexts of education; and educational policy.

Marjorie Faulstich Orellana is Professor of Urban Schooling in the Graduate School of Education and Information Studies at UCLA. She is the author of *Translating Childhoods: Immigrant Youth, Language and Culture* (Rutgers, 2009), *Immigrant Children in Transcultural Spaces: Language, Learning and Love* (Routledge, 2016), and has two forthcoming books: *Language and Cultural Processes in Communities and Schools: Bridging Learning for Students from Non-Dominant Groups* (co-edited with Inmaculada García-Sánchez) and *Mindful Ethnography.*

Uzziel H. Pecina is an Assistant Teaching Professor of Education Administration, PK-12 Education Administration Graduate Program Coordinator, University of Missouri-Kansas City. He is a former principal and Spanish teacher and Kansas City native. His research interests include educational leadership, urban education, multicultural education, and teacher preparation.

Diana Peña coordinates the mental health program and provides counseling for undocumented students at UC Berkeley's Undocumented Student Program. As a licensed psychologist, her areas of focus include immigrant mental health, LGBTQ-affirmative therapy, QTPOC resilience, spirituality, grief/loss, and professional development for Latinx psychologists. Her dedication to serving underrepresented students is rooted in her immigrant-family upbringing and her vision for health and well-being among immigrant and indigenous communities.

Alonso R. Reyna Rivarola is a doctoral student in the Department of Sociology and director of the Dream Center at the University of Utah. Borrowing from his upbringing as an undocumented student in Utah, his research interests are found in the intersections of education, labor, and immigration. Through his doctoral studies, Alonso seeks to explore and develop tools for more accurately capturing and representing the impact of engagement programs in historically underserved neighborhoods and communities.

Ryan Rumpf worked as the Director of English Language Development and World Languages for the Missouri Department of Elementary and Secondary Education at the time of publication. Previously, he has spent 15 years as a teacher and program coordinator in Arizona, Colorado, Missouri, and Vietnam. During his time at the department, Ryan led efforts to improve state- and district-level policies regarding identification and reclassification, enrollment and graduation planning, and supporting ELs with disabilities.

María Teresa (Maite) Sánchez is an Assistant Professor of Bilingual Education at Hunter College of the City University of New York. She's also a Project Advisor for CUNY–NYSIEB, (CUNY–New York State Initiative for Emergent Bilinguals). Her research focuses on language education policy and practice, bilingual education, translanguaging pedagogy, and bilingual education teacher preparation. Further information can be found on her website: www.maitesanchez.org.

Samantha M. Paredes Scribner is an Associate Professor at Indiana University-Purdue University Indianapolis whose research and teaching focus on the organizational and political dynamics within and around urban K-12 schools, and the consequences of leadership and policy practice for constituents of urban school communities, particularly Latinx students and families. Dr. Scribner situates her work in urban schools attended by high percentages of ethno-linguistically and racially diverse students and families.

Chloe Latham Sikes is a doctoral student in the Educational Policy and Planning program at the University of Texas at Austin. Her research interests include the intersections of immigration and educational policy, school–university–community partnerships, education advocacy coalitions, and critical policy analysis.

Kim H. Song is a Professor in the Department of Educator Preparation at University of Missouri-St. Louis. She is the Principal Investigator of the U.S. Department of Education funded project *Strengthening Equity and Effectiveness for Teachers of English Learners*, 2017–2022, in which she directs the professional development activities for content teachers to serve English Learners.

Dawn Thieman is a retired public school district administrator with over 20 years' experience as a teacher and administrator working with immigrant and refugee students. Her interest is in equitable education and educational policy for English Learners and their families. She earned her BS in Elementary and Special Education at Fontbonne College; MA in English with an emphasis in TESOL at Southeast Missouri University; and EdS in Leadership from the University of Missouri-St. Louis (UMSL). She is currently pursuing her PhD at UMSL.

Lina Trigos-Carrillo is an Assistant Professor in the Department of Psychology of Education and Development at the Universidad de la Sabana in Colombia. Her research focuses on critical sociocultural perspectives on writing, the sociology of knowledge, and community/family literacy of minorities and emergent bilinguals across the Americas. In her prior postdoctoral position at the University of Missouri, she facilitated parent engagement initiatives, professional development, and program evaluation.

Guadalupe Vela has an MEd in Educational Administration from the University of Texas at El Paso and currently works as an instructional coach. Her research interests include bilingual education, technology and education, and leadership.

Sarah Yacoub, who recently earned her master's degree from California University of Pennsylvania, teaches Arabic at Northampton Community College and is certified by the American Council on the Teaching of Foreign Language. She volunteers as an interpreter and translator for Interfaith in Action, collaborates with faculty and students at Moravian College, and has translated several Arabic language pieces for the TV program *60 Minutes*. She previously taught Arabic in a Syrian middle school.

Adeli Ynostroza is a doctoral student at the University of Utah, pursuing her PhD in Education, Culture, and Society. She self-identifies as a borderlands Mexican-American woman embracing multiple languages and cultures. Her current research is on biliteracy, bilingual children's literature in the elementary bilingual classroom, and multimodal practices.

Foreword

Marjorie Faulstich Orellana

RESEARCH THAT INFORMS REAL DILEMMAS OF PRACTICE IN USEFUL AND COMPASSIONATE WAYS

Most educational research focuses on problems: it identifies what is wrong with schools, teachers, classrooms, families, or children, or what gets in the way of learning or achieving educational success, however defined. Researchers may conclude their work with recommendations for practice, but these often sound like afterthoughts: obligatory moves to try to make research useful for solving real world problems. Many of the recommendations are not feasible in school contexts. Or they insufficiently grapple with the contradictory demands that are already placed on teachers and administrators in the complicated, messy, daily life of schools.

This book is different. While it uses a "problem" framing, it presents the problems as case studies and as dilemmas of practice. It shows possibilities and successes, along with what might be considered mistakes or uncertainties. It takes seriously the idea that solutions are rarely simple, one-dimensional, or clear cut; they are fraught, nuanced, and complex. People may see things from different perspectives, and bring very different values and assumptions to the conversations. The authors of this book use research and theory to examine how competing demands come together in actual schools, and are grappled with by real teachers, administrators, students, parents, and other school leaders. There are no easy scapegoats here; no person or group is demonized, nor are the identities of teachers, parents, administrators, or students flattened or made into caricatures. The authors take seriously the perspectives, values, and decision-making processes of these agentic, thinking, human beings who operate in complex ecologies, and who are, generally, trying to "do the right thing."

The dilemmas of practice that are addressed in this book cover a wide range of contemporary concerns: anti-immigrant discourse, the needs and experiences of undocumented students, LGBTQ youth, bi-, multi-, and translingualism, and more. They are informed by "cutting edge" theoretical perspectives, including culturally sustaining pedagogies, trauma-informed practice, and translanguaging. They are set within specific policy contexts, with attention both to educational policies and wider state and federal legislation that impact students' and teachers' lives. Authors show how these dilemmas of practice play out in particular local spaces: in large and small schools, within urban and rural school districts, in diverse geographical areas of the U.S., with populations of different ages, races/ethnicities, language backgrounds, gender and religious identifications, and more. Each chapter offers resources for addressing these issues and poses important questions for consideration, without prescribing particular courses of action.

This kind of applied scholarly work is not easy: it is much safer to hide in the realm of theory than to take the risks involved in speaking directly to practice. But it is exactly what we need in order to take the important perspectives that the academy has the luxury and resources to cultivate and see how they play out in the world. This book may help us all advance from "critical" educational research to transformative educational praxis. I only wish I could listen in on the many conversations that this book is sure to spark.

Preface

WHY THIS BOOK AND WHY NOW?

The world is at a unique moment in time. While transnational migration is not a new phenomenon, more people around the globe are moving across regions and countries at greater rates than ever before. While many people move in pursuit of occupational, social, or educational opportunity, others leave their country of origin for a new destination in search of safety and refuge, fleeing civil war, conscription into gangs, and impoverished home economies that offer little opportunity to rise from life circumstances. More people are displaced than ever: the United Nations High Commissioner for Refugees (2017) estimates that, as of 2017, 68.5 million people have been forcibly displaced. Of these, 40 million have been internally displaced, 25.4 million are refugees, and 3.1 million seek asylum. Ten million others are considered stateless.

The mass movement of people has been met with a variety of policy responses and political and social tensions. Though the United States is often touted as a nation of immigrants, historically U.S. immigration policy has cycled through periods of receptiveness and constriction in the acceptable numbers, socioeconomic statuses, and "desirability" of certain immigrants. The election of President Donald Trump in 2016 heralded a new cycle of tightening immigrant policies and anti-immigrant discourse, including a return to large-scale immigration enforcement raids; efforts to ban immigrants from six Muslim-majority countries; attempts to rescind Deferred Action for Childhood Arrivals (DACA); a hyper-focus on extending a multibillion-dollar wall on the U.S.–Mexico border; the criminalization of migrants; and, perhaps most distressing, the separation of parents from their children in detention centers (Chishti & Bolter, 2017). Such proposals signal to 13.5% of the U.S. population, or 44 million immigrants living in the U.S. (Batalova & Alperin, 2018), that their rich heritages and contributions to society are not valued. So what is happening in our nation's schools, which are often the first institution with which immigrants and refugees become deeply involved (Orellana, Meza, & Pietsch, 2002)?

Schools have never been immune to maelstroms of social and policy change, and they are not immune now. Research shows that changes in immigration policy arenas, among others, impact schools. Since 2016, bullying and incidents of hate speech have increased in schools (Vara-Orta, 2018). Communities that have a 287(g) agreement—an accord with federal government immigration agencies to help enforce immigration law—have seen a drop in their Latinx student enrollment (Dee & Murphy, 2018). Some children have had parents deported, with schools stepping in to provide counseling and support (Crawford, 2017). It is essential that school leaders and educators are best prepared in light of these circumstances and ever-changing communities.

PREPARING LEADERS IN TIMES OF CHANGE

The sociopolitical climate is such that schools must work harder to create welcoming climates, ensure that students from different backgrounds feel a sense of belonging and community, and engage families as full participants in their children's education. The troubling incidents noted above are only a few of many that give impetus for school leaders, other educators, and those who care about educational equity to seek opportunities to reflect on their particular contexts, so they develop new ways to navigate and enhance the complex interactions that shape immigrant students' schooling. Building professional skills and cultural competency are urgent tasks as the demographic landscape of schooling is diversifying across rural, suburban, and urban communities. Immigrants increasingly settle in non-traditional destination states and have a growing presence in the South and Midwest regions of the country (Marrow, 2005). Over 20% of households speak more than one language regularly (Census.gov, 2017). It is projected that, between 2005 and 2050, 82% of U.S. population growth will be attributable to immigrants and their families; 23% of this group will be 17 years old or younger (Passel & Cohn, 2008).

Though the term "immigrant" may be used indiscriminately—and we use it as a general term in this book to refer both to foreign-born students who migrate here with family members as well as to those who are children of foreign-born parents—it encompasses related but distinct student groups. These groups may include, but are not limited to, students who are called: culturally and linguistically diverse (CLD), transnational, English Learners (ELs), migrants, refugees, unaccompanied minors, and/or undocumented. Some of these are specific legal terms used by schools, and we define them in the Definition of Terms section below. The fact is, as families move, it means the children attending U.S. schools change. Approximately 7% of K-12 students, or 3.2 million children, have an undocumented parent. Nearly 725,000 students themselves are undocumented (Passel & Cohn, 2016). Nearly 10% of public school students are now labeled "ELs," a growth of 1.4% since 2000 (National Center for Education Statistics, 2018).

While the labeling of immigrant students often suggests that they need help (as "limited" in English, for example), research shows that they come to school with myriad assets, and they want to contribute to their new educational spaces. There has been an explosion of new "dual language" (DL) schools, where children from English-speaking backgrounds mix with those of other language backgrounds to become bilingual and biliterate together (Arias & Fee, 2018). Students and their families bring unique cultural traditions and stories to schools and in turn create dynamic learning opportunities for all (Zapata & Laman, 2016). Meanwhile, educational leaders must have the knowledge and ability to design equitable learning opportunities that respect the backgrounds and practices of newcomers, understand the assets they want to share, work toward humanizing integration, and, when necessary, provide rich English and multilingual development opportunities (Berubé, 2000; López, González, & Fierro, 2006).

BOOK AIMS

The focus of this edited collection is to prepare current and future leaders to: 1) understand how various immigrant groups are classified; 2) distinguish the various needs and experiences of different immigrant student populations; 3) grasp the varying cultural, sociopolitical, legal, and economic contexts that affect students' educational experiences, and 4) know research on best practices and policy options to address immigrants' educational circumstances. This book is specifically designed for current school leaders and central office administrators, those studying to be educational leaders, other educational leaders like counselors and instructional coaches, and community leaders. The aim is to encourage leaders' understanding of how educational practices and discourses around immigration and immigrants can intersect with policies and laws, so they can support K-12 students' educational access and families' participation in schooling. In addition, Chapter 7 includes an extended explanation of various laws and legal cases that have shaped schooling for immigrant youth.

BOOK ORGANIZATION

The volume consists of three sections—*School Leadership*, *Community Leadership*, and *District Leadership*—with chapters in each section focusing on how educational leaders situated in various contexts respond to dilemmas. While the *School* section highlights the leadership of assistant principals, principals, teachers, and counselors, the *Community* section includes cases where school leaders partner with community members from non-profit organizations, universities, and advocacy or parent groups. Meanwhile, the leaders in the *District* section case studies tend to be administrators from the central office level. All chapters include a hypothetical case narrative of a realistic school scenario where the educational leaders interact with immigrant students, families, and other educators, and are challenged to consider ways to promote greater equity in the school community. Often, cases demonstrate how distributed leadership (Spillane, 2006) and teams of educators and community members are key to addressing issues and/or building capacity for immigrant education. Narratives are inspired by real-life events, but the names of most schools, districts, educators, and students are pseudonyms. A pertinent research base and teaching notes follow each case to provide supplemental context, history of legal and ethical issues contained in the case, and support for leader decision making. Suggestions for best practices come from experts in fields such as educational leadership, counseling psychology, educational policy, anthropology, curriculum/instruction, and bilingual education, and others whose work centers on creating inclusive school communities (see contributors' biographies.) Finally, each chapter ends with teaching activities and/or reflective discussion questions, and each section ends with a list of helpful resources, so leaders and future leaders can refine their understanding and practice.

HOW TO USE THIS BOOK

This book is primarily intended for use in pre-service leadership programs and professional development opportunities designed to prepare school administrators and other educational leaders (including teacher leaders). School districts may consider forming book clubs and having small groups of educators work through chapters. Instructors can use the table below to choose readings based on individual contexts and needs. This table includes the following about each case narrative: region of the U.S., geographic context, student demographics, level of schooling, and key actors. Readers can work through chapters independently of the others or approach content thematically (e.g., by schooling level or based on region). However readers use this book, we hope that educational practices shift so that the ideal of equitable education comes closer to reality.

Table 0.1

	Title	*Region and Geography*	*Students*	*Grade Level*	*Key Actors*
SCHOOL LEADERSHIP					
1	Equity and Access for English Learners: Developing Inclusive Advanced Placement Programs	Midwest Suburban Chicago	10% ELs 23% Black 17% Latinx 9% Asian	High school—public	Assistant principal, student
2	Listening to African Muslim Girls: Schooling at the Intersection of Race, Religion, and Gender	Southwest Urban	Somali refugees in historically white context	High school—public	Principal, student
3	"Anil, please tell your dad your report card is really good!" Language Brokering at Parent–Teacher Conferences	Midwest Suburban Missouri	50% diverse ELs including new refugees from Syria	Elementary—public	Teacher, principal
4	Teacher Tensions: Addressing the Impact of Anti-immigrant Discourse on Students	Southwest Urban Texas	40% ELs 87% Latinx	Middle school—public	Teacher
5	Translanguaging: Challenges and Opportunities for School Leaders	Northeast Suburban New York	33% ELs 70% Latinx	Elementary—public	Principal
6	Standardized Testing and Mariachi: Dilemmas of a Culturally Sustaining Dual-Language Principal	West Urban Utah	50% ELs 95% Latinx	Elementary—charter	Principal
7	When ICE Came to Town: Separating Families and Disrupting Educational Trajectories	West Urban Utah	Historically White, now "majority-minority," with recent influx of Latinx, Pacific Islander, Asian undocumented	High school—public	Principal, teacher, student

(continued)

Table 0.1 (Cont.)

	Title	*Region and Geography*	*Students*	*Grade Level*	*Key Actors*
8	Creating a Welcoming Environment of Mental Health Equity for Undocumented Students	Southwest Urban	Predominantly Black (50%), Latinx (30%) Including undocumented	High school—public	Counselor
9	UndocuCollege Access: Addressing Documentation Issues in the College Choice Process	West Urban southern California	Predominantly Latinx, Asian Including undocumented	High school—public	Counselor
10	The Paradoxical Implications of Deported American Students	Midwest Urban Lincoln, Nebraska	Predominantly Latinx Including undocumented	Elementary, middle school—public	Counselor, principals, professor
COMMUNITY LEADERSHIP					
11	Balancing School Priorities on the Border: A Case of School Leadership in Immigrant Communities	Southwest Urban border town, El Paso	80% ELs 93% Latinx	Elementary—public	Principal, mentors, community organizations
12	How School Leadership Influences (and Is Influenced by) Immigration	West Urban, Los Angeles, California	Predominantly Latinx Including undocumented	Middle school—charter	Principal, Executive Director, political advocacy organizations
13	A Principal's Mission to Create Space and Inclusivity for Immigrant Students in a Predominantly Latinx Charter School	Midwest Urban	92% Latinx Including settled Mexican families and Central American newcomers	High school—charter	Principal, community organizations

14	School Choice and Immigrants: Do Families Choose or Do Schools Choose?	Northeast Urban New York (Brooklyn)	Less than 5% ELs, although census tract has 20% ELs	Elementary K-8—charter	Principal, community organizations
15	Negotiating Culturally Responsive Leadership in Remote Rural Settings	Northeast Rural	Less than 5% CLD students, recent influx of migrant workers	High school—public	Principal, community advocates
16	Distributed Leadership in Schools with "Emergent Bilingual Leadership Teams" for Collaborative Decision Making	Northeast Urban New York (Queens, Bronx)	25–30% ELs, many Latinx, newcomers with limited or interrupted schooling	Elementary and high school—public	Principal, university, parent advocates
17	Innovating Practices in New Immigrant Destinations: A University–School District Partnership Focused on Family Engagement	Northeast Urban, Boston	10% ELs 66% White, with growing percentage of newcomers from Central America, Brazil, Pakistan	K-12 District partnership—public	Assistant principal of middle school, university, district EL coordinator
18	Mapping Just Borders of Distributed Leadership: Micropolitics of Engaging Undocumented Latinx Organizing in an Anti-immigrant Climate	Midwest Urban	27% ELs 60% Black 29% Latinx	Elementary—public	Principal, school–community liaison, parent advocates
19	Developing Inclusive and Multilingual Family Literacy Events at Diverse Schools	Midwest Urban	15% ELs 55% Black 15% Latinx	Elementary—charter	Principal, university, teachers

(*continued*)

Table 0.1 (Cont.)

	Title	*Region and Geography*	*Students*	*Grade Level*	*Key Actors*
DISTRICT LEADERSHIP					
20	The Importance of Enrollment and Graduation Planning for Adolescent Newcomer English Learners	Midwest Suburban Missouri	80% White 7% Black 4% Latinx 1% ELs from 16 countries	High school—public	District officials, counselor
21	The Better Immigrant: Seeking Genuine Inclusivity of All Immigrant Youth	Midwest Urban	100% ELs, 50% Latinx, 50% other, including newly arrived Burmese	Elementary—public	Principal, district EL coordinator
22	How Leaders Learn About the Needs of Immigrant Students in a Turbulent Time	Midwest Rural	9% ELs 60% White 20% Latinx 10% Black	High school—public	Superintendent, ESL teacher, principals, paraprofessional
23	Organizing District-wide Change for Equity in a New Immigrant Destination	Southeast Suburb	Historically White, with newcomers: 45% Latinx 10% Asian	High schools—public, magnet	Superintendent
24	Isolating or Inclusive? Educating Refugee Youth in American Schools	Southwest Urban Arizona	Historically White, with 2–3% refugees from 52 countries	District attempt to build a school for newcomers	Assistant superintendent, district refugee coordinator

REFERENCES

Arias, M. B., & Fee, M. (Eds.). (2018). *Profiles of dual language education in the 21st century*. Blue Ridge Summit, PA: Multilingual Matters.

Batalova, J., & Alperin, E. (2018). Immigrants in the U.S. states with the fastest growing foreign-born populations. Washington, DC: Migration Policy Institute. Retrieved from www.migrationpolicy.org/article/immigrants-us-states-fastest-growing-foreign-born-populations

Berubé, B. (2000). *Managing ESL programs in rural and small urban schools.* Alexandria, VA: Teachers to Speakers of Other Languages, Inc.

Census.gov. (2017, September 14). New American community survey statistics for income, poverty and health insurance available for states and local areas. Retrieved from www.census.gov/newsroom/press-releases/2017/acs-single-year.html?CID=CBSM+ACS16

Chishti, M., & Bolter, C. (2017, July 19). The Trump administration at six months: A sea change in immigration enforcement. Migration Policy Institute. Retrieved from www.migrationpolicy.org/article/trump-administration-six-months-sea-change-immigration-enforcement

Crawford, E. R. (2017). The ethic of community and incorporating undocumented immigrant concerns into ethical school leadership. *Educational Administration Quarterly*, *53*(2), 147–179.

Dee, M., & Murphy, T. (2018, September). Vanished classmates: The effects of local immigration enforcement on student enrollment. NBER Working Paper 25080. Retrieved from www.nber.org/papers/w25080

López, G. R., González, M., & Fierro, E. (2006). Educational leadership along the U.S.–Mexico borders/hybridity/building bridges. In C. Marshall & M. Oliva (Eds.), *Leadership for social justice: Making revolutions in education* (pp. 64–84). New York: Pearson.

Marrow, H. B. (2005). New destinations and immigrant incorporation. *Perspectives on Politics*, *3*(4), 781–799.

National Center for Education Statistics. (2018). English Language Learners in public schools. Retrieved from https://nces.ed.gov/programs/coe/indicator_cgf.asp

Orellana, M. F., Meza, M., & Pietsch, K. (2002). Mexican immigrant networks and home–school connections. *Practicing Anthropology (Special Issue on Latinos in the Midwest)*, *24*(3), 4–8.

Passel, J. S., & Cohn, D. (2008, February 11). U.S. Population Projections: 2005–2050. Pew Research Center. Retrieved from www.pewhispanic.org/2008/02/11/us-population-projections-2005–2050/

Passel, J. S., & Cohn, D. (2016, November 17). Children of unauthorized immigrants represent rising share of K-21 students. Pew Research Center. Retrieved from www.pewresearch.org/fact-tank/2016/11/17/children-of-unauthorizedimmigrants-represent-rising-share-of-k-12-students/

Spillane, J. P. (2006). *Distributed leadership*. San Francisco, CA: Jossey-Bass.

United Nations High Commissioner for Refugees. (2017). Global trends report. Retrieved from www.unhcr.org/globaltrends2017

Vara-Orta, F. (2018, August 6). Hate in schools. *Ed Week*. Retrieved from www.edweek.org/ew/projects/hate-in-schools.html

Zapata, A., & Laman, T. T. (2016). "I write to show how beautiful my languages are": Translingual writing instruction in English-dominant classrooms. *Language Arts*, *93*(5), 366–378.

Acknowledgments

Any book is a true labor of love. We have many people to thank for investing their time and expertise to make this book a reality. Each of you has inspired us with your generosity and belief this project can make a difference in the lives of educators, students, and families. We are especially grateful to Edwin Bonney—managing editor extraordinaire—who has worked side by side with us the entire way. We still need to know how you manage each task so efficiently, gracefully, and with a constant smile! We also thank numerous reviewers and school leaders who read chapters and provided valuable feedback: Julia Coggins, Jill Dunlap Brown, Jill Edwards, Arlene Galve-Salgado, Carole Garth, Tony Gragnani, Robert Greenhaw, Connie Hurst-Bayless, Helen Porter, Sara Schmittgens, Dawn Thieman, and Jim Walters. To our authors: we have learned so much through your scholarship, advocacy, and passion to work toward meaningful equal education for all. Thank you also to Heather Jarrow, our editor at Routledge, Rebecca Collazo, and to Matt Friberg, who first advocated for this project. It has been a true pleasure working with you. Finally, our sincere gratitude to all of the immigrant students, families, and educational leaders who provided stories and inspiration for our cases and who daily strive to live up to the ideals of community, love, belonging, and acceptance.

Definition of Terms

1.5 Generation Immigrant. Person who immigrates to another country in their childhood or youth. Distinct from a first-generation immigrant who immigrates as an adult and also from a second-generation immigrant, a native-born child with immigrant parentage.

Asylee/Asylum Seeker. Person who seeks and applies for protection by moving across an international border. Closely related to but different from refugee, as asylum seekers' claims have yet to be reviewed.

Culturally and Linguistically Diverse (CLD). Term used in lieu of "English Learner" to recognize both the linguistic and cultural differences experienced by ELs.

DACA/DACAmented. Reference to a 2012 program, Deferred Action for Childhood Arrivals (DACA), that allowed people who immigrated to the U.S. as minors to receive a two-year reprieve from immigration enforcement actions and who were granted two years' work authorization if they met certain guidelines. "DACAmented" refers to someone with DACA protections. As of March 2019, DACA recipients can renew their applications, but no new applications are accepted.

DREAMERs. Young undocumented immigrants who advocate for the federal government to pass the Development, Relief, and Education for Alien Minors (DREAM) Act, which would provide conditional residency status and access to federal financial aid. Despite several attempts, the DREAM Act has not been passed as of this book's publication.

Emergent Bilingual (EB). Term used in lieu of "English Learner" to recognize that, in learning English, students are becoming bilingual (García, 2009) and draw on home language practices as they learn.

English Learner (EL). Student whose first or home language is not English, and who is learning to read, speak, or write in English. Equivalent to English Language Learner (ELL).

Immigrant. Person who leaves their country of origin with the intent to live permanently in another country. In the new country, the immigrant is considered a first-generation immigrant, while children born to first-generation immigrants are considered second-generation.

Latinx. Term used to describe individuals of Latin American heritage, including those who do not identify with sex and gender binaries.

Migrant. Person who moves within or between states, or even between countries, often for agricultural or fishing work. Migrants may or may not be considered immigrants.

Mixed-Legal Status Family. Family whose members have different legal statuses. For example, a family of four might include one undocumented parent, one parent with permanent residency, and two U.S.-born children/ U.S. citizens.

Refugee. Person who leaves their country of origin for fear of violence, persecution, conflict, or disruption to the public order and who has international protection/status as their claim has been evaluated, per the 1967 Protocol modification of Article 1 of the 1951 UN Convention (United Nations, 2018).

Transnational. Person with ties to two or more countries, who may identify with more than one country.

Unaccompanied Minor. Child below the legal adult age who enters a country without official government authorization and without a parent or legal guardian (U.S. Department of Health and Human Services, 2018).

Undocumented Immigrant. Person who is foreign-born and does not have legal status to live in a host country. Equivalent to "unauthorized immigrant." A related term, "illegals," is considered derogatory as it labels a person, not their actions. Moreover, coming to the U.S. without authorization is a civil, not criminal, offense.

REFERENCES

García, O. (2009). Emergent bilinguals and TESOL: What's in a name? *TESOL Quarterly*, *43*(2), 322–326.

United Nations High Commissioner for Refugees (UNHCR). (2018).What is a Refugee? Retrieved from www.unrefugees.org/refugee-facts/what-is-a-refugee/

U.S. Department of Health and Human Services and Administration for Children and Families Office of Refugee Resettlement. (2018). About the Program. Retrieved from www.acf.hhs.gov/orr/programs/ucs/about

SECTION I

SCHOOL LEADERSHIP

Chapter **1**

Equity and Access for English Learners

Developing Inclusive Advanced Placement Programs

Chris Belcher and Sarah L. Hairston

CONTEXT

This case study takes place in a Chicago suburban comprehensive high school serving grades 9–12 that we call Wilmot High School. In the past ten years, Wilmot's predominately White monolingual student demographics have shifted owing to the influx of a growing immigrant population. Of the 1650 students, 23% are African-American, 17% Latino/Hispanic, 9% Asian, 7% multiracial, and 44% White/non-Hispanic, with 52% of students qualifying for subsidized school lunches. Additionally, the English Learners (ELs) have grown from a handful to approximately 10% of the total school population in the past ten years.

Although the student body has grown increasingly diverse, the faculty and staff remain mostly monolingual and White. Wilmot High School has approximately 100 teachers, of which 87% are White. There are five school administrators, six counselors, and 25 office and support staff, of which 82% are White. There is only one faculty member fluent in Spanish and one part-time teacher specifically designated for EL students. With little district funding for interpreters and EL educators, Wilmot High School must figure out creative ways in which to address the shifting demographics and the unique needs that brings.

Dorothy Roberts, the assistant principal at Wilmot High, works closely with students around issues of discipline, supervision, and academic success. Her rising concern is around ELs receiving adequate academic attention and support. The past five years have shown low academic achievement among ELs, while other student groups have seen moderate to high levels of improvement. A recent "Gap Analysis," conducted for the school as part of a grant program focusing on equitable student enrollment in Advanced Placement (AP) courses by race and income, confirmed her concern. White and Asian middle- to upper-income students were taking AP courses at five times the rate of students of color and economically disadvantaged students. Additionally, less than 2% of ELs were enrolled in an AP course and instead were being placed in lower-level course offerings based on teacher and counselor recommendations.

From Dorothy's work with ELs, and despite their reported low achievement record, she knows they are capable of more rigorous coursework and better academic outcomes, even though many of the students are in various stages of English language fluency. Dorothy's confidence and desire to advocate for EL students go beyond her responsibilities as an assistant principal but also stem from her own experiences as a Black woman who has encountered deficit thinking around her race as a student and adult. Dorothy wants to find a way to address this disparity and advocate for EL students despite a lack of funding from the district.

CASE NARRATIVE

Dorothy starts exploring ways to address the disparity of EL enrollment in AP courses by speaking with a senior student, María, and her parents. María is the only EL in her grade enrolled in AP courses at Wilmot High School. María immigrated with her parents to the United States from Mexico just over three years ago. No one in the family had academic fluency in English upon arriving to the States, though María had studied a little English over the years. María found success in her academic work and quickly integrated into the school culture. María started with AP Spanish in her sophomore year and received a five—the highest possible score—on the AP examination. Subsequently, María took two more AP courses in her junior year with similar success. Through a conversation with María and her parents, Dorothy hoped to find a way to make María's success an expectation for ELs rather than an exception.

At their meeting, Dorothy first learned about the family's immigration story. Through María interpreting, María's parents shared their growing concern for their daughter's success in Mexico, so they spoke with family members living in the Chicago area and then made the difficult decision to move there. María and her family had to say goodbye to rural Mexico and move to the struggling suburban neighborhood where they reside today. María laid bare the emotional toll: "I usually don't cry, but this time was different. I had to leave behind my dog, my friends, the rest of my family, my home." This story is a familiar one for Dorothy. Over the past few years, she has repeatedly had this exact conversation regarding immigrant families' desperate desire to provide the best opportunities for their children, but Dorothy could not help but feel like she and Wilmot High School were letting these families down.

Luckily for María, her parents have siblings who are U.S. citizens, which provided a viable path toward visas for the family. This took some weight off the already heavily burdened immigrant family. From Dorothy's experience, some of Wilmot High School's immigrant families do not have the same safety of legal status, nor the privilege of two parents in a position to be fully available to attend to their child's needs. Many of Wilmot's students are living with one parent or other family members who are working long hours.

María shared that in Mexico she was always in the top three of her class. Before coming to the U.S., her grade point average was 9.8 out of 10 and she received multiple awards for her academic performance. "I did not struggle at all in school; most of the time I understood everything. When I came to the U.S., I truly struggled with my schoolwork for the first time. I struggled everyday translating word-by-word, asking questions. I felt a lot of shame for mispronouncing words." María's parents shared that in the beginning they were afraid they had made a mistake coming here. María was losing her outgoing, happy disposition and no longer spoke of her future. The challenges María encountered were no longer positive but riddled with a sense of failure. Her once glowing report cards turned into points of frustration for both María and her parents. Again, Dorothy sat nodding her head hearing this familiar tale. However, María's story has had a different outcome than that of most ELs at Wilmot High School. So what changed for María? What kept her from giving up and subsequently being successful in AP courses?

Although María's counselors and teachers always spoke positively about her, only one teacher ever encouraged her to consider any courses beyond lower-level offerings. Dorothy suspected that many staff had a bias against ELs, thinking they could not master more difficult course concepts due to their developing English language skills. María shared that she understood her teachers and counselors did not see her like the English-speaking honors students. "Their opinion is very influential. For the whole first year, I believed my teachers and counselors who said that I was not ready to advance, even when I asked. I wanted to be like the honors students—to feel special. They made me feel stupid, my grades made me feel stupid, and so I started to believe I was stupid." María's Spanish teacher saw something different in her, "Ms. Hernandez is the only teacher that believed in me that first year. She celebrated what I considered my slow progress and encouraged me to take AP Spanish." Furthermore, María's parents imparted in her a sense of resiliency. They challenged her to overcome the language and culture barriers despite the lack of active support from the majority of Wilmot High School's faculty and staff. This part of the conversation stung, but Dorothy knew it was important to hear and understand the truth of María's experience so she could better support other ELs and immigrant students.

María's family came to the U.S. with a purpose, and they were not going to have this opportunity wasted. María shared that she had very clear goals when first arriving to the U.S., "My dream is to go to college and become a civil and environmental engineer. Then go back to Mexico to build self-sustainable schools in my community." Ms. Hernandez and her parents never stopped encouraging that dream. Together they demanded that she be enrolled in increasingly advanced courses. Reluctantly the counselors acquiesced.

At first María struggled: "I admit I was a little scared of taking an AP class, because it could lead me to have an even lower GPA, and I didn't want to be seen as a failure." Nevertheless, little by little, she saw success and, as those successes multiplied, so did her desire to challenge herself with additional AP courses. "Being in class, doing the work, studying, and taking the AP tests all changed the way I see myself as a student. I'm taking college-level classes. I see that being an immigrant doesn't handicap me. This confidence makes me work even harder."

After hearing María's story, Dorothy knew that Wilmot High School could change their diversity gap in AP courses without allocating a large amount of resources through a focus on how faculty and administrators see their students. Dorothy requested a chance to speak to the faculty regarding the AP participation gap. She was convinced that the school should have high expectations for all students. She believed high expectations also require greater support and that support starts with no longer perceiving students' language backgrounds as a reason to limit access to rigorous courses.

At the next faculty meeting, Dorothy started by sharing how being a Black woman she experienced deficit thinking around her race as a student and adult. She shared her experience of being spoken about and decisions being made for her based on test scores and not based on her as a learner. "When I told my high school counselor that I wanted to apply to the state university, she told me to not even bother, since my ACT score was not high enough, and I wouldn't get in. Thankfully, I did not follow the advice of my high school counselor. I did end up attending the university, majoring in French and Secondary Education." Dorothy also shared how her first job was specifically given to her based on her minority status, making her feel unworthy of the position despite her advanced degrees. "These experiences and more contribute to my equity journey, and no matter where you are on your own equity journey, it is important to reflect on times when you felt as I did, so that we can better understand and empathize with our current students' situations."

Dorothy also invited María to share her story at the faculty meeting. Dorothy believed a student's voice would help faculty and administration understand the unique experiences of ELs and immigrants at Wilmot High School. As the faculty settled in, María confidently stood in front of the group and began to speak, "I am an immigrant. I am an English Language Learner. I believed you when you said I would never be ready for challenging coursework. I began to doubt my own abilities. I encourage you to choose your words carefully. Many kids like me can be successful when given the opportunity. All we need is for someone to believe in us. Luckily, I have parents that never gave up on me and fought for me to have equal opportunities; Ms. Hernandez never saw my language difficulties as a deficit. This year, as a senior, I am enrolled in my sixth Advanced Placement course."

TEACHING NOTES

English Learners grew by roughly one million students from 2000 to 2015 (NCES, 2018), with a 2025 projection of reaching 25% representation of all public-school students (U.S. Department of Education, 2006). Despite ELs being one of the fastest-growing segment of the K-12 student population (NCES, 2014), nearly half of ELs do not attend a postsecondary institution after high school (Kanno & Cromley, 2015). Furthermore, ELs that do attend a postsecondary institution are overrepresented in community colleges and underrepresented in traditional four-year institutions (Kanno, 2018, p. 2).

College and career readiness is a function of accessing a rigorous high school curriculum. Based on Kanno's (2018) findings, one of the three factors inhibiting ELs from attending a four-year university is limited access to advanced-level courses. The low-track placements, including English as a Second Language (ESL) coursework and the sheltered content areas[1] where ELs often find themselves, tend to focus on self-discipline and basic competency rather than the higher-order thinking necessary for college readiness (Oakes, 2005). Students of all races/ethnicities and socioeconomic status are 10–15% more likely to complete college if they have taken an AP course, regardless of whether or not they took or passed the AP exam (Dougherty, Mellor, & Jian, 2006).

The College Board program offers more than 30 AP courses across multiple subject areas (Theokas & Saaris, 2013, p. 2). As of 2010, 71% of all high schools in the United States have an AP program (Theokas & Saaris, 2013, p. 3). Of those high schools with established AP programs, only 1% have equitable enrollment based on race/ethnicity and socioeconomic status (Equal Opportunity Schools [EOS], n.d.). This inequity further hinders ELs from placement in AP programs due to multiple marginalizations through an intersectionality of racial/ethnicity, low-income, and first-generation statuses (García, Kelifgen, & Falchi, 2008).

According to a survey of over one million students, the most common AP course enrollment barrier reported by underrepresented students is a lack of adult encouragement (EOS, n.d.). Additionally, the survey indicated that underrepresented students are only one-fourth as likely to receive adult encouragement to enroll in an AP course in comparison to their majority peers. Callahan and Humphries (2016) believe that placement of ELs in ESL coursework or sheltered content areas to address limited proficiency adversely signals low expectations to educators. "While English acquisition and achievement are not mutually exclusive, research has documented educators' tendency to view English proficiency as a requirement precluding ELLs' entry into academically rigorous coursework" (Callahan, Wilkinson, & Muller, 2010, p. 3).

In response to the growing research, a number of high schools are creating successful strategic plans to address the inequality gap in AP courses (Belcher, 2017). For example, Federal Way Public Schools in Washington State opened access to AP programs by creating an "opt-out" rather than "opt-in" policy, which assumes that all students meeting basic proficiency standards have the potential to be successful in an AP program (Theokas & Saaris, 2013, p. 9). District and high school leadership must disrupt inequitable practices limiting the success of all students, especially those with multiple marginalization viewed through a deficit lens.

DISCUSSION QUESTIONS

1. Moving to equity in AP courses requires an understanding of the current political and cultural issues that traditionally affect recruitment and enrollment. What current issues should be considered and why?
2. What is the economic impact for students if they do not access a rigorous curriculum? What is the economic and political impact to the greater society if schools fail to provide equitable access to a rigorous curriculum to our underserved students?

3. What available programs and interventions are available throughout K-12 schooling that may address inequities in AP enrollment and access? How can early interventions address these inequities?

TEACHING ACTIVITIES

1. Book Study

For a more holistic understanding of the achievement gap, read the following book and engage in the study guide provided on the ASCD site: www.ascd.org/Publications/Books/Overview/Creating-the-Opportunity-to-Learn.aspx

Boykin, A. W., & Noguera, P. (2011). *Creating the opportunity to learn: Moving from research to practice to close the achievement gap*. Alexandra, VA: ASCD.

2. Gaps Analysis and Strategic Plan

1. Select one high school to research, and break down the student enrollment in AP courses by race, income, and EL status for the past three to ten years, depending on available data. Critically reflect on the data from within the district/school context as well as from a community and national context.
2. Review policies and procedures for AP enrollment. Critically reflect on potential barriers as well as whom these barriers serve.
3. If possible, interview a student, teacher, and administrator regarding their knowledge on AP access and who is "AP material." Reflect on any discrepancies between what is perceived and the school policy/procedure.
4. Create a presentation showing the data collected, critical reflections, and a strategic plan for addressing any gaps found in the data. Questions to consider: How can school administrators engage teachers, counselors, and parents in a discussion about equity of opportunity? How should data drive the discussion?

NOTE

1 According to Markos and Himmel (2016), sheltered content areas deliver "language-rich, grade-level content area instruction in English" (p. 1) toward building language proficiency for transition to mainstream instruction. For more detailed information on instructional components see Markos, A. & Himmel, J. (2016). Using sheltered instruction to support English learners [Brief]. Retrieved

from Center for Applied Linguistics website: www.cal.org/siop/pdfs/briefs/using-sheltered-instruction-to-support-english-learners.pdf

REFERENCES

Belcher, C. (2017). Recruiting our 'missing' students: A superintendent details his mission to enroll underrepresented students in Advanced Placement classes. *School Administrator*. Retrieved from http://my.aasa.org/AASA/Resources/SAMag/2017/Nov17/Belcher.aspx

Callahan, R. M., & Humphries, M. H. (2016). Undermatched? School-based linguistic status, college going, and the immigrant advantage. *American Educational Research Journal*, *53*(2), 263–295. doi:10.3102/0002831215627857

Callahan, R., Wilkinson, L., & Muller, C. (2010). Academic achievement and course taking among language minority youth in U.S. schools: Effects of ESL placement. *Educational Evaluation and Policy Analysis*, *32*(1), 84–117. doi:10.3102/0162373709359805

Dougherty, C., Mellor, L., & Jian, S. (2006). The relationship between Advanced Placement and college graduation (2005 AP Study Series, Rep. No. 1). Austin, TX: National Center for Educational Accountability. (ERIC Document Reproduction Service No. ED519365)

Equal Opportunity Schools (EOS). (n.d.) Retrieved from https://eoschools.org/

García, O., Kelifgen, J. A., & Falchi, L. (2008). From English language learners to emergent bilinguals. Retrieved from http://files.eric.ed.gov/fulltext/ED524002.pdf

Kanno, Y. (2018). High-performing English learners' limited access to four-year college. *Teachers College Record*, *120*, 1–46.

Kanno, Y., & Cromley, J. (2015). English language learners' pathways to four-year colleges. *Teachers College Record*, *117*(12), 1–44.

National Center for Education Statistics (NCES). (2014). The condition of education 2014. Retrieved from http://nces.ed.gov/pubs2014/2014083.pdf

National Center for Education Statistics (NCES). (2018, April). English language learners in public schools. Retrieved from https://nces.ed.gov/programs/coe/indicator_cgf.asp

Oakes, J. (2005). *Keeping track: How schools structure inequality* (2nd ed.). New Haven, CT: Yale University Press.

Theokas, C., & Saaris, R. (2013). Finding America's missing AP and IB students (Shattering Expectations Series, pp. 1–14, Rep.). Washington, DC: The Education Trust. Retrieved from https://1k9gl1yevnfp2lpq1dhrqe17-wpengine.netdna-ssl.com/wp-content/uploads/2013/10/Missing_Students.pdf

U.S. Department of Education. (2006). Building partnerships to help English language learners. Retrieved from http://www2.ed.gov/nclb/methods/english/lepfactsheet.pdf

Chapter 2

Listening to African Muslim Girls

Schooling at the Intersection of Race, Religion, and Gender

Van T. Lac and Nathern S. Okilwa

CONTEXT

Decades of economic and political instability around the world have caused an increase in refugee resettlement in historically racially/ethnically homogeneous communities in recent years. One such community is Andrew Jackson High School (AJHS, pseudonym), the focus of this case study. AJHS is nestled in a tree-lined community in a suburban neighborhood a mile away from a major thoroughfare of a large metropolitan city in the southwestern United States. The city is racially diverse as a whole; however, there are enclaves characterized by socioeconomic status and race, such as the AJHS community, whose residents are predominantly white with deep roots in the area. The neighborhood is served by two elementary schools, one middle school, and one high school, all within a radius of two miles.

The increasing enrollment of refugee students in schools such as AJHS has elicited disparate responses. Some of the responses are grounded in prejudice, intolerance, bigotry, and racism. The heightened intolerance and injustices toward refugees are fueled by a hostile sociopolitical climate in the U.S. and around the world. There are recent cases of injustices in schools across the country that systematically deny refugee youth access to a safe and equitable public-school education (Deppen, 2016; Stuart-Cassell, Bell, & Springer, 2011).

In the case presented here, we learn how a school leader, Cliff Leonard, leverages the voices and perspectives of African Muslim refugee girls to promote welcoming and inclusive spaces at AJHS. In the following sections, we present the case narrative, teaching notes, and, lastly, pertinent resources.

CASE NARRATIVE

Hadija sits, knees twitching, across from her principal, Mr. Leonard, and next to her teacher and advocate, Ms. DeWitt. On a mild Friday afternoon, Hadija, with tears welling in her eyes, details the anxieties and fears she endures at AJHS.

> "It is just endless. Comments made in class," as she looks down at her tissue.
>
> "Like what?" Mr. Leonard inquires with a deep furrowed brow.
>
> Hadija rolls her eyes and states, "Oh, you know, Muslims are terrorists. We don't need any more refugees coming into this country; immigrants are taking all our jobs," Hadija looks up for a moment.
>
> Mr. Leonard asks Hadija, "Well, what do teachers say when students make these comments?"
>
> Hadija looks Mr. Leonard directly in the eyes and utters with frustration, "Nothing."

The principal takes a deep sigh. Weeks after a thwarted terrorist attack in the New York City subway at the hands of a suspected Muslim national from Saudi Arabia, Mr. Leonard and his administrative staff have noticed an uptick in Islamophobic incidents. White students at AJHS have been targeting African Muslim students. Specifically, xenophobic messages have been graffitied on bathroom walls; several Muslim girls have had their hijabs yanked off in the hallways; and the newcomers' room for recent arrivals has been vandalized with graffiti on the door. The principal specifically requested to speak with Hadija, known as an outspoken leader among the Somali youth at AJHS, because many are afraid to speak to administrative staff. Hadija agreed to speak with Mr. Leonard under the condition that Ms. DeWitt could be present as well.

> "My friends and I don't feel safe anywhere at this school."
>
> "What about the newcomers' room?"
>
> Hadija scoffs, "You know, I'm not a recent arrival, right? I've lived in this country since I was five years old."
>
> Mr. Leonard turns pink from embarrassment and replies, "I'm so sorry. I didn't mean to..."

In Hadija's mind, Mr. Leonard represents another clueless white educator with no awareness of the hardships she endures, along with her friends, on a daily basis at school. Life for Hadija holds enough challenges at home. She lives with both her parents, Asad and Kadijah, and ten siblings. As the eldest female daughter in the family, Hadija helps her mother with childcare after school and on the weekends. Hadija would never divulge to school officials the fact that her father has another family in Somalia. Since arriving in the U.S., he could only declare his marriage to one woman, her mom Kadijah.

Lately, home life has been stressful for Hadija; she has been arguing with her parents constantly. Asad and Kadijah want what is best for their daughter: they urge Hadijah to place more effort in the Muslim faith rather than being so fickle. Some days Hadija wears her hijab and other days she does not. Her parents implore her to do better in school: she is currently a B-average student. Hadija has several teachers who believe in her, such as Ms. DeWitt. However, Ms. DeWitt recognizes Hadija's struggles with acquiring academic English. Hadija has expressed a desire to apply for college in the fall and attend the flagship school an hour away; her parents think she should attend the junior college nearby and then transfer to a state school near home. Sometimes Hadijah wants to spend a Saturday afternoon hanging out with her friends; Hadija grows resentful of her older brother who rarely has to do chores, coming and going as he pleases.

"What can we do to make this school safer for you?" Mr. Leonard asks.

"I dunno." Arms crossed, Hadija responds as she looks up from her Black All-Star Converse shoes.

"I mean, if your teachers or I could do anything to help make you and your friends' experiences better at this school, what would it be?" Mr. Leonard wonders.

"For one thing, make your white students stop harassing us," Hadija states with a snicker.

"What else?"

"Teachers need to speak up for us. I sometimes feel either teachers are scared to say something in our defense or they actually believe these comments too," Hadija reveals. The principal scribbles some notes on a clipboard.

"I see. What else?" Mr. Leonard listens intently.

"We don't feel welcomed here, Mr. Leonard," Hadija mutters.

"Who doesn't?" Mr. Leonard seeks further clarification.

"Anyone who is not white. Students who look like me. My parents. Families." She continues, "I don't think you understand how hard it is being Black and Muslim here at this school."

"You're right, Hadija. I have no idea." Mr. Leonard revealed.

This information appears to come as a surprise for Mr. Leonard: for the most part, he just assumed that any absence of tension indicates, inclusion and harmony among individuals at his school. Flyers and notifications are often sent home in English and translated into several home languages, including Somali and Spanish, for non-English speaking households. At school events, such as open house, parent–teacher association meetings, and homecoming games, the school is abuzz with students, parents, and community members; however, Mr. Leonard recognizes participation tends to be dominated by white students and families. He assumes the lack of attendance from racially marginalized families must be due to other obligations, such as parents working multiple jobs.

"Well, do you have any ideas how we could make students and families feel more comfortable and welcome here?" Mr. Leonard wondered.

"Yes, I do. My friends and I talk and think about this often—what we would do if we ran this school," Hadija begins to share her ideas while Mr. Leonard takes notes.

TEACHING NOTES

Multifaceted Challenges for Refugee Students

In the process of settling in their newly adopted home country, refugee students present and face a number of challenges in their schooling endeavors. Challenges emanate from exposure to traumatic events of war, lack of formal or disrupted education, illiteracy in their first language, illiterate parents or guardians, and cultural practices and beliefs (e.g., preference for boys' over girls' education, early marriages, etc.) that are, sometimes, antithetical to the educational dreams of some refugee children, particularly girls. Consequently, refugee students' schooling experiences are further complicated by, just to mention a few, inadequate language support, misconceptions and stereotypes about refugee students' experiences, and unmet psychosocial and emotional needs of students (Dorner, Kim, Floros, & Mujanovic, 2017).

Inadequate language support. Refugee students find it difficult to access the mainstream curriculum due to inadequate language support. Most schools are generally unprepared to handle multiple student languages; they lack the adequate resources (e.g., teacher expertise, curriculum materials, etc.) to support each of their students' language needs (Okilwa, Haupert, Cordova, in press). Particularly, students from non-dominant language groups who are illiterate in their first language (i.e., no basic education) experience educational challenges.

Misconceptions and stereotypes. At times, educators unknowingly entertain and assign misconceptions and stereotypes about refugees as problem kids, intellectually inferior, health risks, and security risks, e.g., future potential terrorists, (Suárez-Orozco, Suárez-Orozco, & Strom, 2017; Wingfield & Karaman, 2001). What it often amounts to is refugee students experiencing differential treatment, marginalization, isolation, and discrimination (Hall, 2017). Also, these stereotypes mask the postmigration realities and conditions of refugees, such as poverty, isolation, racism, and sometimes the uncertainty of their migration status (Rutter, 2006).

Psychosocial and emotional needs. The trauma from the exposure to the horrors of war or natural disasters and the need to adapt to a new homeland have lasting effects on refugee students (McBrien, 2005). These factors often act as barriers that prevent refugees from fully engaging in the learning process. The effects are displayed in psychosocial and emotional behaviors and needs that vary in scope and magnitude. For some students, the effects may manifest themselves inwardly (i.e., tending toward endangering themselves) or outwardly (i.e., turning to others and society). With the selected challenges highlighted here, the following section explores how school leaders could support refugee students to be successful in their educational endeavors.

Parent Engagement of Refugee Families

A robust body of scholarship suggests that parent engagement with the school is associated with positive educational outcomes for students (Banerjee, Harrell, & Johnson, 2011; Henderson, Mapp, Johnson, & Davis, 2007; McNeal, 2001). However, schools are known to favor mainstream or traditional parent engagement practices such as parent teacher conferences, classroom volunteers, fundraisers, and parent–teacher association meetings (Henderson et al., 2007; Tutwiler, 2005). Refugee parents, in particular, may not fully participate in school-centric activities due to lack of transportation and confidence to interact with schools due to limited educational skills, and language barriers.

Epstein (1995) proposed a framework for parent engagement that, if reconceptualized and applied in non-mainstream ways, has potential to reach out to marginalized parents. The typology of parent engagement calls for practices related to parenting, communicating, volunteering, learning at home, decision making, and collaborating with community. When trying to engage refugee parents in these practices, it is worth accounting for cultural diversity and the specific needs and desires these parents bring with them.

a) **Parenting**—Schools should strive to help all families establish home environments to support children as students. It is important for refugee parents to learn the norms and expectations of parenting in their new homeland and to avoid negative encounters with agencies such as Child Protective Services. Through partnerships with community organizations, classes are offered to parents on campus or in the communities where they reside.

b) **Communication**—School leaders should design effective forms about school programs and children's progress. The principal has to know the parents to establish communication preferences. For instance, some non-English speakers may prefer text messages, because they can use phone applications to translate the messages into their languages, thus avoiding having to find a translator.

c) **Volunteering**—Schools recruit and organize parent help and support in ways that are comfortable to the parents. It begins with schools creating positive environments where parents are willing to participate. First, reaching out to parents in such ways as hosting meetings (e.g., parent–teacher conference, home visits) in their residential communities draws parents into authentic partnerships and willingness to volunteer. This may call for reconceptualizing volunteering and initiating non-intimidating ways of engagement, such as schoolwide cultural events or curriculum-based cultural activities in the classroom, allowing parents to showcase their cultural wealth and experiences. Such non-threatening volunteer opportunities, instead of "othering" certain parents, would acknowledge and celebrate differences.

d) **Learning at home**—School leaders should provide information and ideas to families about how to support students to complete homework. Schools have collaborated with community organizations to provide tutoring services to students in their residential communities, especially those who live in the same apartment complexes.

e) **Decision making**—It is important for school leaders to engage parents in educational decisions that impact their children's academic trajectories. Most refugee students and their parents truly perceive education as a path to social mobility. They have hopes and dreams that require the support of educators. In turn, listening to students and families helps to empower their voices. Educators may have to set aside deficit perceptions of refugees and embrace the potential rooted in students' resiliency in order to engage them in charting a successful future for themselves.

f) **Collaborating with the community**—Schools should seek to identify and integrate resources and services from the community to strengthen school programs. Principals who seek community partnerships recognize that schools alone cannot address the diverse needs of refugee students and that every community comprises assets and wealth that can benefit students.

Preparing and Training Educators to Listen to Students

School leaders must prioritize preparing and training teachers to ensure the success of refugee youth. In the case of Hadija and her peers, African Muslim refugee girls, we cannot adequately support their challenges without gaining insights into their lived experiences on issues of race, religion, gender, and immigration status (Cho, Crenshaw, & McCall, 2013).

There are multiple ways school leaders can honor and value the voices of students from marginalized backgrounds, moving beyond treating refugee youth like a monolithic group. Fielding (2001) developed a typology of student voice and identified four ways educators can incorporate student perspectives into their experiences in school. We elaborate on each category and then offer suggestions on how school leaders may develop new practices with refugee youth (Fielding, 2001).

a) **Student as Data Source** encourages educators to learn more about their students through data. Moving beyond standardized testing, teachers of refugee youth should use formal and informal assessments to learn more about how refugee youth learn in school and their histories within the education system.
b) **Student as Active Respondent** requires educators to hear the thoughts and perspectives of students. Educators might ask students about their thoughts and perspectives on a topic. In terms of refugee youth, we recommend teachers and school leaders foreground building relationships with students, so they can learn about their lived experiences. This form of learning requires looking beyond traditional metrics and facilitating conversations to hear the stories from youth.
c) **Student as Co-researcher** considers pupils as collaborators on inquiry-based learning focused on an issue identified by adults. With this form of student voice, teachers and school leaders may ask refugee youth to be co-researchers; refugee youth may conduct surveys or interview fellow refugee students about their experiences in schools. Educators may use research findings to inform instructional practices or school climate and culture.
d) **Student as Researcher** prioritizes students as the drivers of their own learning, where students are actively engaged in every step of a social inquiry. In this case, educators create the conditions to support refugee youth in social inquiry that matters to them. Perhaps refugee youth will want to conduct a research project about how refugee students experience Islamophobia. A crucial distinction between "students as researchers" and previous recommendations is

centralizing marginalized students as the sources and producers of knowledge. Educators could use students' research findings to further professional development for teachers or engage the student body on a critical social issue.

Scholars in the field have written extensively about the power of student voice and the ways adults can support youth. This will require adults intentionally carving out opportunities for youth to exercise their voices in schools (Lac & Mansfield, 2018; Osberg, Pope, & Galloway, 2006) and positioning students as agents of change (York & Kirshner, 2015).

DISCUSSION QUESTIONS

1. Mr. Leonard assumed that the absence of palpable tension represented a sign of inclusion and acceptance at his school. In what ways does Mr. Leonard's assumption represent a misstep in his thinking about marginalized populations at his school?
2. Mr. Leonard made the assumption that Hadija and her friends were newcomers. Where should Mr. Leonard start his learning about the refugee population in his school? What suggestions would you have for Mr. Leonard for his own professional development regarding African Muslim girls at AJHS?
3. Reflecting on Mr. Leonard's actions, what did he do well to address the needs of African Muslim girls at his school?
4. What are the barriers to conversations focused on marginalized populations, such as refugees, at your school? What are some ways to address these challenges?
5. Please reflect on the demographics at your school. Which populations tend to be marginalized or silenced? Which populations hold privilege and power?

TEACHING ACTIVITY

1. Drawing from Fielding's typology of student voice, choose one of the ways to incorporate student perspectives into an issue facing your school/district. For this activity, please 1) define the issue; 2) describe the type of student voice you want to elicit; 3) justify your choice; 4) analyze what resistance you may experience in this activity and how you will address it.

REFERENCES

Banerjee, M., Harrell, Z. A. T., & Johnson, D. J. (2011). Racial/ethnic socialization and parental involvement in education as predictors of cognitive ability and achievement in African American children. *Journal of Youth and Adolescence*, *40*, 595–605.

Cho, S., Crenshaw, K. W., & McCall, L. (2013). Toward a field of intersectionality studies: Theory, applications, and praxis. *Signs: Journal of Women in Culture and Society*, *38*(4), 785–810.

Deppen, C. (2016). "Traumatized" refugee students sue Lancaster school district over treatment. Pennsylvania Real-Time News. Retrieved from www.pennlive.com/news/2016/07/refugee_students_prompt_aclu_l.html

Dorner, L., Kim, S., Floros, A., & Mujanovic, M. (2017). "Everybody kind of looked at me like I was from Mars:" Preparing educators through qualitative service-research projects. *International Journal of Qualitative Studies in Education*, *30*(7), 669–687.

Epstein, J. L. (1995). School/family/community partnerships. *Phi Delta Kappan*, *76*(9), 701–712.

Fielding, M. (2001). Students as radical agents of change. *Journal of Educational Change*, *2*(2), 123–141.

Hall, C. (2017). Sudanese refugee Ayan Macuach fights to change stereotypes and study law. ABC News. Retrieved from: www.abc.net.au/news/2017-12-16/sudanese-refugee-ayan-macuach-fights-to-go-to-university/9264050

Henderson, A. T., Mapp, K. L., Johnson, V. R., & Davies, D. (2007). *Beyond the bake sale: The essential guide to family–school partnerships*. New York: New Press.

Lac, V. T., & Mansfield, K. C. (2018). What do students have to do with educational leadership? Making a case for centering student voice. *Journal of Research on Leadership Education*, *13*(1), 38–58.

McBrien, J. L. (2005). Educational needs and barriers for refugee students in the United States: A review of the literature. *Review of Educational Research*, *75*(3), 329–364.

McNeal, R. B. (2001). Differential effects of parental involvement on cognitive and behavioural outcomes by socioeconomic status. *Journal of Socio-Economics*, *30*, 171–179.

Okilwa, N. S., Haupert, K., & Cordova, A. (in press). Learning in the new land: School leadership in support of refugee students. *Journal of School Leadership*.

Osberg, J., Pope, D., & Galloway, M. (2006). Students matter in school reform: Leaving fingerprints and becoming leaders. *International Journal of Leadership in Education*, *9*(4), 329–343.

Rutter, J. (2006). *Refugee children in the UK*. Maidenhead: Open University Press.

Stuart-Cassel, V., Bell, A., & Springer, J. (2011). Analysis of state bullying laws and policies. Retrieved from http://www2.ed.gov/rschstat/eval/bullying/state-bullying-laws/state-bullying-laws.pdf

Suárez-Orozco, C., Suárez-Orozco, M., & Strom, A. (2017). Immigrant students are internalizing stereotypes: Educators can help. *Education Week*, *37*(5), 27.

Tutwiler, S. W. (2005). *Teachers as collaborative partners: Working with diverse families and communities*. Mahwah, NJ: Erlbaum.

Wingfield, M., & Karaman, B. (2001). Arab stereotypes and American educators. American-Arab Antidiscrimination Committee. Retrieved from www.adc.org/fileadmin/ADC/Educational_Resources/ArabStereotypesandAmericanEducators.pdf

York, A., & Kirshner, B. (2015). How positioning shapes opportunities for student agency in schools. *Teachers College Record*, *117*(13), 103–118.

Chapter 3

"Anil, please tell your dad your report card is really good!"

Language Brokering at Parent–Teacher Conferences

Lisa M. Dorner, Shu-Sha Angie Guan, and Dawn Thieman

CONTEXT

Determination. Smart. Good. Strong Foundations. Diversity Is Our Strength. Running along the homepage of its website, these words define the Beauton School District in small-town Missouri. Over the past 30 years, this district of only 1500 students has become one of the most diverse in the state. Seemingly overnight, Beauton's student population changed from majority U.S.-born to almost 50% foreign-born, the majority of whom are designated by the state as "English Learners" (ELs). Most of the children with this designation receive English language support within their elementary or middle school classrooms from an expert EL co-teacher, while the high school offers some sheltered courses designed just for ELs. In a relatively short time, the Beauton community has embraced the demographic shift, and school leaders and teachers together have created a welcoming, culturally responsive context.

Families come from all over—including Mexico, Vietnam, and Korea—and over time the school has hired bilingual personnel who speak Spanish, Vietnamese, and Korean. However, most recently, an increasing number of students at the elementary school are refugees from Syria. These Syrian families were originally settled in the nearby city, but eventually moved to this quieter area; they had heard that Beauton was an excellent district with good resources for newcomers like themselves. While the district has been able to build up multilingual staff in families' other languages, no one at the elementary school speaks Arabic. This makes parent–teacher interactions a challenge, especially for first-year teacher Ms. Sally Newport.

CASE NARRATIVE

It's October 10th, and Beauton Elementary School is buzzing with activity for parent–teacher conferences. Because it's a warm fall day, the principal and assistant principal are greeting families outside. There is also a welcome table set up in the lobby, where high school students earn service hours as they direct parents to the correct part of the school. The art, physical education, and music teachers are stationed at tables in the cafeteria to have one-on-one conversations with any parents that so desire. Representatives from the Parent–Teacher Organization have arranged a book and resource fair in the library. And the classroom teachers are anxiously waiting for their first family conference to begin in their respective rooms.

Fifth-grade teacher Ms. Newport has arranged everything meticulously. She finished grading all her students' assignments, filled out each student report card with letter grades and personal comments, and made one pile of classwork from each student to showcase their current writing. She plans to show parents around the classroom, to describe how she encourages collaboration as students work in small groups as part of "centers," where themes and core activities change weekly. Ms. Newport knows that a number of her students' parents speak Spanish, but this does not cause her any concern, as she studied Spanish in college and feels comfortable using both Spanish and English to communicate. She had also heard from the other fifth-grade teacher that most of the Syrian refugee families speak some English.

She's nervous, but Ms. Newport finishes her first three conferences without any difficulty. Only once did she have to explain the idea of the "centers" in Spanish—to Mariana's mom—and she appreciated when Mariana herself jumped in with additional information on this week's project focused on designing their own classroom governance structure.

Her next student, Anil Hadi, however, is from Syria. He has been in the school for the past two months and has been doing an excellent job learning the class routines. He studied English before arriving here and can generally understand basic conversations; she assumes that his parents will understand her well enough, too. As Anil, his dad, and younger brother walk into the room, she greets them with a cheerful, "Hello," to which his dad merely looks down and nods. She motions to the chair she set up for parents and invites Anil and his younger brother to sit on the other side of the table.

Ms. Newport launches into her talk about Anil's report card, class activities, and progress. After a breathless three minutes, she realizes she has not heard one response from Mr. Hadi, so she looks up, a bit apprehensive, and realizes that he's been looking at Anil, questioningly. She asks if he has any questions and he shrugs, and says something to Anil that she cannot understand. Anil, looking down and perhaps embarrassed, says, "I'm sorry,

Ms. Newport, my dad can't hear—um, can't understand—you." "Oh, I'm so sorry, Anil," she says slowly, thinking about what to do. "Do you want to explain to him what I just said? Can you tell him about your report card?" Anil looks back and forth between his father and his teacher, and says something in Arabic, gesturing at the grades on the table. Mr. Hadi brightens a bit, leans forward, and responds to his son. Anil then looks at Ms. Newport and says, "He wants to know what these letters mean, here," and he points at the B and C he has in Math and English Language Arts. Ms. Newport continues the conversation, speaking more slowly and carefully explaining how she determines the letter grades and what they mean. The conference goes over their allotted time by 15 minutes, but she ends it feeling good about working with Anil to communicate with his dad.

During the break time in the teachers' room, Ms. Newport runs into the principal, Ms. Ronner, excited to tell her about her success with this first set of conferences. She mentions the struggle, but then the recovery, in her conference with Anil's father. Ms. Ronner listens attentively and congratulates Ms. Newport on working through the communication issue with Anil's father. However, she shares her concern regarding the school district policy based upon federal guidelines that state that an interpreter must be offered for all conferences (U.S. Department of Education, 2015). Ms. Ronner asks Ms. Newport if she knew the procedure for arranging for an interpreter, but Ms. Newport said she was unaware. Ms. Newport feels defeated and upset; she did not know about the policy or the process for requesting an interpreter, and now she wonders if she's done something detrimental to Anil or his father.

As a result of this conversation, Ms. Ronner recognizes the need for establishing a written interpreter request process in her school. Reflecting on Ms. Newport's experience, she also presents her with an idea she's recently learned about: student-led conferences (SLCs). She asks Ms. Newport if she would consider piloting this idea in her classroom based upon her initiative in using the student as a language broker to bridge the communication gap with Anil's father. Ms. Newport is eager to learn more about SLCs and agrees to work with Ms. Ronner to pilot them during her spring conferences. Equally inspired, Ms. Ronner promises to research more about child language brokering to share with the rest of Beauton's team.

TEACHING NOTES

Schools are one of the most frequently cited contexts outside of the home for children's translation and interpretation work (Tse, 1995). While this is variously called language brokering, child translating, family interpreting, and natural translation, Orellana, Reynolds, and colleagues (2003) coined the term *para-phrasing* to highlight that child language brokers "use their knowledge of the English language and of U.S. cultural traditions to speak *for* others and *in order to* accomplish social goals" (p. 508). Language brokering is a fact of daily life in multilingual immigrant communities across the United States and the globe (Orellana, 2017), and it is important for educators to honor and build upon such unique skills.

Perspectives on Language Brokering

Teacher and administrator concerns about the use of child language brokers (CLBs), especially in schools, often reflect the discomfort that arises when children's responsibilities are not aligned with cultural beliefs about what is appropriate for their developmental stages and ability levels (Titzmann, 2012). For example, concerns of "parentification" or role reversal arise in parent–teacher conferences where brokers are given active, expert positions rather than passive ones. Indeed, researchers have found a link between language brokering and poor mental health outcomes, parent–child conflict, and exposure to discrimination that may result from the stress, (re)negotiation of relationships, and contact with institutional personnel experienced by CLBs in a variety of situations (Benner & Graham, 2011; Shen, Tilton, & Kim, 2017).

That said, language brokering has also been associated with positive academic, socioemotional, and transcultural outcomes (Crafter, Cline, & Prokopiou, 2017; Dorner, Orellana, & Li-Grining, 2007; Shen et al., 2017). This has been attributed to the fact that language brokering is complex work that requires language, cognitive, memory, social, and intercultural skills (García-Sánchez, Orellana, & Hopkins, 2011). Contrary to concerns that children may be mistranslating information, in fact examination of CLB communication during parent–teacher conferences suggests youth often (a) downplay teachers' praise; (b) highlight criticism and take on more responsibility than teachers assign; and (c) faithfully translate teachers' cause-and-effect explanations for their academic performances (García-Sánchez, et al., 2011). Moreover, within certain families and cultural traditions, "helping out" through translation is an expected and regular, daily practice (Dorner, Orellana, & Jiménez, 2008), and with appropriate support can be rewarding as opposed to stressful.

Working with Language Brokers

When professional interpreters assist with family–school communication, they must have appropriate training and understanding about families' languages and cultures, school policies and requirements, as well as responsible ethical and confidential conduct (Tuttle & Johnson, 2018). Similarly, there are ways to support child language brokers through positive feedback, promoting education and collaboration of school and community stakeholders (e.g., teachers, counselors, social workers), and continued assessment of the needs and outcomes of CLBs and their families (Orellana & Guan, 2015; Shen et al., 2017; Tuttle & Johnson, 2018). Student-led conferences are one way to engage CLBs (and in fact all students) in developmentally appropriate and ethical family–school communication, meeting an important goal to support all families' participation in school life, regardless of cultural or linguistic differences (Bang, 2009).

Student-Led Conferences

Research on students leading their own "parent–teacher" conferences has appeared in the literature for nearly two decades. SLCs have been shown to have a number of positive effects for both students and parents, including increased student achievement, greater student involvement in and responsibility for their own learning, increased parent-conference participation, and improved relationships between parents and schools (Borba & Olvera, 2001; Hackmann, 2010; Verlaan, Shull, Meredith Mims, & Nelson, 2016). The successful use of SLCs requires whole-staff training and preparation for both students and their parents (Bailey & Guskey, 2000). Typically, teachers work with students prior to the conferences to reflect on their work, compile their portfolios, and practice or role-play what they will say. Teachers also reach out to parents to let them know what to expect, and they should plan for special circumstances, such as children with special needs or parents who cannot attend.

Villanueva and Buriel (2010) observed that immigrant students are already acting as language brokers between teachers and parents, so a formal student-led process provides a systematic format for communication. SLCs also support immigrant parents, students, and their teachers by providing a unique avenue for school–family communication in the parents' home language.

Do SLCs with students as language brokers negate the need for interpreters? To some degree, yes. However, parents have a right under federal law to receive professional language assistance if requested, and districts must provide information to parents in a form that they understand (U.S. Department of Education, 2015). Thus, districts should still be prepared with trained interpreters, whether in person or over the phone, and teachers must continually assess when the presence of the student may not be appropriate or desired by either the parent or the teacher. Speaking to parents about their expectations and assessing cultural traditions and family practices are likewise important to determine when and how to work with child language brokers in schools.

TEACHING ACTIVITIES

1. Read this article about the legal and ethical challenges of providing translation and interpretation in schools: https://hechingerreport.org/schools-federal-pressure-translate-immigrant-families/. Then discuss which circumstances in the article could be resolved by student-led conferences, and when professionally structured translation/interpretation would be necessary.
2. Write a proposal to develop student-led conferences in your school. Address these questions:
   - What are the learning objectives for students?
   - What are the expected outcomes for parents? Teachers?
   - What activities can be used to prepare students?
   - What student artifacts will be in the student portfolio?
   - What type of training can prepare teachers and staff?
   - What are some challenges that might arise and approaches to address them?
   - How will you assess the SLCs?
3. Read the *Child Interpreting in School: Supporting Good Practice* guide: http://child-language-brokering.weebly.com/uploads/1/4/9/3/14938884/clbis_support_good_practice_guide_v.3.1.pdf. Create an action plan (including a diagram of program leadership, steps of operation and activities, and outcomes) or a "tip sheet" for how to involve children in conferences to ensure ethical, effective communication. Your action plan or tip sheet may be part of a School Improvement Plan or other strategic planning process.
4. Describe how administrators like Ms. Ronner can promote better communication practices with immigrant parents. You may use the following resources: *Schools' Civil Rights Obligations to English Learner Students and Limited English Proficient Parents*, https://www2.ed.gov/about/offices/list/ocr/ellresources.html, or background information on refugees, found here: www.culturalorientation.net/learning/backgrounders.

REFERENCES

Bailey, J. M., & Guskey, T. R. (2000). *Implementing student-led conferences.* Thousand Oaks, CA: Corwin Press.

Bang, Y. (2009). Helping all families participate in school life. *Young Children, 64*(6), 97–99.

Benner, A. D., & Graham, S. (2011). Latino adolescents' experiences of discrimination across the first 2 years of high school: Correlates and influences on educational outcomes. *Child Development, 82*(2), 508–519.

Borba, J. A., & Olvera, C. M. (2001). Student-led parent–teacher conferences. *Clearing House, 74*(6), 333–336.

Crafter, S., Cline, T., & Prokopiou, E. (2017). Young adult language brokers' and teachers' views of the advantages and disadvantages of brokering in school. In R. Weisskirch (Ed.), *Language brokering in immigrant families: Theories and contexts* (pp. 224–244). New York: Taylor & Francis.

Dorner, L. M., Orellana, M. F., & Jiménez, R. (2008). "It's one of those things that you do to help the family": Language brokering and the development of immigrant adolescents. *Journal of Adolescent Research, 23*(5), 515–543.

Dorner, L. M., Orellana, M. F., & Li-Grining, C. P. (2007). "I helped my mom" and it helped me: Translating the skills of language brokers into improved standardized test scores. *American Journal of Education, 113*, 451–478.

García-Sánchez, I. M., Orellana, M. F., & Hopkins, M. (2011). Facilitating intercultural communication in parent–teacher conferences: Lessons from child translators. *Multicultural Perspectives, 13*(3), 148–154.

Hackmann, D. G. (2010). Student-led conferences. In *Encyclopedia of cross-cultural school psychology* (pp. 943–944). Boston, MA: Springer.

Orellana, M. F. (2017). Dialoguing across differences: The past and future of language brokering research. In R. Antonini, L. Cirillo, L. Rossato, & I. Torresi (Eds.), *Non-professional interpreting and translation: State of the art and future of an emerging field of research* (pp. 65–80). Philadelphia, PA: John Benjamins Publishing Company.

Orellana, M., & Guan, S. A. (2015). Immigrant family settlement processes and the work of child language brokers: Implications for child development. In C. Suárez-Orozco, M. Abo-Zena, & A. K. Marks (Eds.), *Transitions: The development of children of immigration* (pp. 184–200). New York: NYU Press.

Orellana, M. F., Reynolds, J. F., Dorner, L. M., & Meza, M. (2003). In other words: Translating or "para-phrasing" as a family literacy practice in immigrant households. *Reading Research Quarterly, 38*(1), 12–34.

Shen, Y., Tilton, K. E., & Kim, S. Y. (2017). Outcomes of language brokering, mediators, and moderators. In R. Weisskirch (Ed.), *Language brokering in immigrant families: Theories and contexts* (pp. 47–72). New York: Taylor & Francis.

Titzmann, P. F. (2012). Growing up too soon? Parentification among immigrant and native adolescents in Germany. *Journal of Youth and Adolescence, 41*(7), 880–893.

Tse, L. (1995). Language brokering among Latino adolescents: Prevalence, attitudes, and school performance. *Hispanic Journal of Behavioral Sciences*, *17*(2), 180–193.

Tuttle, M., & Johnson, L. V. (2018). Navigating language brokering in K-12 schools. *Journal of Mental Health Counseling*, *40*(4), 328–340.

U.S. Department of Education (2015). Information for limited English proficient (LEP) parents and guardians and for schools and school districts that communicate with them [fact sheet]. Retrieved from https://www2.ed.gov/about/offices/list/ocr/docs/dcl-factsheet-lep-parents-201501.pdf

Verlaan, W., Shull, M., Meredith Mims, M., & Nelson, G. (2016). Using portfolios and student-led conferences to increase student motivation and parental engagement. *Literacy Summit Yearbook*, *2*, 43–51.

Villanueva, C. M., & Buriel, R. (2010). Speaking on behalf of others: A qualitative study of the perceptions and feelings of adolescent Latina language brokers. *Journal of Social Issues*, *66*(1), 197–210.

Chapter 4

Teacher Tensions

Addressing the Impact of Anti-immigrant Discourse on Students

Chloe Latham Sikes and Andrea Chevalier

CONTEXT

Hannah Brookstone is a White eighth-grade social studies teacher in a large urban school district in Texas. Her middle school campus serves grades six to eight, with a student body of over 750 students that is 87% Hispanic, 4% Black, 7% White, 1% Asian, and less than 1% each of Native students and students of two or more races. Furthermore, the student body is 85% economically disadvantaged and 40% English Language Learners, and over 13% of students are served through special education. In this narrative, she visits the Texas State Capitol in Austin, Texas, and witnesses a political display that is based on true events.

CASE NARRATIVE

Hannah has been with the district for four years and enjoys teaching social studies, because she believes that knowing where we come from shows us how far we have to go as a society. She loves her students' tenacity but often finds that they are disinterested in the eighth-grade social studies' focus on early United States history through Reconstruction. Many of Hannah's students are of Mexican descent, but she also has students from El Salvador, Honduras, and Puerto Rico. The longer Hannah teaches her curriculum, the more she realizes that nearly every picture shown, every story told, is about a person that bears no resemblance to her students or their stories.

Hannah works to improve her lesson content delivery, but she knows she has to do more to make social studies meaningful to her students. She resolves that this year she will take her students to the Texas Capitol to observe government firsthand. She hopes that the presence of Texas' Mexican-American legislators will dispel some of the disenchantment the students feel about American democracy and the political system, and close the distance between the America they see in the classroom and the one they live in.

Hannah secures funds for the student trip to the Texas Capitol, including a long bus ride to and from Austin. Her students are excited to have time on the bus to chat, play games, and show off their phones and tablets to each other. Hannah brings all of her classes, totaling about 60 students, and five parent chaperones. As the students near Austin, Hannah already feels victorious and excited to witness diversity and civic engagement. When the bus parks, she raises her hand to signal silence and tells her students that they will be heading straight to the Texas House of Representatives chamber floor to observe the legislative session. She reminds the students that the House gallery—the viewing area for the House chamber—maintains specific rules, like no eating or drinking, no standing, and no heckling or cheering. Cheering jokingly in response, the students stand up and file off the bus with their chaperones as Hannah leads the way into the Capitol.

As Hannah directs her students through the main entry floor of the Capitol building, she wonders if they notice that all of the Texas governors' portraits lining the circular wall depict White faces. Soon, the students take their seats in the House gallery and stretch their necks to watch the bustle of the legislators. Hannah hopes her pre-field trip lesson prepared the students for what is taking place and who the key Mexican-American legislators are. These include a formerly undocumented Latina representative, the chairman of the Mexican American Legislative Caucus (MALC), and the vice chair of MALC and first openly LGBTQ representative. One student recognizes a legislator and looks back at Hannah with a smile, mouthing, "Look, miss! It's that one!"

The legislators debate proposed amendments to a bill related to kinship care payments, a source of state monetary assistance for adult relatives of foster children who become their caregivers. Hannah listens intently as various representatives present their amendments to the bill, but her mind starts to wander. She scans her students and wonders if any of them were foster students who would benefit from this bill.

The next proposed amendment is presented by Representative Kent a White legislator. He begins by discussing the specific details of the bill and its creation of a monthly payment for kinship caregivers. Hannah performs a periodic visual survey of her students when she hears the representative clarify that his amendment demands the caregiver must be in the country legally to receive the payment. She whips her head around and feels the mood stiffen. She recognizes the chairman of MALC, Representative Alvarez as he approaches the other microphone on the House floor. Rep. Kent continues, stressing that only *documented* citizens should receive the funding. As legislators opposed to the amendment boo, the students pick up on the tension and lean in to listen.

Rep. Kent justifies his amendment. He says the state tries to "handle" its children, but that the bill as written creates an "entitlement" for undocumented residents. Some of the students murmur and whisper to each other. Hannah's eyes shift to one of her star students, Brenda, a Latina eighth grader. Recently, Hannah has worked closely with Brenda and her parents to discuss her high school plan, and she suspects some of Brenda's family members may be undocumented. As Hannah's heartbeat quickens, she wonders what Brenda and her other students are thinking and feeling. Rep. Kent exclaims, "Why would we include an entitlement for people who are here illegally and unaccounted for?" A loud groan of disapproval echoes, further drawing the students into the spectacle. Hannah worries. With every mention of the word "illegal," she feels a jolt of adrenaline. Should she signal to the students that they would be leaving? How will she address this exchange with the students later?

Hannah notices numerous legislators of color congregating at the microphone in support of Rep. Alvarez. She feels a wash of hope and gambles that this could turn out to be a good teaching moment, perhaps an inspiring display of the importance of racial diversity in political representation. Her students scoot to the edges of their seats as Rep. Kent mentions legality and immigration several more times, his voice rising. He passionately argues that anybody in the room would help a child even if they were "illegal," but that the question is "what are they doing here? They're not here legally!" Hannah's heart races and she nervously fiddles with her school badge as Rep. Alvarez opposes the representative's amendment.

Rep. Alvarez a lawyer and seasoned legislator, coolly questions Rep. Kent on the amendment. As he grills his colleague on the legal aspects of his amendment, Hannah notices a few students putting their fists to their mouths and looking to each other with wide eyes to say "Oh!", while another student smiles and makes a "drop the mic" motion. Rep. Kent again uses phrases like "the home of an illegal" and "all these kids that came across the border" in his refute to the MALC chairman. Rep. Alvarez's calm demeanor transforms into heated defense as he charges Rep. Kent with equating children in desperate need with "lawbreakers." Assured by the turn in events, Hannah settles in, determined to have her students witness the debate's outcome.

After a heated back-and-forth, just before the final vote on the amendment, Rep. Alvarez launches into a speech that captivates the students. His volume increases as he decries the failure of the state legislature to protect foster children, averring that they end up as "whores," "pimped out," and "used like a piece of meat." As a growing group of legislators flank the Chairman with every impassioned word, he asserts: "As a son of immigrants to this country, and as a proud Latino, this feels really racist, and I'm using that word, members." Hannah hears a few quiet gasps from her students and looks back at them. Their eyes are wide, fixed on the chairman as he reprimands his fellow legislators for using immigrant kids as a prop—a spectacle—to display how tough they are on immigration issues. Defeated, Rep. Kent offers, "I am not a racist, I love all people," and withdraws the amendment. Hannah breathes a sigh of relief. The contentious amendment is defeated by the strength and skill of other legislators. She begins the process of escorting her students out of the Capitol building to journey back to their school.

TEACHING NOTES

The case narrative showcased how political speech displays opposing narratives and ideologies about social issues, in this case immigrant families, children, and state welfare. Political speech and actions that emphasize a viewpoint, rather than a specific policy goal, can be characterized as "political spectacles" (Koyama, 2013; Wright, 2005). Political spectacles are intended to align with particular values, ideologies, and political positions through the use of strategic language, behavior, and expressions—or discourse—to make a "spectacle." The case narrative focused on the political spectacle created by the proposal of an amendment to a bill for child welfare that displayed an anti-immigrant and racially charged political position through associated discourse (i.e., the language and expressions used).

Over the past several decades, federal immigration policy has used alternating discourses of immigrants as "deserving" of public assistance, services, and paths to citizenship, in contrast to "undeserving," such as contemporary narratives of immigration as a national security threat (Abrego, Coleman, Martínez, Menjívar, & Slack, 2017; Schneider & Ingram, 2005). These competing discourses have veered toward associating immigrants with criminals over the last 30 years (Abrego et al., 2017), which allows for policies that position children and families coming to the United States as a threat, rather than as people seeking better opportunities and safety.

Because the overwhelming majority of families that immigrate without authorization to the United States arrive from Mexico and Central American countries (Rosenblum & Ruiz Soto, 2015), anti-immigrant discourse also reflects a racially targeted anti-immigration strategy. The use of anti-immigrant discourse to defend and justify cruel policies, such as family separation and immigration detention, has revealed an intent to criminalize and discriminate against Hispanic/Latino immigrant children and their families (Dorner, Crawford, Jennings, Sandoval, & Hager, 2017). Policymakers adopt the same discourse and rhetoric to advance other policies that are not directly connected to immigration policy, but that can still marginalize and discriminate against immigrant families. As in the case narrative above, anti-immigrant rhetoric influenced how children in the foster care system with immigrant family members were positioned as undeserving of state assistance.

For educators and school leaders, the political realities of anti-immigrant detention and deportation policies that impact children and families present urgent issues of concern. Even if children are U.S.-born citizens, they may have parents, siblings, and family members who are undocumented or have mixed statuses, meaning some family members hold U.S. citizenship or other forms of legal residency while other members in the same family may live without legal documents (Suárez-Orozco, Yoshikawa, Teranishi, & Suárez-Orozco, 2011). Between 2012 and 2016, nearly 700,000 U.S.-born children residing in Texas had at least one unauthorized immigrant parent (Gelatt & Zong, 2018).

Family separation of adults and children occurs when any member of a family faces detention or deportation. Research shows that families' fear of detention and deportation policies has a negative impact on family financial security and social-emotional well-being and has negative implications for children's behavior and performance in school (Brabeck & Xu, 2010; Lovato, 2018; Romero, 2008). Intense fear of family separation constitutes ongoing trauma with serious implications for academic disruptions in children's education (Lovato, 2018). Furthermore, the pressures associated with being undocumented negatively impact children at various levels of cognitive and social-emotional development, from their stress levels and sense of security to affordability of housing and education (Suárez-Orozco et al., 2011).

In order to better support immigrant students, educators must become familiar with how "parents' legal status affects their children's academic performance," and how increased hostility toward immigrant families in political discourse impacts children's emotional well-being and school success (Brabeck & Xu, 2010, p. 356). Since all children, regardless of immigration status, have protected access to public schools per the 1982 Supreme Court decision *Plyler v. Doe* (Crawford & Hairston, 2017), educators should be able to cultivate conducive learning environments for students' academic success. Outside of the classroom, school leaders must be prepared to respond to Immigration and Customs Enforcement (ICE) patrols and raids near school campuses and know other safe adult family members or caregivers who can care for a child in this situation (Negrón, Carter, Burns, & Patterson, 2017).

In this case narrative, children in the foster care system may be placed with kinship caregivers (relatives) who have mixed legal status, so schools must be aware of how ICE policies and anti-immigrant political discourse can impact a student's development and their family well-being both in and out of the classroom. The more that educators understand how the larger sociopolitical context impacts their students' lives, the easier it is to build relationships and strong school cultures for students' learning.

TEACHING ACTIVITIES

1. Deciding between Protection and Exposure

School leaders and teachers must work to recognize how exposure to policy environments occurs and how to address resulting student discomfort. Using the narrative, walk through Hannah's numerous on-the-spot decisions, and guide your discussion with the following reflection questions:

1. What are the most difficult conversations to have with students that arise from the policy environment?
2. How do different kinds of discomfort generated by the policy environment affect students in different ways?
3. How can teachers navigate exposure and discomfort to confront sensitive issues such as race and immigration in ways that empower students?
4. What programs, practices, or policies can school leaders engage in to prepare teachers for difficult situations created by the policy environment?

2. Values and Ideas

Use the following activity to spark meaningful conversation about the interaction between the legal-political system, society, and human conditions.

1. Create a line on the floor in your room that is long enough for all participants to see. Each side of the line will represent support or opposition to a value statement.

2. Create an agreed-upon set of norms for participants, and return to the norms should any participants break from them. Facilitation of this activity must be safe and respectful.
3. Create five topic-relevant value statements. For example: "Education is a public good," or "A fundamental role of school leaders is to protect school children."
4. For each value statement, participants will physically move to a side of the line. Participants on either side, or who abstain from choosing, will be invited to share their perspective.
5. At the end, facilitate a group debrief (e.g,. what was hard, where there was agreement) and provide time for private, silent journaling.

3. Race and Immigration Discourse

Language provides a window into the understanding of the speaker. It is particularly important that we carefully choose our words concerning political issues.

1. Word dump: As a whole group, choose a topic (e.g., immigration, school choice) and allow participants to say whatever words come to their mind. Write these down in a place visible to all members. For instance, "school choice" words might include "charters, parents, opportunity, private, lost resources," etc.
2. In small groups, categorize the words based on the understanding they convey and the contexts they create.
3. Using these contexts and word categorizations, create a letter home to parents that explains the event at the Capitol and what your administration/classroom will do to support healing and growth in its aftermath.

REFERENCES

Abrego, L., Coleman, M., Martínez, D. E., Menjívar, C., & Slack, J. (2017). Making immigrants into criminals: Legal processes of criminalization in the post-IIRIRA era. *Journal on Migration and Human Security*, *5*(3), 694–715. https://doi.org/10.14240/jmhs.v5i3.105

Brabeck, K., & Xu, Q. (2010). The impact of detention and deportation on Latino immigrant children and families: A quantitative exploration. *Hispanic Journal of Behavioral Sciences*, *32*(3), 341–361. https://doi.org/10.1177/0739986310374053

Crawford, E. R., & Hairston, S. L. (2017). He could be undocumented: Striving to be sensitive to student documentation status in a rural community. *Journal of Cases in Educational Leadership*, *21*(1), 3–15. https://doi.org/10.1177/1555458917718008

Dorner, L. M., Crawford, E. R., Jennings, J., Sandoval, J. S. O., & Hager, E. (2017). I think immigrants "kind of fall into two camps": Boundary work by U.S.-born community members in St. Louis, Missouri. *Educational Policy*, *31*(6), 921–947. https://doi.org/10.1177/0895904817719529

Gelatt, J., & Zong, J. (2018). *Settling in: A profile of the unauthorized immigrant population in the United States*. Washington, DC: Migration Policy Institute.

House Chamber: Debate on the House Floor of the Texas State House of Representatives, 85th Legislature. (March 1, 2017). Retrieved from http://tlchouse.granicus.com/MediaPlayer.php?view_id=39&clip_id=12815

Koyama, J. (2013). Global scare tactics and the call for US schools to be held accountable. *American Journal of Education*, *120*(1), 77–99. https://doi.org/10.1086/673122

Lovato, K. (2018). Forced separations: A qualitative examination of how Latino/a adolescents cope with parental deportation. *Children and Youth Services Review*. Advance online publication. https://doi.org/10.1016/j.childyouth.2018.12.012

Negrón, F., Carter, T., Burns, T., and Patterson, J. (2017). Lifting the lamp beside the schoolhouse door: A legal guide to serving undocumented students in public schools (p. 32). National School Boards Association. Retrieved from https://cdn-files.nsba.org/s3fs-public/reports/107114917_NSBA_Immigration_Guide_Web_FINAL.pdf?9z5l0X54LS_gdm_9tG1wxPbWMgSecrpn

Romero, M. (2008). The inclusion of citizenship status in intersectionality: What immigration raids tell us about mixed-status families, the state and assimilation. *International Journal of Sociology of the Family*, *34*(2), 131–152.

Rosenblum, M. R., & Ruiz Soto, A. G. (2015). *An analysis of unauthorized immigrants in the United States by country and region of birth*. Washington, DC: Migration Policy Institute.

Schneider, A. L., & Ingram, H. M. (Eds.). (2005). *Deserving and entitled: Social constructions and public policy*. Albany, NY: SUNY Press.

Suárez-Orozco, C., Yoshikawa, H., Teranishi, R., & Suárez-Orozco, M. (2011). Growing up in the shadows: The developmental implications of unauthorized status. *Harvard Educational Review*, *81*(3), 438–473. https://doi.org/10.17763/haer.81.3.g23x203763783m75

Wright, W. (2005). The political spectacle of Arizona's Proposition 203. *Educational Policy*, *19*(5), 662–700. https://doi.org/10.1177/0895904805278066

Chapter 5

Translanguaging

Challenges and Opportunities for School Leaders

Dina López and Ofelia García

This case narrative is inspired by CUNY–NYSIEB's professional development work with many schools in New York. However, Principal Hudson and Springvale Elementary are a fictional character and school.

CONTEXT

Springvale Elementary is a K-5 elementary school situated in a suburban district outside of New York City. Due to changing demographics in the local community over the past ten years, the school now serves a predominantly Latinx student population. (Latinx is a gender-neutral term referring to those of Spanish-speaking and/or Latin-American heritage.) Close to 70% of students are from Spanish-speaking households, with many having immigrated from Central and South American countries. The rest of the student body is 20% Black, 7% White, 2% Asian, and 1% multiracial. About one third of the students at Springvale have been classified as English Language Learners (ELLs, also called EBLs, emerging bilingual learners). Though the majority of these students (95%) speak Spanish at home, other languages, such as Arabic, Bengali, Pashto, and Polish, are also represented in the school.

Springvale Elementary offered three programs for their classified ELLs: a Two-Way Spanish–English Dual Language Bilingual Education (DLBE) program; Transitional Bilingual Education (TBE); and an English as a Second Language (ESL) push-in/pull-out program. Students with home languages other than English and Spanish were placed in the ESL program (now called English as a New Language, ENL, in New York State). The Dual Language Bilingual program was a 50/50 side-by-side model; that is, one teacher taught only in English and another one only in Spanish. The DLBE program went from kindergarten through fifth grade. The program aimed to develop bilingualism and biliteracy, as well as cross-cultural understanding among its students.

The surrounding community is made up of a mix of working-class, middle-class, and higher income residents. However, students with higher socioeconomic status tend to go to Catholic or private schools. Students who do enroll in the public elementary schools are lower or middle class, and the DLBE program was seen as a way to attract and retain more local middle-class families. Half of the students in the program were from English-speaking families and the other half were from Spanish-speaking families. The Transitional Bilingual Education program at Springvale targeted EBLs with "entering" or "emerging" proficiency in English, and instruction was mainly in English with some Spanish language supports; however, there was no explicit instruction in Spanish. The ESL program at Springvale was mainly a push-in program, meaning that an ESL-certified teacher supported EBLs in some mainstream classrooms, although the school also provided some pull-out ESL services for these students.

Over the past ten years, student performance on state Math and ELA tests had been dismal (hovering at 23–25% proficiency), and Springvale Elementary had been identified as a low-performing school. Principal Hudson had taken over the school about three years ago and had been charged with getting scores up. The first order of business had been to overhaul the English Language Arts and Math curricula and make them more uniform across the grades. Teachers had gotten professional development on the balanced literacy approach and on the new common core-aligned state Math curriculum. She felt that the school was making strides, just not fast enough.

CASE NARRATIVE

It was a rainy fall Friday afternoon, and Principal Laura Hudson was in her office wrapping up some emails before heading home. It had been a trying week at Springvale Elementary—including a grueling quality review visit from New York State—and she was anxious to get home to her family. After putting the finishing touches to a couple of emails to parents and one to the assistant superintendent, she came across an unopened message with the subject heading "Upcoming Translanguaging Workshops." She read about a series of workshops for school leaders and teachers that would be offered at The Graduate Center of City University of New York over the next couple of months with the focus on improving practice for "emergent bilinguals" by "using bilingualism as a resource" and implementing *translanguaging* strategies in varying classroom contexts. The workshops were part of a professional development project between New York State and City University of New York called CUNY–NYSIEB (City University of New York–New York State Initiative on Emergent Bilinguals, www.cuny-nysieb.org). Principal Hudson was not so sure what *translanguaging* meant exactly, but she was intrigued. And the email seemed incredibly timely since one of the main issues identified by the state visit had been the underperformance of those classified as ELLs at Springvale. No, she couldn't do this, she thought; she already had so much on her plate. But she couldn't shake the feeling that she could be missing out on an important opportunity. After mentally debating it for several minutes, she decided to go ahead and register.

When Principal Hudson sat down on the morning of the first workshop focused on bilingual students and translanguaging, the most recent state visit and quality review was on her mind. The evaluator had identified the performance of students labeled as ELLs on state tests as particularly worrisome and had suggested that working with teachers on how to better serve ELLs be one of Principal Hudson's top priorities. As someone who was woefully undertrained in bilingual education and TESOL, she hoped that these workshops would provide her with tools to help her begin this work.

The CUNY–NYSIEB workshops on bilingualism and translanguaging did not disappoint. After every session, Principal Hudson left feeling inspired and energized. What she was learning at the workshops was also shifting her understandings of bilingualism and the strengths and needs of her bilingual students and families. Following lectures and discussion, the participants were engaged in a process of Collaborative Descriptive Inquiry, where they were asked to describe their experiences in their school around a question focused on some specific aspect of teaching these students.

Principal Hudson first learned to view ELLs as emergent bilinguals, as students who in developing English were also becoming bilingual (García & Kleifgen, 2010). She understood then that bilingualism, and not just English learning, were important topics for her and all her teachers, since they were indeed developing the bilingualism of their emergent bilingual students. Principal Hudson began to realize that the learning of English in that community always resulted in the development of bilingualism. Bilingualism, she started understanding, couldn't be resisted, but had to be leveraged.

Through the focus on "emergent," Principal Hudson also started understanding that it was impossible to simply move her emergent bilingual students so that they "had" English. Instead, in shifting the focus to people "doing" language, she became convinced that what was important was to provide her students with appropriate affordances and opportunities so that they could "do" English for different tasks, including academic ones.

Principal Hudson had thought that bilingualism was simply additive, and that what was important was to "add" English as a second language to her "ELLs" so that they could become "English proficient." But through participation in the CUNY–NYSIEB workshops, she started understanding bilingualism as much more than simply the addition of a second language to a first language. First, she realized that many of her emergent bilingual students had been born in the United States, and they were growing up with two languages simultaneously. She started seeing that English was not simply their "second" language, just as Spanish was not simply their "first" language. The concept of additive bilingualism was being challenged! She started understanding the concept of dynamic bilingualism that was introduced in the workshops. And she started to realize that if she indeed wanted to ensure that her emergent bilingual students performed/did English competently in different academic tasks she would have to let go of the idea of "English" as a "second" or even "new" language. English had to become part of the students' communicative repertoire, not as an add-on, not as second, but as an integral part that was simply theirs.

Once the concept of translanguaging was introduced in the workshops, Principal Hudson struggled. She had started to understand bi/multilingualism, but how was she to understand multilingualism through a translanguaging perspective? She could grasp the idea that her bilingual students used Spanish and English dynamically, that is, responding to the context, the situation, and their audience. But she had always understood bilingualism as simply being English and a language other than English, in the case of her students, mostly Spanish. But now she was being asked to "trans-cend" her understandings of bilingualism by focusing on the "trans." That is, she was asked to understand bilingualism not from the perspective of the named languages, but from the perspective of the children themselves. "What exactly did this mean for her students, her programs for emergent bilinguals, and her curriculum?" Principal Hudson wondered.

Principal Hudson started to understand that the way in which bilingualism was being conceptualized, through a translanguaging lens, meant that all of her instructional programs, whether they were ESL/ENL, TBE, or DLBE, had to leverage the multilingualism of her students. Even in bilingual programs where only two languages of instruction were used, there were students with other languages and many diverse language practices. CUNY–NYSIEB proposed that the first step would be to develop a multilingual ecology for the school. Principal Hudson learned that the visible usage of language in a school said a lot about how a school valued multilingualism.

She had the sudden realization that her school, except for the Dual Language and TBE classroom hallways, was largely an English monolingual environment. In between two workshop sessions, she took a walkthrough around Springdale to analyze the languages that were displayed and used in and around the school. She was amazed and disappointed to see English-only signage in the main entrance, main office, and in the majority of the school's hallways and bulletin boards. Almost 80% of the school's students spoke languages other than English, but they were nowhere to be found in the visible landscape of the school. During this time, Principal Hudson also conducted classroom visits and noticed that the home languages of students were rarely used as resources for instruction and—more disturbingly—that, sometimes, bilingual students were reprimanded for using Spanish during classroom activities in ESL and TBE classrooms, and for using the "wrong" language in DLBE classrooms.

Principal Hudson started coming to terms with the fact that not only her ESL and TBE programs had to leverage bilingualism, but that the structure of her DLBE program had to be made more flexible and to allow for the dynamic and flexible use of languages. How was this to happen?

It was at this point that Principal Hudson decided to share her newfound knowledge with her teachers. She brought in a university-based teacher educator affiliated with the CUNY–NYSIEB project to do a presentation on translanguaging to her full faculty. From her perspective, the presentation had been dynamic and informative, so Principal Hudson expected mostly positive feedback from the teachers. However, this was far from the case. The presentation seemed to resonate with her ENL and bilingual teachers, as some even stayed after the presentation to talk to the presenter. A fourth-grade ENL teacher admitted that she had thought she was doing her students a favor by requiring them to speak only English, but that the presentation had made her rethink this stance. TBE and Dual Language teachers expressed how refreshing it was to hear that using the home language flexibly in strategic ways was actually an effective practice. One kindergarten DLBE teacher admitted that she had been using translanguaging for years, but always felt guilty because of the prevailing notion that you must maintain strict separation of the languages. But some Dual Language bilingual teachers were wary. They wondered how translanguaging could be used strategically to help bilingual students' linguistic performances and identity-building, without destroying the important space for Spanish instruction. "If I let them speak English in my classroom, they will not want to learn or speak in Spanish," argued a third-grade DL teacher.

Principal Hudson's close colleague, a second-grade TBE teacher, informed her that many of the general education teachers did not seem convinced about the concept of translanguaging. From what Principal Hudson could gather, there were many assumptions being made about emergent bilinguals and their families. One 16-year veteran teacher had been heard saying, "They come here and they want to learn English. I don't think the parents want us using Spanish in the classroom." Another had complained that it did not make sense to use home languages since, "They are only going to be tested in English." Another gripe expressed by teachers was the idea that since they were not bilingual themselves, there was no way they could effectively use translanguaging in their classrooms. Thus, many believed that the presentation was not useful for monolingual teachers: "I don't know why we all had to participate in this workshop. This should have been only for the bilingual teachers."

Principal Hudson was disheartened by some of these responses. She knew it pointed to larger issues, including the disconnect between school and home and the undervaluing of the linguistic and cultural resources of her emergent bilingual students. After the full faculty presentation, she decided she needed to address these issues by putting a team of teachers together to deepen their knowledge of translanguaging and using bilingualism as a resource in their instruction. Yet when she presented this opportunity to her faculty, the only ones who volunteered were the bilingual and ENL teachers. Principal Hudson knew that to effect school-wide change, she would need buy-in from her general education teachers and the rest of the school leadership and staff. However, at the moment, she was at a loss as to how to best go about this. How could she get buy-in from the whole school staff?

TEACHING NOTES

Dynamic Bilingualism and Translanguaging

Bilingualism has long been thought of as the use of two separate and bounded language systems. An additive understanding of bilingualism assumes a simple (1+1=2) equation in which a person starts with one language and simply adds another—one that does not relate to or interact with the "first" language. The concept of dynamic bilingualism, which the CUNY–NYSIEB workshops expounded, completely shifts this perspective (García, 2009). Dynamic bilingualism posits that bilinguals can never be two monolinguals in one (Grosjean, 1982) and that their language performances are always the result of using language in different contexts and for various tasks. Thus, it is not a matter of having teachers "add" more to their emergent bilingual students—more vocabulary, more phrases, more texts disconnected from what they already know. Instead, teachers are challenged to teach differently, taking into account the students' full linguistic repertoire, and providing them with the different contexts and tasks that will engage them in "doing" language authentically and meaningfully (García & Li, 2014; Li, 2011).

Translanguaging theory postulates that, from the internal perspective of the bilingual, the speaker does not simply have two named languages, but has one unitary communicative repertoire. This communicative repertoire includes linguistic and multimodal features with which speakers make meaning. Translanguaging posits that for bilinguals this repertoire is not compartmentalized into two discrete linguistic systems. Rather, the linguistic cognition of bilinguals is not dual but unitary (Otheguy, García, & Reid, 2015, 2018).

These theoretical perspectives on dynamic bilingualism have important implications for schools that are interested in better serving their emergent bilingual students and families. One is that the school environment and landscape must reflect the linguistic diversity of the students and families and the ways in which they use language. As described in the case narrative, one way to achieve this is for a school to develop a multilingual school ecology (García & Kleyn, 2016). Another implication is that schools must engage in a process of self-reflection and analysis in order to understand how students' bilingualism is being leveraged (or not) through curriculum, instruction, and programming. For schools that already offer DLBE programs, there must be an awareness that just as students need a space to perform in English and to perform in Spanish in a DLBE program, they also need a space in which they can experience their bilingual performances as unitary and reflective of their *bilingual* identities, and not just a Spanish language identity and an English language identity (Lee, Hill-Bonnet, & Gillispie, 2008; Sánchez, García, & Solorza, 2018).

Collaborative Descriptive Inquiry as a Tool to Engage Entire School Community

The purpose of Collaborative Descriptive Inquiry, which we describe below, is twofold. First, educators' stances about bilingualism are one of the most important shifts that must occur. However, school leaders must not impose this through a top-down approach. Only through being engaged in a collaborative process in which staff have the opportunity to listen to each other generously and gather data collaboratively is there a possibility of shifting their stance toward the students' and the community's multilingualism.

Second, school leaders cannot change school structures or demand pedagogical changes by dictating it so. The Collaborative Descriptive Inquiry process engages educators themselves in acting on their reflections and their new understandings. In this way, transformations in structures and practices can happen organically in distributed and collaborative ways.

The overall purpose of the Collaborative Descriptive Inquiry process is to create a community of learners and agents—teachers and staff curious about their students and their community and the ways in which languages and literacies are used in those communities. Teachers are able to learn deeply and firsthand about the linguistic and cultural resources of their students in order to build lasting relationships and draw on these funds of knowledge in their school and classrooms. Only a curious, committed, and engaged community of educators-as-learners can then effect school transformations that serve well a diverse multilingual community.

One of the first steps toward changing instruction and curriculum for emergent bilinguals is to develop understandings of dynamic bilingualism and translanguaging among staff and faculty. Unless teachers hold a positive stance toward bilingual students' language and cultural practices, as well as their histories, instruction for these students will always remain poor. However, effective school leaders know that they cannot just exert that shift in attitudes simply by declaring it to be so. A distributive school leadership model, in which teachers take leadership roles within the process, is thus necessary (Leithwood, Mascall, & Strauss, 2009; Spillane, 2006), especially to transform schools to work with emergent bilinguals (Ascenzi-Moreno, Hesson, & Menken, 2015). With an understanding that many educators and staff have little experience with bilingualism, the process of Collaborative Descriptive Inquiry offers a productive approach to shifting educators' stances. Collaborative Descriptive Inquiry (García & Ascenzi-Moreno, 2012) is a process derived from the descriptive processes developed by Carini (2000) and Traugh (2000).

TEACHING ACTIVITIES

Steps for Collaborative Descriptive Inquiry

- School leaders or university instructors can use professional development opportunities, weekly staff meetings, or class meetings over a period of at least three to four months to engage groups of students or school staff in reflecting on bilingualism. In this process, everyone must take a turn describing how they have answered a predetermined focusing question, without interruptions. The group selects the chair, whose main role is to listen, keep order, and restate the most important threads in the conversation. After each participant has answered a focusing question, the chair asks whether anyone has any clarifying questions, with others offering responses as directed. Then, there is another round where one-by-one, each person in the group gives a recommendation or shares a reaction. Over time, this builds a collaborative space to acknowledge differences, live with tensions, and alleviate some of them.

- Chairs can then group participants into teams of five to seven people. Ideally, these groups should be diverse across roles (administrator, teacher, staff, parent), teaching experiences (ESL, bilingual, grade level), and language/immigrant background. Because there are generally more monolingual than bilingual personnel in a school, and because families are important stakeholders, there should be a bilingual parent on each team.
- During a preliminary meeting, the team members get to know each other more deeply and select a project to explore over six weeks:
  - Week 1: Choose a project.
  - Weeks 2–4: Conduct Collaborative Descriptive Inquiry sessions about the project; see focusing questions below.
  - Week 5: Reflect on what you have learned and what this means for your school.
  - Week 6: Develop an Action Plan and share it with school leaders.

Focusing Questions for Initial Sessions

1. What has been your experience learning language(s), as well as learning how to read and write? What did you grapple with during those processes?
2. Watch an episode of *Jane the Virgin* or *One Day at a Time*. How are Spanish and English being used? By whom? When? What are you struggling with as you watch these shows?

Focusing Questions for Subsequent Sessions

1. Conduct observations of two different neighborhoods in the school community. Make sure that each neighborhood is diverse socioeconomically, racially, and ethnically. Spend some time on a main street where stores are located. Take pictures of signage in languages other than English. Listen for languages other than English. What languages are represented in the signage and the sounds in the different communities? For what purposes? How are the different languages being used? What does that tell you?

2. Conduct an oral history with four bilingual/multilingual parents. Make sure that one is the im/migrant parent of an emergent bilingual; you may have to ask for assistance with interpretation. Ask them about their experiences with im/migration and multilingualism. Focus on their use of language and literacy in the U.S. and in their particular communities. What do their stories tell you about the function of bilingualism for these families and their communities?

REFERENCES

Ascenzi-Moreno, L., Hesson, S., & Menken, K. (2015). School leadership along the trajectory from monolingual to multilingual. *Language and Education, 30*(3), 197–218.

Carini, P. (2000). Prospect descriptive processes. In M. Himley and P. Carini (Eds.), *From another angle: Children's strengths and school standards. The Prospect Center's descriptive review of the child*, pp. 8–20. New York: Teachers College Press.

García, O. (2009). *Bilingual education in the 21st century: A global perspective.* Malden, MA, and Oxford: Wiley-Blackwell.

García, O., & Ascenzi-Moreno, L. (2012). How to use this translanguaging guide: The collaborative descriptive inquiry process. In C. Celic & K. Seltzer (Eds.), *Translanguaging: A CUNY–NYSIEB guide for educators* (pp.7–10). New York: CUNY-NYSIEB, The Graduate Center, the City University of New York.

García, O., & Kleifgen, J. A. (2010). *Educating emergent bilinguals policies, programs and practices for English Learners.* New York: Teachers College Press.

García, O., & Kleyn, T. (Eds.) (2016). *Translanguaging with multilingual students.* New York and London: Routledge.

García, O., & Li, Wei. (2014). *Translanguaging: Language, bilingualism and education*. London, UK: Palgrave Macmillan Pivot.

Grosjean, F. (1982). *Life with two languages.* Cambridge, MA: Harvard University Press.

Lee, J. S., Hill-Bonnet, L., & Gillispie, J. (2008). Learning in two languages: Interactional spaces for becoming bilingual speakers. *International Journal of Bilingual Education and Bilingualism, 11*(1), 75–94.

Leithwood, K., Mascall, B., & Strauss, T. (Eds.) (2009). *Distributed leadership according to the evidence.* New York: Routledge.

Li, Wei. (2011). Moment analysis and translanguaging space: Discursive construction of identities by multilingual Chinese youth in Britain. *Journal of Pragmatics*, 43, 1222–1235.

Otheguy, R., García, O., & Reid, W. (2015). Clarifying translanguaging and deconstructing named languages: A perspective from linguistics. *Applied Linguistics Review*, 6(3), 281–307.

Otheguy, R., García, O., & Reid, W. (2018). A translanguaging view of the linguistic system of bilinguals. *Applied Linguistics Review*. doi:10.1515/applirev-2018-0020
Sánchez, M. T., García, O., & Solorza, C. (2018). Reframing language allocation policy in dual language bilingual education. *Bilingual Research Journal*, *41*(1), 37–51.
Spillane, J. (2006). *Distributed leadership*. San Francisco, CA: Jossey-Bass.
Traugh, C. (2000). Whole-school inquiry: Values and practice. In M. Himley and P. Carini (Eds.), *From Another Angle: Children's strengths and school standards. The Prospect Center's Descriptive Review of the Child* (pp. 182–198). New York: Teachers College Press.

Chapter 6

Standardized Testing and Mariachi

Dilemmas of a Culturally Sustaining Dual-Language Principal

Sandra Leu Bonanno, Adeli Ynostroza, and Eulogio Alejandre

CONTEXT

Perla Elementary (K-5), an urban charter school located in Utah, was founded in 2014. Here, a recent Senate bill provided funding to develop foreign language skills, spur economic growth, and exponentially expanded a network of dual language schools (Boyle, August, Tabaku, Cole, & Simpson-Baird, 2015). In contrast to the predominantly White, middle-class student population of surrounding Dual Language Immersion (DLI) programs (Valdez, Freire, & Delavan, 2016), Perla Elementary serves approximately 50% of students whose heritage language is Spanish, 50% whose heritage language is English, and overall 95% students identifying as Latinx, a gender-neutral term referencing Latin American cultural identity.

Uniquely operating outside the state network and its funding, the school implements a 90/10 dual-language program in Spanish and English that emphasizes bilingualism and multiculturalism. Most of the students immigrated from Mexico or Central and South America or were born in the United States to first-generation immigrant parents. Approximately 73% of students are enrolled in the free and reduced lunch program, though the principal estimates that a higher percentage come from lower income backgrounds. These numbers fluctuate because numerous families are unwilling to participate in any federally funded food or enrichment programs due to their immigration status. These nuances facing Perla students and their families form a stark comparison to the affluent districts that overwhelmingly house dual-language programs in this state.

CASE NARRATIVE

The beginnings of Perla relied heavily on *hope* and *cope*. José Cervantez, a Mexican-American bilingual male and the principal of Perla Elementary, had always dreamt of a school less constricted by district policies. After working in traditional, public-school systems as a teacher and administrator for 27 years, Cervantez felt that education, and especially dual language immersion programs, needed to be better at sustaining students' cultural and linguistic histories and pluralistic identities. Originally, Mr. Cervantez was hesitant to leave public education. However, when he researched the possibilities for working at a charter school, he was shocked to read that Perla's vision was identical to his own: "I looked and their vision was my vision almost word for word...all Latino kids will be bilingual or biliterate and will be affecting their lives in a positive way...They will be ready...to serve the local and global community."

Cervantez was hired in February 2014 to open Perla Elementary on August 24th, 2014. The school already faced several hurdles even before construction. The principal had only six months to find children, teachers, curriculum in two languages, and effective professional development that would build on the strengths of the community. Furthermore, the original plot the school board had found was allotted for tax-generating businesses, not for non-profit entities. Finding a suitable piece of land for a charter school became a temporary obstacle, but José Cervantez and Perla Elementary's school board were able to persist and *cope* through the challenges by holding onto *hope* for an inclusive learning environment for Latinx communities.

The Fiscal Responsibility of Social Justice

A welcoming symbol in the community, Perla Elementary eventually found its home in a new brightly-colored building that often served as a gathering space for both families and students. As its business manager, in addition to instructional leader and accountability supervisor, Cervantez oversaw the operational budget. Rent for the building was one of the school's greatest financial costs. In its first year, Cervantez had negotiated rent at approximately 45,000 dollars per month. But the amount was set to increase by 3% each year, meaning that their operational budget continued to grow and take away from other funding categories such as curriculum and instructional materials. It became apparent that keeping the vision of student success was not separate from financial stress. In light of the steady increase in interest, Cervantez decided to begin the process of acquiring a loan and purchasing the building to build equity.

Mr. Cervantez and the school board had to act quickly. If they did not obtain a loan within the first four years of opening the school, the building would be appraised at its most current valuation, a two-million-dollar increase. However, numerous banks required a three-year track record of the school's student assessment scores to demonstrate that it would be a reliable investment and should receive a lower interest rate. In theory, if a school applying for a loan had low standardized testing scores, the state could close down the charter; the banks did not want to lose their investment! Thus far, Cervantez had focused on strengthening students' dominant language, Spanish, and creating an inclusive environment through invitational education rather than standardized test scores. However, he recently received a letter from the state warning him that 56% of the school's third-grade students were not meeting the state reading level goals. The stakes were high. If the students did not subsequently meet the English reading proficiency goal, the school would transition to probationary status, lose potential funding, and have difficulty authorizing a loan for future programs.

Cervantez immediately asembled a leadership team and assessed that third-grade students were only one percentage point from reaching the minimum state-wide score. He worried that implementing a targeted tutoring program for testing would objectify students and categorize them based on standardized proficiency levels. He was specifically concerned that an emphasis on standardized assessments contradicted the mission of the school to serve Latinx students and communities by affirming their identities in a safe environment. And yet, the school could not afford an increase in rent that would detract from funds for curricular and extracurricular experiences that centered around *cultura*. How was Perla Elementary to maintain a safe environment for Latinx students while ensuring state funding for all the culturally sustaining curriculum and activities?

The leadership team began by communicating the necessity of standardized testing to all stakeholders while maintaining the critical ideology of their school mission. Not willing to compromise their dedication to bilingualism and biliteracy, they decided to protect the dual-language structure of their day program and supplement tutoring after school. Volunteers from the community offered tutoring sessions for an hour after all extracurricular programs to avoid interfering with students' music, dance, and athletics. To enlist the support of families, the principal clearly emphasized through meetings and memos that the standardized test represented less than 10% of the knowledge and abilities of students. But that students needed to excel in this 10%, just as they did in bilingualism, banda, and the arts, and participating in the tutoring program was a support to better these testing skills.

Surprisingly, parents were in full support and enrollment in the tutoring program was near 100%.

"You're Not Musicians, You're Magicians"

Amidst the pursuit of loans, Perla Elementary continued to cultivate the arts programs, including a mariachi band and modern and *folklórico* dance. These programs were all core components of how the school maintained ties to the community and fostered students' mental and emotional strength. Cervantez framed these programs as opportunities for students to develop a shared story of belief in oneself and to promote an environment of belonging. Cervantez explained that he believed there were components or guidelines that might help serve Latinx communities, but there was no perfect recipe or scripted curriculum. "We don't think we are saving kids," he conveyed, "we are creating a space where they can feel it's theirs."

Notably, the mariachi band was not only for the Mexican-American student population but also intended to appeal to all students. For example, the music teacher invited parents to send songs from their home country such as Colombia, Japan, and Venezuela. Cervantez and his staff were deliberately shaping cultural traditions to be more inclusive opportunities for all the students. Through this cultural synergy, Cervantez expressed, "You create magic. You create hope and you create pride."

Giselle, an upper-grade student enrolled at Perla, was an example of this magic. Giselle frequently struggled with standardized testing. Teachers at Perla were adamant that Giselle was meeting grade-level requirements, but each year standardized testing made her feel anxious. In her panic, the stress would cause Giselle's neck to be covered in red blotches; her nervousness brought an inability to concentrate. More recently, Giselle was encouraged to enroll in the mariachi band and fell in love with the trumpet. One day, the mariachi teacher asked Mr. Cervantez to join one of their weekday practices in the hallways. As Giselle began to play with immense pride and passion, the principal and other onlookers nearby were floored and some had tears in their eyes.

Giselle had become an integral part of the mariachi band and her self-efficacy had grown, especially when playing for crowds as large as 20,000 people. Mr. Cervantez recalled, "When you see this group of kids, they stand taller when they blow the trumpet." Giselle became one of the best trumpet players in the mariachi band and she knew it. She felt it. This time, during the state standardized test, Cervantez logged into the system to monitor student scores. Giselle had scored proficient in all tests; Giselle's confidence in herself and her abilities had translated to her academic performance.

"Worth 6.25%"

Altogether, the third-grade students had surpassed the state proficiency goals by 20% in their reading scores. Now, in their fourth year of operation, Cervantez submitted a cumulative overview of the students' standardized scores that spanned over three years to determine the overall interest rate. Based on the continual growth in student scores, and subsequent projections, the bank agreed to a 6.25% interest rate for the next five years. The contract also included an arrangement to potentially renegotiate the rate based on subsequent review of the students' standardized test scores.

In framing standardized testing, Mr. Cervantez adopted a similar approach to the one adopted for cultivating the school-wide culture. When the horns and trumpets of the mariachi resounded, students took pride in their culture and selves. Cervantez fervently believed that the self-efficacious attitudes on stage can also translate off stage. When "the kids...know they can create Magic—why can't they take a test?" expressed Cervantez. He underscored that the students' ability to be their best selves translates to multiple aspects of their performance and academic endeavors.

TEACHING NOTES

Context of Standardized Testing and Bilingual Education

Under No Child Left Behind (NCLB) and now the Every Student Succeeds Act (ESSA), there have been and continue to be tensions between the goals of bilingual education and federal accountability measures. Bilingual and bicultural student outcomes can be difficult to realize when DLI schools are held to stringent and time-sensitive standardized achievement measurements (Palmer, Henderson, Wall, Zúñiga, & Berthelsen, 2016). Mandated accountability measures such as NCLB and ESSA have placed higher pressure on schools with larger populations of emergent bilinguals to meet testing proficiency in English, which has inadvertently led to the dissolution of numerous bilingual programs (Abedi, 2004; Menken, 2006). Because of the high stakes linked to student scores, some schools have also narrowed their curriculum and instruction for these populations by aligning them to the test and de-emphasizing higher order learning (Cammarota & Romero, 2009; Wright, 2002). This unintended effect of school accountability has created a disadvantageous environment for principals leading bilingual schools. Those that continue to build and sustain DLI programs, such as Mr. Cervantez, must be sensitive to both external financial and accountability pressures as well as their mission to sustain students' cultures and languages.

Understanding leadership approaches that attempt to balance standardized achievement and social justice initiatives is crucial because Achinstein and Ogawa (2011) found that teachers who resisted alone against inequitable testing policies often experienced professional isolation. Therefore, under leadership dedicated to implementing more socially just policies, teachers and leaders alike are able to collaboratively provide equity-oriented academic access for underserved students. This case study focused on a leadership perspective that emphasized "both and" by raising academic achievement indicators through a culture and climate that actively sustained students' identities. Here, "both and" signifies that students are able to access traditional routes of academic excellence while still having the skills to critique the system itself and simultaneously cultivate a strong and healthy concept of self-worth (Bucholtz, Casillas, & Lee, 2017).

Culturally Sustaining School Leadership (CSSL)

A culturally sustaining approach is a central component of leadership for social justice (Brooks & Miles, 2010; Cooper, 2009). Such approaches develop a culture of achievement for immigrant communities by encompassing more than just indicators of standardized testing. In the case study, Cervantez drew from culturally sustaining pedagogies (CSP; Paris & Alim, 2014) in order to emphasize both academic rigor and healthy student identities as educational outcomes. Based in culturally relevant (Ladson-Billings, 1995) and responsive pedagogies (Gay, 2000), CSP moves beyond leveraging students' culture to meet traditional academic standards; rather, this theoretical shift adopts a decolonized approach where academic excellence is redefined as simultaneously sustaining identities of students of Color and providing them educational access (Paris & Alim, 2017). Building upon the cultural focus of culturally sustaining pedagogies and an equity orientation from social justice leadership, culturally sustaining school leadership does the following: 1) challenges the rigid framing of students' identities, 2) underscores leadership decisions that promote multilingualism and multiculturalism, and 3) adopts a critical consciousness that spans across cultures (Larson & Murtadha, 2002; Paris, 2012). In the case study, the principal of Perla Elementary encountered numerous hurdles to enacting a culturally sustaining school for immigrant populations. Especially within the first years of development, he negotiated a balance between the tenets of CSSL and meeting external school requirements in his decision-making.

First, leaders who utilize a CSSL approach recognize the multifaceted nature of student identity, including culture and language, knowledge worthy of sustaining in the whole school culture (Paris, 2012). Under this framework, leaders understand that students' identities and ways of knowing are influenced by both heritage and evolving community practices and draw from both in order to create a sense of belonging so that students feel more competent, motivated, and connected to a school's culture (Osterman, 2000; Scanlan & López, 2014). In this case study, the school leader avoided utilizing a set language, curriculum, and instruction to serve the students. Mr. Cervantez emphasized that "we can't tell them what culture is." For immigrant populations specifically, culturally sustaining principals recognize the progressively complex nature of how students see themselves between or amongst cultures and incorporate that complexity into building school culture. In practice, schooling should be contextually bound and based on the lived experiences of students (Irizarry, 2007), which requires a school leader to reevaluate and reenvision each academic year based on the evolving student populations.

Second, culturally sustaining school leaders understand that, in America's increasingly interconnected society, the ability to relate and communicate across communities and identities is a valuable skill set that deserves to be cultivated in schools (Paris & Alim, 2014). For Perla Elementary, bilingualism and biliteracy are foundational values to the mission of the school which also guide managerial and financial leadership decisions. Immigrant students' multilingual and multicultural abilities are sustained and carry equal organizational weighting to that of national learning standards. Students are also encouraged to have tools and skill sets to thrive across and within both worlds, languages, and still challenge dominant norms. These critical skills support students in simultaneously achieving institutional access and practicing counter-hegemonic activism.

Finally, CSSL necessitates that leaders develop an awareness of societal injustice and foster this awareness or critical consciousness amongst all community members (Brown, 2004). For example, Cervantez challenged the normalized emphasis on standardized testing and its labels such as "proficient" and "not proficient" that affected students' self-image. In practice, he carried out this organizational belief by also evaluating cultural indicators of student success and hiring teachers who wholeheartedly believed that students are more than their score on a test. Under CSSL, principals promote critical consciousness amongst school communities and challenge stakeholders to inwardly reflect and act against educational or cultural practices that reify genderism, sexism, ableism, and other oppressions.

These three CSSL tenets are useful guidelines for leaders operating within traditional systems of schooling and acting as social justice advocates for immigrant populations. As school leaders balance external mandates within their own school vision, often commitment to meeting accountability or district standards must be weighed against the school goals of the local community. Many of the dilemmas faced by school leaders such as Cervantez are indicative of the ethical decision making necessary to provide students the tools to develop a healthy identity and a critical lens as well as access to institutional power. From a CSSL perspective, this case study explores how both initiatives can be achieved so long as students are engaged in critical conversations about power, race, and language as they continue to strive within colonized academic systems.

DISCUSSION QUESTIONS

1. In addition to test scores, what other indicators did Mr. Cervantez and the staff at Perla Elementary use to gauge school and student success?
2. In your institution, how is standardized testing currently framed to teachers, students, and their families?
3. Mr. Cervantez acknowledged how complex student identity can be and avoided prescriptive curriculum or instruction. How do you, as a school leader, invite student voice in the school's academics and climate?
4. There were numerous financial hurdles to establishing Perla Elementary. How did Mr. Cervantez meet the budgetary demands and simultaneously foster a culturally sustaining school vision?

TEACHING ACTIVITIES

1. Analyze or write a letter of communication to families and students about standardized testing, carefully considering the wording of the notice. Think about: What is the narrative that you want the surrounding community to believe and value in academics?
2. Cervantez utilized multiple indicators for student success, including standardized testing, school climate surveys, and students' understanding of cultural selves. Take a look at how a local school evaluates success and imagine additional data points that foster holistic student growth.

3. In reviewing a local school's budget and master schedule, think about how resources such as time and finance are allocated. What tasks, events, and instructional periods are given the most weight and resources? What does that say about what this school values most?

REFERENCES

Abedi, J. (2004). The No Child Left Behind act and English language learners: Assessment and accountability issues. *Educational Researcher*, *33*(1), 4–14.

Achinstein, B., & Ogawa, R. T. (2011). *Change(d) agents: New teachers of color in urban schools*. New York: Teachers College Press.

Boyle, A., August, D., Tabaku, L., Cole, S., & Simpson-Baird, A. (2015). *Dual language education programs: Current state policies and practices*. Washington, DC: American Institutes for Research.

Brooks, J. S., & Miles, M. T. (2010). Educational leadership and the shaping of school culture: Classic concepts and cutting-edge possibilities. In Horsford, S. (Ed.), *New perspectives in educational leadership: Exploring social, political, and community contexts and meaning* (pp. 7–28). New York: Peter Lang.

Brown, G. T. (2004). Teachers' conceptions of assessment: Implications for policy and professional development. *Assessment in Education: Principles, Policy & Practice*, *11*(3), 301–318.

Bucholtz, M., Casillas, D. I., & Lee, J. S. (2017). Language and culture as sustenance. In D. Paris & H. S. Alim (Eds.), *Culturally sustaining pedagogies: Teaching and learning for justice in a changing world* (pp. 43–60). New York: Teachers College Press.

Cammarota, J., & Romero, A. F. (2009). A social justice epistemology and pedagogy for Latina/o students: Transforming public education with participatory action research. *New Directions for Student Leadership*, 123, 53–65.

Cooper, C. W. (2009). Performing cultural work in demographically changing schools: Implications for expanding transformative leadership frameworks. *Educational Administration Quarterly*, *45*(5), 694–724.

Gay, G. (2000). *Culturally responsive teaching: Theory, practice and research*. New York: Teachers College Press.

Irizarry, J. G. (2007). Ethnic and urban intersections in the classroom: Latino students, hybrid identities, and culturally responsive pedagogy. *Multicultural Perspectives*, *9*(3), 21–28.

Ladson-Billings, G. (1995). Toward a theory of culturally relevant pedagogy. *American Educational Research Journal*, *32*(3), 465–491.

Larson, C. L., & Murtadha, K. (2002). Leadership for social justice. *Yearbook of the National Society for the Study of Education*, *101*(1), 134–161.

Menken, K. (2006). Teaching to the test: How No Child Left Behind impacts language policy, curriculum, and instruction for English language learners. *Bilingual Research Journal*, *30*(2), 521–546.

Osterman, K. F. (2000). Students' need for belonging in the school community. *Review of Educational Research*, *70*(3), 323–367.

Palmer, D., Henderson, K., Wall, D., Zúñiga, C. E., & Berthelsen, S. (2016). Team teaching among mixed messages: Implementing two-way dual language bilingual education at third grade in Texas. *Language Policy*, *15*(4), 393–413.
Paris, D. (2012). Culturally sustaining pedagogy: A needed change in stance, terminology, and practice. *Educational Researcher*, *41*(3), 93–97.
Paris, D., & Alim, H. S. (2014). What are we seeking to sustain through culturally sustaining pedagogy? A loving critique forward. *Harvard Educational Review*, *84*(1), 85–100.
Paris, D., & Alim, H. S. (Eds.). (2017). *Culturally sustaining pedagogies: Teaching and learning for justice in a changing world*. New York: Teachers College Press.
Scanlan, M., & López, F. A. (2014). *Leadership for culturally and linguistically responsive schools*. New York: Routledge.
Valdez, V. E., Freire, J. A., & Delavan, M. G. (2016). The gentrification of dual language education. *Urban Review*, *48*(4), 601–627.
Wright, W. (2002). The effects of high stakes testing on an inner-city elementary school: The curriculum, the teachers, and the English language learners. *Current Issues in Education*, *5*(5), 1–23.

Chapter 7

When ICE Came to Town

Separating Families and Disrupting Educational Trajectories

Liliana E. Castrellón, Alonso R. Reyna Rivarola, and Gerardo R. López

INTRODUCTION

To understand the current political climate affecting undocumented immigrants in the United States, it is important to outline how and why immigration became a critical issue within our contemporary political discourse. Although immigration has been a contentious topic since the early waves of European immigration, it took a unique tone in the mid-1990s, when California voters passed Proposition 187: a state ballot initiative that prohibited non-U.S. citizens from accessing social, health, education, and other services in the state. Until then, immigration was largely seen as a federal concern and state-level interventions were atypical (Pabón López & López, 2009). Over time California voters passed two other ballot initiatives, and similar anti-immigrant, anti-Latinx[1] "copycat" laws were afoot in the states of Washington, Arizona, Florida, and Oregon (Quiroga, 1995).

Adding more fuel to the anti-immigrant fire, the 2001 attacks on the World Trade Center ignited a tremendous backlash against cultural and religious others, and set off a national discourse focused on securing the borders from possible foreign invaders. Indeed, the 9/11 attacks reinforced the belief that the borders were porous and that more resources were necessary to crack down on immigration. After these terrorist attacks, the country's attention focused on the border as a national security concern (USA Patriot Act, 2001).

As images of a broken border proliferated in the media, a dangerous slippage and elision was taking shape in the popular discourse:

that terrorists could easily enter the country in much the same way as immigrants from Latin America. The sense of fear, vulnerability, and panic—coupled with the problematic union of the "undocumented" and "terrorist" tropes—led to a rise in anti-immigrant legislation at both the federal and state levels (Santa Ana, 2002). The rise in "287(g) Agreements," which deputized state and local law officials to enforce federal immigration laws, unleashed a wave of local immigration sweeps and targeted enforcement practices across the nation (Olivas, 2012). By 2005, anti-immigration sentiment in the U.S. was widespread, often parading under the banner of "national security" (American Civil Liberties Union [ACLU], 2018). Although federal legislators tried to pass draconian immigration bills, such as the Border Protection, Anti-terrorism, and Illegal Immigration Control Act of 2005 (H.R. 4437), they largely failed due to significant pushback from pro-immigration and advocacy groups across the country (Engler & Engler, 2016).

Soon thereafter, the stock market crash of 2008 reinvigorated the immigration debate, and there was a renewed push from states to clamp down on the perceived immigration "problem." Arizona's anti-immigration bill Support Our Law Enforcement and Safe Neighborhoods Act, popularly known as S.B. 1070, sparked a new round of anti-immigration "copycat" laws in Georgia, Indiana, Alabama, Utah, and South Carolina (National Immigration Law Center, 2014).

After the election of President Barack Obama in 2008, the number of undocumented people who were identified and deported topped 400,000 in 2012 alone, despite the fact that Obama's deportation efforts explicitly targeted criminals and individuals who were known national security threats (Rosenblum & Meissner, 2014). While the number of deportations declined in the last three years of the Obama administration, the election of Donald J. Trump in 2016 unleashed an anti-immigrant fervor throughout the country. Trump not only launched his campaign on an anti-immigrant/anti-Latinx platform—referring to Mexican immigrants as criminals, drug dealers, and rapists (White House, 2018)—but he also kept up his anti-immigrant rhetoric by referring to certain immigrants as dangerous and even "animals" (Davis, 2018).

Adding to this anti-immigrant political climate is the sharp increase in Immigration and Customs Enforcement (ICE) raids since Trump entered office. In fact, Trump's chief of the ICE division actually promised a quadrupling of workplace crackdowns at a 2017 press conference (Kopan, 2017). Unfortunately, his promise came true, as this country witnessed an increase in large-scale ICE crackdowns in cities across the U.S. following his announcement (Kopan, 2018). This increase in workplace raids has placed enhanced demands on schools, as students whose families are at risk of detention and deportation must wrestle with the psychological and emotional toll of being separated from their families in this manner.

CONTEXT

This case study takes place in the Jordan River neighborhood, which is located in a mid-sized city in the Wasatch Front in the Rocky Mountain West. The economic boom of the 1990s led to unprecedented demographic shifts in the ethnic and racial compositions of Jordan River (Perlich, 2004). The demand for developing infrastructure during the 2002 Winter Olympics served as a catalyst for incentivizing people from Mexico, Central, and South America to migrate north to fill jobs the local workforce could not fill (Perlich, 2004). Additionally, Jordan River is home to one of the largest populations of Pacific Islanders outside of Oceania, as well as a significant population of people of refugee background from Southeast Asia and West Africa, among other regions in the world, who have resettled in the state of Utah. The ethnic and racial demographic shifts since the 1990s in the Jordan River community have impacted the vibrancy of diversity in its neighborhood and schools.

Jordan River Neighborhood Schools

The vast majority of students in Jordan River attend one of five neighborhood schools. The feeder public high school for Jordan River students is located five miles away in a predominantly White suburban area. Jordan River neighborhood students who attend the public high school must commute not only far away from home, but also to a neighborhood that is not reflective of the demographic makeup of their own community. The four public K-8 schools and feeder public high school, the administration, and the teachers all have a similar demographic makeup, which is not reflective of the student demographics at each of the schools or the overall Jordan River neighborhood. However, the school district has institutionalized community learning centers (CLCs), particularly in Title I schools that serve predominantly communities of color, to offer during-and-after-school full cycle programming and services for children, youth, young adults, adults, and the elderly. The undocumented immigrant community of Jordan River is primarily comprised of three racial/ethnic populations: Latinx, Pacific Islander, and Asian. It is clear the Jordan River neighborhood is a very diverse community, which is one of the reasons it was targeted by ICE raids multiple times over the past ten years.

CASE NARRATIVE

To capture the vast complexity and impact of ICE raids on our students, schools, and communities, the narratives below illustrate multiple interconnected storylines to provide us with a macro-level snapshot of events. Weaving together these narratives, we aim to present a more nuanced account of one story from different vantage points to better understand how this scenario unfolded for the communities involved.

School Leadership

Principal Johnson. Rosemarie Hunter High School (RHHS) has recently become a minority-majority school, and Principal Johnson knows students are falling through the cracks, despite a string of recommendations and best-practices from the district. As she brainstorms next steps, a CLC liaison and parent, Señora García, walks into her office. "Principal Johnson!" she exclaims. "There has been an ICE raid! LOOK!" Señora García hands Principal Johnson her phone to show her social media alerts and updates from local non-profit organizations. While ICE raids have happened in the past, the community was not prepared for something of this magnitude. Unsure of how to respond, yet knowing that many students at RHHS have family members who work at the raided meat-processing plant, Principal Johnson begins collecting as much information as she can to inform teachers and students of the unfolding event and plan of action. She asks Señora García to call another local non-profit to find out more information and what her school can do to support students and families, while she proceeds to call the school district lawyers for guidance and specific protocols. Realizing the end of the school day is fast approaching, and not hearing back from the district, Principal Johnson calls an urgent, yet voluntary, after-school faculty meeting.

Ms. Romero. Ms. Romero is watching the clock as she is finishing her AP Physics lecture. She is thinking about winter break, which is around the corner, and she is just as anxious as the students for a break when she notices students in the class have their phones out and are speaking to one another. Annoyed, she calls for the attention of the distracted students and quickly realizes that students are worried and putting away their items ready to leave. "What's going on?" she asks, but no one responds to her question. The bell rings and the students rush out. After the students clear the classroom, Principal Johnson makes an announcement over the intercom: "Teachers, this is Principal Johnson. I am calling a faculty meeting in the library at

2:40 PM. You are not required to attend, but the nature of this meeting is of utmost importance. We appreciate your participation. Thank you."

The meeting. Principal Johnson frantically paces back and forth while teachers enter the library. As the teachers file in, some are speculating about the nature of the meeting, while others are discussing the strange behavior of their students. Principal Johnson announces that there has been an ICE raid at a local meatpacking plant where many family members of RHHS students work. Immediately, teachers begin asking questions: "Do we know if any of our parents were detained?" "What are we supposed to do?" "Can ICE come to the school?"

Principal Johnson did not have many answers. However, she elaborates on what teachers should expect: 1) a decline in attendance; 2) students' distrust of government officials, including teachers; 3) psychological and emotional stress among students; and 4) offensive language and targeted bullying toward students of immigrant and refugee backgrounds.

Since the 2016 presidential election, targeted racialized bullying has become a problem at RHHS. Although a diverse community, the larger surrounding area is predominantly White and local residents still harbor anti-immigrant ideologies. For example, some students with immigrant backgrounds have been targeted with "build the wall" taunts and posters, and have been victims of other racial microaggressions[2], even on school grounds.

Despite these incidents, Principal Johnson never imagined that in her own school neighborhood an ICE raid of this magnitude could happen. Before ending the meeting, Principal Johnson leaves teachers with information about several community agencies that could help families. She added that she is currently working with Señora García to learn more information and will disseminate this information as soon as it becomes available.

The next couple of days. As Principal Johnson predicted, school attendance dropped following the ICE raid. Among the missing is a sizeable number of Latinx, Asian American, and Pacific Islander students. During the lunch break, the teachers' lounge is abuzz: "Did you hear about Raúl's parents?" "What about Kehaulani's sister?"

Ms. Romero ignores the chatter, her thoughts still on the students running out of her class the previous day. Like most of her colleagues, Ms. Romero felt powerless. Nothing in her teacher preparation program has prepared her for such an incident. When the last school period arrives, the majority of the seats are empty in her class. Unsure of how to address the matter with the few remaining students in the class, Ms. Romero decides to stick to her curriculum.

After a few days, students return to class. Abel, a Latinx student, seems distant, which is unlike him. After class she asks him, "Abel, how are things going for you? I noticed that you are not coming to class every day and are not as engaged as you normally are. I also know about what happened last week. How can I support you?" "I don't know," he replied. Ms. Romero waited a little longer for Abel to elaborate. His face then turned red and his eyes began to water. "You can't support me, Miss! I have to quit school to take care of my family," he says and runs out the door. Shocked, she yells, "Abel!" But he ignores her.

Abel was not the only student who had not attended school the final week before break. Ms. Romero wonders if students would return in January. She walks into Principal Johnson's office to express her interaction with Abel.

Student Experiences

Abel. "Beep, beep..." 18-year-old high school senior Abel turns off his phone alarm, glaring at the 5:15 AM wake up call. As usual, his parents had already left for work and he has to get his younger siblings ready for school. He finishes his homework while making breakfast for the children. At 6:45 AM he wakes up his 12-year-old and seven-year-old siblings, gets them ready, walks them to school, and speed walks to RHHS. He cannot afford another tardy.

As the end of the school day nears, Abel thinks about the events planned for tonight; it is December 12, *Día de La Virgen de Guadalupe.*[3] and his church planned a celebration. As he waits for the school bell to ring, he receives non-stop notifications on his phone. He tries to ignore them until he observes the panic sweeping the classroom. He pulls out his phone and finds multiple warnings: ICE has been spotted in town. He scrolls through the thread of text messages and alerts, and sees a local non-profit tweet: *Confirmed—ICE RAID in Jordan River Meatpacking Plant, 70 people detained.* In the distance, he hears his teacher, Ms. Romero, ask, "Class, what's going on?" However, rather than responding to Ms. Romero, Abel is thinking about his parents who were on shift that day. The bell rings and Abel rushes out to pick up his siblings and make sure his family is safe.

> "Abel, why are we going so fast?!" asks seven-year-old Azucena.
> "I heard *la migra* is here, is that true?" 12-year-old Arturo inquires.
> "Where are *mami y papi*?" Azucena whimpers.

Abel hears them, but cannot provide answers. He has not yet received a single call or text message from his parents, and they are not home when Abel and his siblings arrive. His thoughts are interrupted by his phone ringing. He frantically answers, hoping it is his parents. But it is his cousin Esperanza, whose parents also work at the plant. Crying, she explains that her mother just arrived home; Tía Francisca was able to get away as ICE detained many other employees, including her father and Abel's parents. Shaken, he hangs up the phone, glaring at his younger siblings. *I need to find out if my parents are OK. I need to take care of the kids. I need to work. I cannot let them separate my family even more.*

Abel does not currently have a job. He is in school full-time with hopes of going to college. His parents asked that he focus on school and help with his younger siblings. Now, Abel knows he has to step up as a guardian and has to find at least a temporary retail holiday position to afford daily living expenses for the family. Fortunately, Abel is DACAmented[4], which affords him a temporary deferment from deportation and a work permit.

The next day, Abel and his siblings do not go to school. Instead, they spend the day waiting for a call from their parents that never comes. Abel thinks about stories of Child Protection Services (CPS) separating mixed-status families; he knows his younger siblings are U.S. citizens, and he is not. His goal is to make sure CPS does not further separate his family. Being 18 years old, he is of age to find a full-time job. However, he faces a conundrum: he wants to go to college but he needs to care for his siblings now. Throughout the day, he and Esperanza talk with friends from RHHS, many of whom also stayed home as they waited to hear from loved ones and were scared that ICE may still be out there.

Later that week. One week has passed and all Abel knows is that his parents and uncle are being held in an ICE detention center in a neighboring state. The children have returned to school, yet all of them are having a hard time concentrating. Azucena cries whenever her brothers leave her, Arturo keeps getting into trouble, and Abel cannot maintain his focus.

Ms. Romero mentions to Abel that she has heard about the raid and since that day has noticed that he has been checked out. "How could I support you?" she asks. "I don't know" he responds. "You can't support me. I have to quit school to take care of my family." The rest of the exchange with Ms. Romero seems like a blur. Overwhelmed, he storms out of the classroom.

While walking the children to school on their first day back, Arturo mentions, "You know *mami y papi* wouldn't want you to quit school, right?" Abel responds, "I know. But I have to make the decision that is best for us now." As Abel walks home, he sees an email alert from the University of Jordan River, with the subject line *Admissions Decision*. The email reads: "Congratulations Abel! You have been granted early admission to University of Jordan River Honors College!"

TEACHING NOTES

Plyler v. Doe and the Equal Protection Clause

It is popularly believed that the 1982 Supreme Court decision in *Plyler v. Doe* gave undocumented children the "right" to go to school. This is an inaccurate reading of the court case because education in the U.S. is not a fundamental "right" but a privilege that is afforded to students by each state within our Union (*San Antonio Independent School District v. Rodriguez*, 1973). Rather, the Supreme Court decided that undocumented children are guaranteed a free public education and cannot be treated differently than their U.S. citizen and/or documented non-citizen counterparts (Pabón López & López, 2009).

The Plyler case focused on a student fee that was imposed on undocumented students for attending schools in the Tyler Independent School District (TISD) in Texas in 1977. The Mexican American Legal Defense and Educational Fund (MALDEF) filed a class action suit on behalf of 16 undocumented students, arguing that the TISD fee violated the Equal Protection Clause of the U.S. Constitution (Olivas, 2012). In this regard, the lower court case was not about education, per se, but about treating one "class" of students differently from another class or group. The case was eventually decided in favor of the plaintiffs and appealed to the U.S. Supreme Court along with another consolidated lower court case. Although the Supreme Court justices overhearing the case did debate whether education was a fundamental right that should be afforded to all students regardless of their background, they stopped short of drawing this conclusion, deciding instead that restricting educational opportunities to a population that was in this country "through no fault of their own" was a surefire way to create a permanent underclass in this country (*Plyler v. Doe*, 1982).

The Plyler case is truly groundbreaking because the Supreme Court found that undocumented students are protected under the Equal Protection Clause of the Fourteenth Amendment (Olivas, 2012). This was the first time in U.S. history when a court formally acknowledged the Equal Protection rights of undocumented individuals under the U.S. Constitution (Olivas, 2012; Pabón López & López, 2009).

Equal Protection Means Equal Protection

As a result of the Plyler decision, school officials must play a critical role in ensuring that undocumented students have the same opportunities to learn as any other student. Undocumented students cannot be treated differently because of their citizenship status (Pabón López & López, 2009). Schools must ensure that students attend schools free from the fear of deportation, and where there is not a "chilling" climate with respect to their undocumented status (U.S. Department of Justice & U.S. Department of Education, 2014). Moreover, students should generally not be asked—either in person or on paper—whether or not they are U.S. citizens and/or be required to show "proof" of their citizenship status by the school, as this can have a chilling effect on undocumented students and families (Borkowski & Soronen, 2009).

Therefore, school officials must play a critical role in ensuring students feel safe while at school. This means monitoring for the presence of immigration officials at or near the school's boundaries, while also ensuring that their presence on school premises only happens with the proper warrant and under close scrutiny. The Department of Homeland Security has a history of respecting schools and churches as "sensitive locations," and schools officials must ensure that immigration enforcement officials do not intervene with the day-to-day functioning of schools (Pabón López & López, 2009). This means respecting the physical boundaries of the school, as well as the walking routes that children and parents take to perform typical school functions (e.g., dropping off/picking up children, back to school nights, school performances, parent–teacher conferences, etc.).

Should an ICE agent, or a deputized officer, arrive at school during school hours, the principal or ranking administrator should inspect the warrant carefully to ensure that it is an official judicial arrest warrant signed by a judge of the court. If there is no judicial warrant, or if there is not an active pursuit underway which requires the officer to cross into school boundaries, it may be permissible to ask the officer to leave and return once a proper warrant has been issued (American Civil Liberties Union [ACLU], 2017). School officials are not required to affirmatively assist federal immigration authorities or their deputized local officers if they do not have a judicial warrant to enter the school. The principal's duty is to maintain a calm and orderly demeanor, and ensure that the presence of the officer does not cause a chilling effect on other students or a substantial disruption of the school environment (Borkowski & Soronen, 2009).

If an ICE agent or deputized officer arrives at a school event during non-school hours, such as a PTA meeting or sporting event, the lead administrator should always ask for a search warrant from the officer. All parents and students should know that it is their right not to answer questions if they are approached by ICE enforcement officials, and that they have a right to an attorney should they be picked up by the officers. Parents and students should be reminded to never lie to officers under any circumstance or provide agents with false documents. School officials cannot stop a lawful investigation, but they do have a duty to inquire whether the active investigation is lawful, as well as the responsibility to ensure that all students and parents feel safe while at the school.

Under no circumstances should a child—or any school information pertaining to that child—be turned over to immigration law enforcement agents without consulting school attorneys. Students have a right to privacy under FERPA (Family Educational Rights and Privacy Act, 20 USC 1232g), and a failure to protect a student's privacy rights may subject the school to legal liability under the law. Such practices should be made part of the formal policy of the school and distributed to stakeholders.

TEACHING ACTIVITIES

1. It is important to be prepared for a potential ICE raid in school communities, and know what resources are available—both at the school and in the community—that can assist impacted students with social, legal, economic, psychological, and spiritual support. One activity is to perform a resource "treasure hunt" at a local school, identifying organizations, support groups, non-government, and legal assistance organizations that can assist students, should an ICE raid happen in the community. Once organizations have been identified, create an action plan—such as a phone tree or "group text"—so that organizations can effectively communicate and disseminate information during times of crisis.
2. In small groups or individually, find out who are the attorneys for your current or local school district, and encourage the district to host professional development for building leaders specifically focused on the unique needs of undocumented and DACAmented students. This information should be readily available from the district and disseminated widely to all schools. If such information does not currently exist, do a "reconnaissance" of information and/or policies that do exist, and then discuss these findings with school attorneys to identify whether the existing information is still current.
3. Read, review, and/or listen (www.oyez.org/cases/1981/80-1538) to the *Plyler v. Doe* case and explore the legal thinking of the Supreme Court Justices in the case, particularly around the idea of "Equal Protection." Discuss what this term means—legally, practically, ethically, and politically—and its implications for working with and supporting undocumented students at schools and as they transition to postsecondary settings.

4. Educators must understand how language shapes and frames perceptions surrounding immigration. For example, if immigration is framed in terms of "legal" and "illegal" activity, this shapes how people understand both the causes and solutions to address a "problem." In this activity, please break into groups and brainstorm the various connotations of the term "illegal." Then read Lakoff and Ferguson's (2006) *The Framing of Immigration* and discuss how the term "illegal" shapes your understanding surrounding this phenomenon. Finally, discuss why certain activities, such as driving over the speed limit, making multiple copies of copyrighted materials, or using commercial software that has not been paid for, are rarely framed in terms of "illegality," although they are examples of breaking the law.

NOTES

1 According to Salinas and Lozano (2017), the "term *Latinx* emerged recently as a gender-neutral label for Latino/a and Latin@" (p. 1). This term makes space for incorporating Latinx individuals who span the gender spectrum—including, but not limited to, individuals of queer and trans* experience.

2 Racial microaggressions are subtle verbal and non-verbal insults/assaults directed at people of color. They can be layered based on race, phenotype, immigration status, language, accent, name, gender, class, or sexuality. These subtle insults/assaults could have a profound effect on the lived experiences of people of color (Kohli & Solórzano, 2012).

3 The Day of the Virgin of Guadalupe is a day of celebration for the Virgen de Guadalupe who is the Mexican patron saint.

4 Nienhusser, Vega, and Saavedra Carquín (2015) define DACAmented as beneficiaries of Deferred Action for Childhood Arrivals. DACA permits a temporary reprieve from deportation, and permission to work legally in the U.S.

REFERENCES

American Civil Liberties Union. (2017). FAQ for educators on immigrant students in public schools. Retrieved from: www.aclu.org/sites/default/files/field_document/2017-11-16_faq_for_educators_immigrants_final_with_logo.pdf

American Civil Liberties Union. (2018). How the USA-Patriot Act expands law enforcement "sneak and peek" warrants. Retrieved from: www.aclu.org/other/how-usa-patriot-act-expands-law-enforcement-sneak-and-peek-warrants

Borkowski, J. W., & Soronen, L. E. (2009). Legal issues for school districts related to the education of undocumented children. Retrieved from: https://cdn-files.nsba.org/s3fs-public/reports/Undocumented-Children.pdf?z7FPI9ZVydzCAmZq1GgB_mDWu9Z.jIvX

Davis, J. H. (2018, May 16). Trump calls some unauthorized immigrants "animals" in rant. *New York Times*. Retrieved from: www.nytimes.com/2018/05/16/us/politics/trump-undocumented-immigrants-animals.html

Engler, M., & Engler, P. (2016, March 4). The massive immigrant-rights protests of 2006 are still changing politics. *Los Angeles Times*. Retrieved from: www.latimes.com/opinion/op-ed/la-oe-0306-engler-immigration-protests-2006-20160306-story.html

Kohli, R., & Solórzano, D. G. (2012). Teachers, please learn our names! Racial microaggressions and the K-12 classroom. *Race Ethnicity and Education*, *15*(4), 441–462.

Kopan, T. (2017). ICE chief pledges quadrupling or more of workplace crackdowns. CNN. Retrieved from: www.cnn.com/2017/10/17/politics/ice-crackdown-workplaces/index.html

Kopan, T. (2018, March 2). How Trump changed the rules to arrest more non-criminal immigrants. CNN. Retrieved from: www.cnn.com/2018/03/02/politics/ice-immigration-deportations/index.html

Lakoff, G., & Ferguson, S. (2006). The framing of immigration. Rockridge Institute. Retrieved from: https://escholarship.org/uc/item/0j89f85g

National Immigration Law Center. (2014). SB 1070 four years later: Lessons learned. Retrieved from: www.nilc.org/issues/immigration-enforcement/sb-1070-lessons-learned/

Nienhusser, K. H., Vega, B. E., Saavedra Carquín, M. (2015). Bridging the gap: Guiding the college search of undocumented students. *Journal of College Admission*, *229*, 31–34.

Olivas, M. A. (2012). *No undocumented child left behind:* Plyler v. Doe *and the education of undocumented schoolchildren*. New York: NYU Press.

Pabón López, M. P., & López, G. R. (2009). *Persistent inequality: Contemporary realities in the education of undocumented Latina/o students*. New York: Routledge.

Perlich, P. S. (2004). Immigrants transform Utah: Entering a new era of diversity. *Bureau of Economic and Business Research*, *64*(5), 1–16.

Plyler v. Doe, 457 U.S. 202 (1982).

Quiroga, A. (1995). Copycat fever: California's Proposition 187 epidemic spreads to other states. *Hispanic*, *8*(3), 18–24.

Rosenblum, M. R., & Meissner, D. (2014). *The deportation dilemma: Reconciling tough and humane enforcement*. Washington, DC: Migration Policy Institute.

Salinas, S., & Lozano, A. (2017). Mapping and recontextualizing the evolution of the term Latinx: An environmental scanning in higher education. *Journal of Latinos and Education*, 1–14. doi:10.1080/15348431.2017.1390464

San Antonio Independent School District v. Rodriguez, 411 U.S. 1, (1973).

Santa Ana, O. (2002). *Brown tide rising: Metaphors of Latinos in contemporary American public discourse*. Austin: University of Texas Press.

USA Patriot Act (Uniting and Strengthening America by Providing Appropriate Tools Required to Intercept and Obstruct Terrorism Act), H.R. 3162, 107th Cong. (2001).

U.S. Department of Justice & U.S. Department of Education. (2014, May 8). Joint "dear colleague" letter. Retrieved from http://www2.ed.gov/about/offices/list/ocr/letters/colleague-201405.pdf

White House. (2018). Remarks by President Trump at a California sanctuary state roundtable. Retrieved from www.whitehouse.gov/briefings-statements/remarks-president-trump-california-sanctuary-state-roundtable/

Chapter 8

Creating a Welcoming Environment of Mental Health Equity for Undocumented Students

Germán Cadenas, Diana Peña, and Jesus Cisneros

CASE NARRATIVE

Yesenia's case represents a compilation of real stories shared by undocumented students with the authors. Yesenia is a 15-year-old, undocumented, Afro-Latinx[1], English Language Learner who begins to display post-traumatic stress symptoms after witnessing increasing immigration enforcement in her community. She attends a large public high school located in a major metropolitan city in a diverse southwestern U.S. state that borders Mexico. She migrated to the U.S. from a Central American country when she was 13 years old. Her family left their home country due to growing violence and safety concerns. When Yesenia's family migrated, they did not fit into any of the existing migration-related categories and conventions that would make them eligible for admission into the U.S. They did not have ties to a U.S. citizen to qualify through a family preference system; they did not have a job offer based on advanced education, wealth, or unique qualifications for employment-based migration; and they did not come from an underrepresented country to qualify for the Diversity Visa lottery program. Consequently, Yesenia's family's only option for entry into the U.S. was to overstay a tourist visa.

Approximately 30% of Yesenia's state's population is of Latinx[2] origin, while people of color make up about 46% of the metropolitan area where they live. State-wide, conservatives maintain a slight political majority, which has led to the election of state lawmakers who perpetuate anti-immigrant rhetoric and have passed hostile laws that target immigrants for detention in privatized prisons (Ackerman & Furman, 2013). Some of these laws allow local law enforcement to collaborate with Immigration and Customs Enforcement (ICE) on raids and increased detainment operations, which have heightened Yesenia's family's fear of detention and deportation.

As an Afro-Latina, Yesenia has struggled to find a sense of community in the predominantly Latinx neighborhood where she and her family live. She sees herself as a minority in this community. Few students at her school look like her and also identify as Latinx. While her cultural background facilitates her relationship with both Latinxs and African-Americans, her immigration status imposes limitations on her ability to completely connect with either based on differing levels of privilege and oppression. For this reason, she tends to keep information regarding her immigration status to herself.

At school, Yesenia has befriended a couple of Black students in her science class. She has begun adjusting slowly to cultural norms in her school and is making progress as an English Language Learner (ELL). She has found the support from her teachers to be particularly invaluable, especially as she navigates a new educational system that still feels very new to her. She has developed an interest in science and begun to consider whether to pursue it further—maybe after she graduates from high school. She feels very comfortable with her biology teacher, Mrs. Chavez, and she has found it inspiring to see a Latina teach about science so passionately and in a way that makes sense to her.

One day at school, Yesenia's friends bring up the changes to immigration laws that the U.S. president posted in a tweet. Yesenia becomes very uncomfortable during this conversation and "shuts down." On her social media news feed, she hears about raids in different parts of the city and the ways that local police can act as federal immigration agents to detain and deport undocumented immigrants. Conversations with her Black friends during lunch additionally heighten Yesenia's anxiety, as there is news about the shooting of an unarmed and innocent Black teenager in another part of town. These conversations have become all too common in her neighborhood and elevate the sense of fear.

Walking home from school, Yesenia cannot help but think about the conversations she had with her peers. Seeing police cars drive by, she feels hyper-vigilant and rushes home. She locks herself in her room for the remainder of the afternoon until her parents get home from work. Later that night she has trouble sleeping. She worries that immigration agents will raid her apartment complex in the middle of the night. Yesenia feels scared, but is unable to express her emotions because she knows that her parents will worry.

The next day, Yesenia experiences heightened levels of anxiety, particularly during Mr. Smith's class. Mr. Smith is a vocal supporter of anti-immigrant policies. Yesenia becomes particularly nervous when he calls on her during class. Struggling to communicate her thoughts in English, Yesenia feels nervous and shaky. As she develops comfort speaking in front of the class, a couple of students snicker to one another behind her back and laugh out loud. Feeling self-conscious, Yesenia experiences racing thoughts and almost faints. She is taken to the nurse's office, where she learns that she experienced a panic attack. Consequently, Yesenia is referred to the school counselor, Miss Thompson.

While Yesenia thinks that Miss Thompson is very nice, she is initially doubtful that she could open up to her; can Miss Thompson truly understand everything that is going on? However, Miss Thompson's welcoming and non-judgmental demeanor helps Yesenia feel comfortable. Yesenia opens up crying, finally able to tell someone about everything she has been holding in. She trusts that Miss Thompson is there to help. While Miss Thompson listens empathically and is affirming, she later shares with the principal that she feels unprepared to meet Yesenia's needs. The principal confides that she too was feeling at a loss. Staff school-wide have been witnessing the impact of changes in immigration policy on students' academic performance and attendance. A significant portion of their student body is undocumented, lives in a mixed-status family, or knows someone who is undocumented. Miss Thompson and the principal recognize that it is imperative for them to seek new ways to support their students and families.

TEACHING NOTES

Training Mental Health Providers on Best Practices with Undocumented Youth

Youth agencies and mental health providers working in K-12 schools may find that their training insufficiently prepares them for working with undocumented students. This student community experiences distress related to the immigration process, acculturation difficulties, trauma histories, discrimination, and racism (American Psychological Association, 2013). Undocumented youth may additionally be subjected to distress caused by marginalization along intersecting identity domains, as illustrated in Yesenia's narrative. In addition to several existing frameworks that help guide clinical sensitivity toward sociopolitical stressors (American Psychological Association, 2012, 2013; Arredondo et al., 1996; California

Psychological Association, 2018), our extensive clinical practice with this population informs the following recommendations when counseling undocumented youth.

Centering trauma-informed practice. Given higher rates of exposure to traumatic events and the chronic stress associated with fear of family separation/deportation, undocumented students may be coping solely with survival-based responses including hyper-vigilance, distrust of public institution representatives, and difficulty regulating emotions. Trauma Informed Care (Substance Abuse and Mental Health Services Administration, 2014) offers an approach to counselors, educators, and institutions-at-large that emphasizes survivors' strengths, recognizes the signs of trauma in students and their families, and responds by fully integrating knowledge of trauma into procedures and settings. Counselors and other school staff may work to educate the community on common reactions to trauma and sociopolitical stress, normalize difficulties, and offer tools to regulate emotion.

Establishing trust. With a rise in anti-immigrant policy across institutions, including government, establishing trust within institutional services such as counseling may require additional efforts on the counselor's behalf. Posters, ally stickers, and other visual markers of an immigrant-friendly space offer a clear indication of institutional intention to serve, regardless of immigration status. Familiarity of and relationships with local community resources (e.g., legal aid clinics, housing advocacy groups, etc.) additionally demonstrate that a counselor is aware of oppressive conditions facing families.

Protection of confidentiality. Given increased vulnerability and risk of exposure, clarity about confidentiality, including the limits thereof, is of paramount importance. K-12 providers should consider the implications of their charting practices, and omit a student's immigration status when it is impertinent to the objectives of documentation. Providers may also discuss with clients the state and federal laws protecting students' health and educational records.

Awareness of privilege and cultural humility. All counselors should understand their power and privilege in relation to students, refrain from perpetuating microaggressions, and approach cultural differences through a strength-based lens. Given collectivist and community-oriented values (common among many Latinx immigrant groups), counselors should be aware of Western-individualistic biases surrounding individual vs. family well-being (American Psychological Association, 2012) and provide culture-specific coping tools for managing stress (e.g., spiritual and indigenous healing practices).

Practical Steps to Support Students' Mental Health

Systemic challenges impacting undocumented students' mental health, as in the case of Yesenia, can be overwhelming to any school leader, particularly as most of these challenges are located outside of an administrator's control. However, there are many practical steps that K-12 leaders can take to create a welcoming environment of mental health equity for their students. While the challenges faced by undocumented students may not be fully resolvable on school campuses, the right conditions may serve to buffer many negative outcomes.

Training to promote ally development, cultural competencies, and intergroup contact. A large body of research documents that prejudicial attitudes are changeable under the right conditions for positive intergroup contact (Pettigrew & Tropp, 2006, 2008). In particular, friendships among groups have the most potent effect in changing prejudice (Pettigrew, Tropp, Wagner, & Christ, 2011). When in-person contact is not possible, vicarious contact (e.g., videos, workshops, knowing someone who is friends with the marginalized group) can also be effective (Miles & Crisp, 2014).

Many educational programs exist to cultivate cultural sensitivity, improve attitudes, and support educators and students in becoming allies of undocumented immigrants (e.g., Undocu-Peers, Undocu-Ally, and DREAMzone). Such programs tend to center their curriculum around the narratives of undocumented students, allowing participants to connect with students' lived experiences through in-person video testimony, and provide updated information regarding laws and policies affecting immigrants' well-being. Research on said programs (Cadenas, Cisneros, Todd, & Spanierman, 2018; Cisneros & Cadenas, 2017; Cisneros & Lopez, 2016) provides evidence of effectiveness in decreasing anxiety, lowering prejudice, boosting empathy, and increasing practitioners' competence and self-efficacy for working with undocumented students. Educational leaders may consider offering similar programs to their staff and students as a first step toward inclusivity.

Holistic institutional supports. Student support services may additionally increase undocumented students' sense of belonging and persistence within educational contexts (Cisneros & Valdivia, 2018; Southern, 2016; Suárez-Orozco, Teranishi, & Suárez-Orozco, 2015). Institutions of postsecondary education have been at the forefront of devising innovative programs to serve undocumented students holistically, such as University of California Berkeley's Undocumented Student Program (USP; Sanchez & So, 2015), a first-in-the-nation model that offers specialized academic counseling, legal counsel, and mental health support for undocumented students. USP's trauma-informed mental health program offers individual counseling, anonymous drop-in consultation, psycho-educational workshops (e.g., coping tools for deportation anxiety), crisis oriented "Healing Circles," psychological evaluation for trauma-based legal adjustment (e.g., U-Visa), and financial relief for psychiatric and pharmaceutical mental health costs.

Beyond these services, the program also fosters strategic partnerships with campus departments that interface with undocumented students at critical junctures, including the campus police department and the career center. Collaboration with staff at the career center, for example, has led to workshops on entrepreneurial options for those that do not qualify for work authorization, and the creation of a weekly career counseling drop-in hour for undocumented students. Though different in developmental age and resources as compared to postsecondary education environments, K-12 institutions may adapt models such as USPs to address existing gaps in emotional support and reduce barriers to academic persistence.

TEACHING ACTIVITIES

Research suggests that activism can boost individuals' abilities to cope with marginalization (Watts, Diemer, & Voight, 2011) and is related to higher community connectivity, stronger sense of identity, lower mental health distress, and higher educational persistence for undocumented students (Cadenas, Bernstein, & Tracey, 2018; Perez, Espinoza, Ramos, Coronado, & Cortes, 2009). The following are activities for educators to foster healthy activism and critical consciousness among undocumented students.

1. Develop and write a rationale for a platform (e.g., a school club, rally, or "know your rights" workshop) that supports student demonstrations, events, and programs addressing immigration issues. Defend how undocumented students could partake in such activities without feeling pressure to disclose their status and while maintaining a sense of safety.
2. Watch the documentary film *The Dream Is Now* (Guggenheim, 2013). Using evidence from the film, discuss how immigration policy impacts undocumented students' wellbeing.
3. Write up a plan, from a school leader perspective, for inviting community organizers to speak on campus, with the goal to increase students' access to mobilizing efforts and role models who can ignite hope for students otherwise isolated and fearful.
4. Look up local resources and organizations on dealing with stress/trauma. Drawing from these resources, create a resource folder for counseling/advising offices that provides culturally-relevant handouts

for students and families coping with immigration stress and/or trauma-related symptoms. For example, such a folder might include a list of low-cost counseling centers, tips on difficulty sleeping, or strategies to manage excessive worry or sadness.

NOTES

1 The term Afro-Latinx describes someone with Latin American background and African ethnicity.
2 The term Latinx is used to describe individuals of Latin American heritage, including those who do not identify with sex and gender binaries reflected in the Spanish language (Santos & VanDaalen, 2016).

REFERENCES

Ackerman, A. R., & Furman, R. (2013). The criminalization of immigration and the privatization of immigration detention: Implications for justice. *Contemporary Justice Review*, *16*(2), 251–263.

American Psychological Association, Presidential Task Force on Immigration. (2012). Crossroads: The psychology of immigration in the new century. Retrieved from www.apa.org/topics/immigration/report.aspx

American Psychological Association. (2013). Working with immigrant-origin clients: An update for mental health professionals. Based on crossroads: the psychology of immigration in the new century. Retrieved from www.apa.org/topics/immigration/immigration-report-professionals.pdf

Arredondo, P., Toporek, R., Brown, S. P., Jones, J., Locke, D. C., Sanchez, J., & Stadler, H. (1996). Operationalization of the multicultural counseling competencies. *Journal of Multicultural Counseling and Development*, *24*(1), 42–78.

Cadenas, G. A., Bernstein, B. L., & Tracey, T. J. (2018). Critical consciousness and intent to persist through college in DACA and US citizen students: The role of immigration status, race, and ethnicity. *Cultural Diversity and Ethnic Minority Psychology*, *24*(4), 564.

Cadenas, G. A., Cisneros, J., Todd, N. R., & Spanierman, L. B. (2018). DREAMzone: Testing two vicarious contact interventions to improve attitudes toward undocumented immigrants. *Journal of Diversity in Higher Education*, *11*(3), 295–308.

California Psychological Association. (2018). Recommendations for Psychological Practice with Undocumented Immigrants in California. Retrieved from: www.cpapsych.org/news/390363/CPA-Immigration-Task-Force-Releases-Practice-Recommendations.htm

Cisneros, J., & Cadenas, G. (2017). DREAMer-ally competency and self-efficacy: Developing higher education staff and measuring lasting outcomes. *Journal of Student Affairs Research and Practice*, *54*(2), 189–203.

Cisneros, J., & Lopez, A. (2016). DREAMzone: Educating Counselors and Human Service Professionals Working with Undocumented Students. *Journal for Social Action in Counseling and Psychology*, *8*(2), 32–48.

Cisneros, J., & Valdivia, D. (2018). Undocumented student resource centers: Institutional supports for undocumented students. *Penn Center for Minority Serving Institutions*. Retrieved from https://cmsi.gse.upenn.edu/sites/default/files/USRCs.pdf

Guggenheim, D. (writer and director). (2013). *The Dream Is Now* [documentary film]. United States: Emerson Collective. Retrieved from www.thedreamisnow.org/

Miles, E., & Crisp, R. J. (2014). A meta-analytic test of the imagined contact hypothesis. *Group Processes & Intergroup Relations*, *17*(1), 3–26.

Perez, W., Espinoza, R., Ramos, K., & Cortes, R. (2009). Academic resilience among undocumented Latino students. *Hispanic Journal of Behavioral Sciences*, *31*, 149–181.

Pettigrew, T. F., & Tropp, L. R. (2006). A meta-analytic test of intergroup contact theory. *Journal of Personality and Social Psychology*, *90*(5), 751.

Pettigrew, T. F., & Tropp, L. R. (2008). How does intergroup contact reduce prejudice? Meta-analytic tests of three mediators. *European Journal of Social Psychology*, *38*(6), 922–934.

Pettigrew, T. F., Tropp, L. R., Wagner, U., & Christ, O. (2011). Recent advances in intergroup contact theory. *International Journal of Intercultural Relations*, *35*(3), 271–280.

Sanchez, R. E. C., & So, M. L. (2015). UC Berkeley's undocumented student program: Holistic strategies for undocumented student equitable success across higher education. *Harvard Educational Review*, *85*(3), 464–477.

Santos, C. E., & VanDaalen, R. A. (2016). The associations of sexual and ethnic–racial identity commitment, conflicts in allegiances, and mental health among lesbian, gay, and bisexual racial and ethnic minority adults. *Journal of Counseling Psychology*, *63*(6), 668.

Southern, K. G. (2016). Institutionalizing support services for undocumented students at four-year colleges and universities. *Journal of Student Affairs Research and Practice*, *53*(3), 305–318.

Suárez-Orozco, M. M., Teranishi, R., & Suárez-Orozco, C. E. (2015). In the shadows of the ivory tower: Undocumented undergraduates and the liminal state of immigration reform. UndocuScholar Project. Institute for Immigration, Globalization & Education, UCLA.

Substance Abuse and Mental Health Services Administration. (2014). Trauma-informed care in behavioral health services. Treatment Improvement Protocol (TIP) Series 57. HHS Publication No. (SMA) 13–4801. Rockville, MD: Substance Abuse and Mental Health Services Administration.

Watts, R. J., Diemer, M. A., & Voight, A. M. (2011). Critical consciousness: Current status and future directions. In C. A. Flanagan & B. D. Christens (Eds.), *Youth civic development: Work at the cutting edge. New Directions for Child and Adolescent Development*, *134*, 43–57.

Chapter 9

UndocuCollege Access

Addressing Documentation Issues in the College Choice Process

Marco A. Murillo

CONTEXT

Over the past decade, undocumented youth have gained visibility in American politics as they've mobilized to advocate for a pathway to citizenship and access to higher education. They represent a diverse body of individuals who seek to gain legal documentation to work, give back to their community, and lead normal lives. Unlike undocumented immigrants who arrived as adults, undocumented youth are in a peculiar legal position. Although they are not authorized to reside in the United States because they lack birthright citizenship or legal documentation, they have the legal right to a public K-12 education (see Chapter 7 for legal definitions). Approximately, 1.1 million undocumented immigrants are under 18 (Warren, 2013), and about 100,000 undocumented students graduate from high school each year (Zong & Batalova, 2019). Many of them navigate the K-12 system with plans to pursue higher education. To them, college represents an opportunity for upward mobility and a way to demonstrate that their family's sacrifices have been worthwhile. However, fulfilling this dream is a challenge.

Undocumented students' pathway to college, like that of many of their peers, depends on having enriching educational opportunities, but also supportive relationships with school personnel (Gonzales, 2010). These relationships are particularly important in helping them make sense of a confusing and ever-changing immigration and educational context. As such, this chapter focuses on the role high school educators play in supporting undocumented students' college choice process.

CASE NARRATIVE

City School is a high school located in a densely populated southern California immigrant neighborhood. The school opened in 2010 and comprises predominantly low-income Latina/o and Asian students who will be the first in their family to attend college. Its first cohort of 12th-grade students graduated in 2012. To ensure students are prepared to enter and succeed in postsecondary education, everyone has access to a college preparatory curriculum that meets the enrollment requirements of the state's four-year university system. However, City School staff recognize that academic qualifications are not sufficient to ensure college enrollment. Most students and their families depend on the school to guide them through the college application and enrollment process. For this reason, City School has instituted one-on-one counseling meetings with students, hosts workshops with parents and students about financial aid, provides students opportunities to participate in extracurricular activities (e.g., internships, clubs, and summer enrichment programs), and coordinates college trips. Each year, the number of students applying and being admitted to two- and four-year colleges has steadily increased. One contributing factor to City School's high college admission rate has been its attention to its undocumented student population.

Lisa has served as City School's college counselor since 2011. In her role, she helped develop and implement the school's college-going culture. One facet of this work includes assisting 12th-grade students to complete college and financial aid applications. During her first year, Lisa realized many of her students were undocumented and needed additional support. At the time, the California DREAM Act, which allows undocumented students to qualify for state and institutional financial aid, had recently passed and was set to be implemented by 2013. Many students and families were aware of the new law but were confused about when and how to apply.

In 2012–13, Lisa was eager to share information about the California DREAM Act and the Deferred Action for Childhood Arrivals (DACA) program created in 2012 by the Obama administration. At the time, DACA provided qualifying undocumented youth reprieve from deportation and a work permit. Initially, she asked students during college counseling sessions if they were U.S. citizens. Because some students were confused by the question, Lisa clarified that she wanted to know in order to provide them with the correct and proper college access support. However, feeling concerned about exposing students or making them feel forced to answer a citizenship question, she stopped asking.

Lisa was unsure of how to provide support to undocumented students so she approached Roberto, an English teacher who every year helped students write personal statements and apply to college. They talked about Luis, a bright young man, who had disclosed to Roberto that he was undocumented. Roberto believed Luis felt comfortable revealing his legal status because of his pro-immigrant rhetoric during class discussions and classroom imagery. One day after class, Luis asked Roberto about college. Roberto answered some of Luis's questions but could not answer all of them, so he suggested that Luis meet with Lisa. Sensing Luis's hesitation, Roberto assured him that Lisa would be a great support system. After giving it some thought, Luis agreed to meet with Lisa at the end of his 11th-grade year to talk about his college aspirations and options. Lisa explained the process for completing college and financial aid applications and assured Luis that she would work with him and his family to make sure his applications were properly completed.

When Luis returned in the fall, Lisa did not ask him about citizenship, because she already knew his documentation status. She did ask if he would be applying for DACA and offered to connect him with a local organization that reviewed application forms before they were submitted. In reflecting on their experience with Luis, Lisa and Roberto concluded that it was important to create a campus climate where the decision to disclose legal status was left to the discretion of students and their families, and also to ensure that the information remained private. During a professional development workshop about college-going with their colleagues, they addressed the need to support undocumented students. Lisa touched on the following points:

(1) Include pro-immigrant imagery in classrooms.
(2) Avoid directly asking students about their documentation status.
(3) Consider potential barriers (e.g., legal status) during the early high school years and provide information, support, and resources to address these challenges.
(4) Discuss in-state tuition and California DREAM Act during all financial aid workshops (i.e., provide information regardless of students' legal status) and work with college representatives to address documentation issues during school visits.
(5) Provide information about DACA and acknowledge that not all students qualify for the program and provide additional supports. In addition, clarify to DACA recipients that their Social Security number does not make them eligible to receive federal financial aid.
(6) Share scholarships that do not require a Social Security number.
(7) Encourage parents to sign up for one-on-one support to complete college and financial aid forms as well as provide resources in the family's home language.

(8) Maintain students' privacy by not keeping documents that connect students' personal information to their legal status, and do not share students' legal status with other school personnel unless the student has agreed.

Teachers appreciated the information. Some commented that they had students approach them about applying to college and being undocumented. Although they knew it was possible, many lacked the expertise to help them navigate the process. While they still had many questions and concerns, they felt better knowing that Lisa was building her expertise on the issue.

Responding to Changes in the Political Climate

A few years into helping students navigate the California DREAM Act and apply for DACA, Lisa had a system in place to help undocumented students and their families. Each year, Lisa held financial aid workshops that included information about the California DREAM Act and other funding sources; she met one-on-one with families who had questions about completing financial aid forms, and she encouraged students to apply for DACA if they were eligible. Things were fairly calm until the 2016 presidential election. The day after the election, many students arrived at school visibly upset. City School teachers spent the day conducting community circles to acknowledge students' fears and concerns. In particular, undocumented students and a few parents who were present expressed concern about going to college and applying for DACA. With only a few weeks before college applications were due, Lisa took immediate action.

Lisa informed students that the election results would not affect their eligibility to attend college. Through her ongoing efforts, she ameliorated some concerns but expected additional questions pertaining to the completion of financial aid forms. When students returned from winter break, Lisa hosted a financial aid workshop and invited Ulises, an organizer and policy analyst from a local immigrant rights organization, to talk directly about being undocumented and completing financial forms. Ulises acknowledged people's fears but clarified that California's student financial aid system was separate from the federal government. In addition to the workshop, Lisa met one-on-one with families who had additional concerns. These efforts eased some of the trepidation felt by students and their families about submitting a California Dream Act application.

Despite alleviating some concerns about financial aid, DACA presented another obstacle. When DACA was first announced, Lisa actively informed students and encouraged them to apply. With the Trump administration threatening to end the program, Lisa became cautious. She continued to inform students about DACA but noted that with the new administration the program could end at any moment and their information would be accessible to the federal government. Although Lisa understood DACA's benefits, she also recognized the risks associated with the program should it be eliminated and recipients' information ever used as a means for deportation. City School's fear became a reality in September 2017. The Trump administration announced its intent to phase out DACA by March 2018 and called on Congress to legislate a solution before the date. Lisa followed the political proceedings but felt overwhelmed by the constant changes. Numerous judicial filings in support of and against DACA made it difficult to understand DACA's current status, such as whether current DACA recipients can reapply and if new applications will be accepted. Although uncertain of what will happen with immigration policy, Lisa continues to prepare and support undocumented students to enter college. She is working with teachers and students to create a DREAMer club at City School to address social, educational, and emotional issues among immigrant-origin students and allies.

TEACHING NOTES

Immigration Policy and Education

Not since the Immigration Reform and Control Act (IRCA) of 1986 has the federal government provided a pathway to citizenship to undocumented immigrants. Since 2001, multiple proposals of the Development, Relief and Education for Alien Minors Act (DREAM Act) have sought to provide a pathway to citizenship for undocumented immigrants who graduate from high school or have earned a high school equivalency certificate, possess good moral character, and obtain a postsecondary degree or serve two years in the military. Although intensely debated, no bill has ever passed. Similarly, comprehensive immigration bills have failed to garner enough support in Congress.

In response to congressional inaction and pressure from undocumented youth and immigration advocates, President Barack Obama announced DACA on June 15, 2012. The benefits include temporary relief from deportation, a Social Security number, and a two-year work permit for undocumented immigrants who arrived to the U.S. before the age of 16, were under the age of 31, and had been present in the country for five years (before June 15, 2007) (Passel & Lopez, 2012). Five years into the program, nearly 800,000 undocumented youth had obtained DACA (Krogstad, 2017). Some positive outcomes from having DACA include reenrolling in school and improving job and career prospects (Gonzales et al., 2017). Despite DACA's success, President Trump rescinded the program in September 2017 with the intent to phase it out in early 2018. However, legal challenges and judicial rulings in response to Trump's decision maintained the program in operation. As of December 2018, current DACA recipients could renew their application, but applications from new applicants were not being accepted.

Some states have also answered the call to act by proposing policies that promote access to higher education for undocumented students. Currently, 19 states and Washington, DC allow undocumented students to qualify for some form of in-state tuition, including ten that also grant financial assistance (National Immigration Law Center, 2018). Specific requirements to qualify for in-state tuition and financial aid vary across each state; however, those who qualify are typically undocumented students who attended high school in the state for a specified number of years and graduated from high school or have earned a high school equivalency certificate. For example, in 2001, California became the second state to allow undocumented students to qualify for in-state tuition (AB 540). Then, in 2011, it granted access to institutional and financial aid to individuals who qualified for in-state tuition through AB 130 and 131, better known as the California DREAM Act. Flores (2010) found that states where undocumented students are eligible for in-state tuition have seen an increase in college enrollment. Unfortunately, the reach of such measures is sometimes stifled, because information is poorly disseminated and many undocumented students are unaware of college access resources and opportunities.

Undocumented Students from K-12 to Higher Education

Per the Supreme Court's decision in *Plyler v. Doe* in 1982, all children, regardless of immigration status, have the right to equally access public education (see Chapter 7). School districts cannot determine district residency based on immigration status, and the Family Educational Rights and Privacy Act (FERPA) prohibits schools from releasing personal records to outside agencies (National School Board Association & National Education Association, 2009). However, the ruling made no claims about higher education. The end of high school and transition to adulthood represent a transition into "illegality" (Gonzales, 2011). During this transitional stage, undocumented youth experience dramatic changes, such as coming to terms with the fact that their legal status will limit their financial support to pursue higher education, constrain work opportunities, and exclude them from many of the activities their U.S.-born and legally residing peers partake in

(Abrego, 2006; Gonzales, 2011). They also have difficulty finding support in school because legal status is not something readily addressed by educators (Nienhusser, 2013).

Emerging research has described the unique educational challenges and barriers undocumented students encounter because of their legal status (Gonzales, 2016). These include dealing with a stigmatized identity, finding little support from K-16 educators and personnel, paying out-of-state tuition rates in most states, lacking safe spaces, and having limited access to financial support (Contreras, 2009; Gonzales, 2010). Even with the passage of in-state resident tuition policies (ISRTPs), college continues to be a significant financial burden because many undocumented youth are disqualified from most forms of financial aid, including scholarships; as a result, they may feel discouraged by the limited reach of these laws (Martinez, 2014).

Given the complexity of federal immigration policies and differences in opportunities across states, educators are key figures in helping students navigate a complex system. They can help undocumented youth move beyond the spotty "patchworks" of college access information (Enriquez, 2011) to excel academically and, ultimately, build their futures.

TEACHING ACTIVITIES

The following activities will help educators delve into issues of immigration and documentation, and their intersection with education. Educators working in sociopolitically conservative contexts may be restricted in addressing documentation issues in school and may need to take additional measures to protect students and their families. Educational leaders may be able to connect with national, state, and/or local organizations and leaders to create safe spaces and offer support for undocumented youth in their particular context.

1. Immigration and Documentation in Your Community

In groups of three or four, discuss the role of immigration and immigrants in your lives, and how documentation issues play a role in your educational context and community, make connections to the case narrative, and identify knowledge gaps.

Questions to consider:

(1) Please share some aspects of your or your family's history of immigration/arrival (if applicable) to the U.S. What were some challenges?

(2) In what ways, if any, does your story intersect with current conversations about immigration and immigrants?
(3) What are your initial thoughts on the case narrative? How do you feel about Lisa's approach in working with undocumented students? How does this relate to your own experience and interactions with students who might be undocumented or facing other documentation issues?
(4) How often do you talk with a student, family, and/or colleague about legal status issues? How comfortable do you feel talking about legal status issues?
(5) Immigration and education policy is complex and constantly changing. What questions do you have about working with undocumented students? What type of resources and support would be helpful moving forward?

2. Here's What, So What, Now What?

To delve into the issues undocumented students encounter in school and as they prepare for college, groups of three or four individuals should address the following prompts.

Here's What? Explain the political and social climate undocumented students face at your school, community, or organization. Write some factual statements, data, or observations.

So What? Write your interpretation of the context, data, or observations relating to undocumented students at your school, community, or organization. What patterns do you see? What do the data mean? Why is this issue important to your school, community, or organization?

Now What? Write a plan of action including new ideas, new questions, or next steps to support your school, community, or organization. What can be done? Who can do it? How can it be sustained?

REFERENCES

Abrego, L. J. (2006). "I can't go to college because I don't have papers": Incorporation patterns of undocumented Latino youth. *Latino Studies*, *4*(3), 212–231.
Contreras, F. (2009). Sin papeles y rompiendo barreras: Latino students and the challenges of persisting in college. *Harvard Educational Review*, *79*(4), 610–631.
Enriquez, L. E. (2011). "Because we feel the pressure and we also feel the support": Examining the educational success of undocumented immigrant Latina/o students. *Harvard Educational Review*, *81*(3), 476–499.

Flores, S. M. (2010). State dream acts: The effect of in-state resident tuition policies and undocumented Latino students. *Review of Higher Education*, *33*(2), 239–283.

Gonzales, R. G. (2010). On the wrong side of the tracks: Understanding the effects of school structure and social capital in the educational pursuits of undocumented immigrant students. *Peabody Journal of Education*, *85*(4), 469–485.

Gonzales, R. G. (2011). Learning to be illegal: Undocumented youth and shifting legal contexts in the transition to adulthood. *American Sociological Review*, *76*(4). doi:10.1177/0003122411411901

Gonzales, R. G. (2016). *Lives in limbo: Undocumented and coming of age in America*. Berkeley: University of California Press.

Gonzales, R. G., Murillo, M. A., Lacomba, C., Brant, K., Franco, M. C., Lee, J., & Vasudevan, D. S. (2017). *Taking giant leaps forward*. Washington, DC: Center for American Progress.

Krogstad, J. M. (2017). DACA has shielded nearly 790,000 young unauthorized immigrants from deportation. Washington, DC: Pew Research Center. Retrieved from www.pewresearch.org/fact-tank/2017/09/01/unauthorized-immigrants-covered-by-daca-face-uncertain-future/

Martinez, L. M. (2014). Dreams deferred: The impact of legal reforms on undocumented Latino youth. *American Behavioral Scientist*, *58*(14), 1873–1890. doi:10.1177/0002764214550289

National Immigration Law Center. (2018). Laws and policies improving access to higher education for immigrants. Washington, DC. Retrieved from www.nilc.org/wp-content/uploads/2017/10/table-access-to-ed-toolkit.pdf

National School Board Association & National Education Association. (2009). *Legal issues for school districts related to the education of undocumented children*. Alexandra, VA: National School Board Association.

Nienhusser, H. K. (2013). Role of high schools in undocumented students' college choice. *Education Policy Analysis Archives*, *21*(85), 1–32.

Passel, J., & Lopez, M. H. (2012). Up to 1.7 million unauthorized immigrant youth may benefit from new deportation rules. Washington, DC: Pew Hispanic Center.

Warren, R. (2013). US-born children of undocumented residents: Numbers and characteristics in 2013. New York: Center for Migration Studies. Retrieved from http://cmsny.org/publications/warren-usbornchildren/

Zong, J., & Batalova, J. (2019). *How many unauthorized immigrants graduate from U.S. high schools annually?* Washington, DC: Migration Policy Institute.

Chapter **10**

The Paradoxical Implications of Deported American Students

Edmund T. Hamann and Jessica Mitchell-McCollough

> If we don't understand the everyday lived experiences of people, we can't really think of immigration policy or reform.
>
> (Tileva, 2018, p. 30)

CONTEXT

Principals and teachers throughout the United States (and world) have students with transnational ties. Sometimes students were born in another country. More commonly, one or both parents were. Sometimes that means students and/or parents lack documentation, which creates anxiety and ambiguity in students' lives that schools need to negotiate. Suro and Suárez-Orozco (2015) recently estimated that one in 15 schoolchildren were from mixed-status households (meaning one or more members of that household could be deported), but five-sixths of these students were themselves U.S. citizens.

Given these conditions, U.S. schools must consider the possibility that some of their students may move somewhere else, even to a different country, often with little notice. In turn, they need to plan for how those prospectively mobile students can be best served. They also need to think about how to keep those possible departures from disrupting the schooling of the students who remain. Departures can be sudden and traumatic, but they can be less traumatic if action plans have been developed.

The case that follows comes from Lincoln, Nebraska, which Mary Pipher (2003) called "the middle of everywhere" in her book, noting Lincoln's role as a refugee resettlement area, as well as the hub of much new migration. Some of the details have been changed to protect anonymity.

CASE NARRATIVE

In a recent spring, two school principals and several teachers in Nebraska were faced with agonizing decisions about what to do, both educationally and humanely. They had just learned that two of their students, Maria de la Luz, a middle school student, and her younger brother, Norberto, an elementary school student, were about to move to Mexico. They were leaving the United States for a land neither child knew because their father was being deported and their mother wanted to keep their family together. As such, they were joining the roughly 600,000 children in Mexican schools with prior experience in the United States (Zúñiga & Hamann, 2015).

The educators had a week to intentionally ready their students for departure, as the father was seen as sufficiently unthreatening that he was allowed a week before he would be sent away. Still, a week is not much time to reorient entire lives. One task at hand for the principals and teachers in this case was how to best facilitate the educational transition the family would be facing. An email from a guidance counselor at one of the children's schools captures the improvisational nature of figuring out what to do. Serendipitously, the counselor remembered that a professor she knew had studied the circumstances of students in Mexico with prior experience in the U.S. Her email (below) wondered if he might be able to help.

> Say, I have a 6th grade student, U.S. born, whose parents are being deported to Mexico next week and she is going with them. I know that you worked with an institution in Monterrey, Mexico on a project involving cross-country immigration. I'm wondering if you have any tips for this student who is essentially immigrating to a foreign country. She wants to take some books so she won't forget her English. I assume she'll be behind the Mexican students academically and may face teasing because of her accent. In the past U.S. born students have reported not being accepted by peers—too "gringa." Do you have any thoughts or advice? The little girl is leaving on Friday. I have another 6th grade girl whose dad was apprehended by ICE; it was a big mess and the incident rippled throughout our school district's Hispanic community.
>
> Hope all is well with you...

Less than a day after that email's crafting, the professor and counselor had a chance to talk and then, later in the week, for 30 minutes, both met with Maria de la Luz herself. It was during that 30-minute conversation that they learned about Norberto, as Maria de la Luz clarified that both she and her younger brother were headed to Mexico. She said it would be their first plane ride and the first time that they would meet their grandparents in person. She also conceded she was nervous about what they would find in Mexico.

Given the short time frame—one week—that the school community had to support these children as they prepared for the transition to their next school and community environment, two things stood out as priorities. The first was to ask what generally would make the prospect of moving less daunting? The second was to consider what would make moving specifically to Mexico less daunting? That is where the discussion of the adventure of plane travel and the prospect of meeting close kin for the first time fit in. The idea was to focus on known upsides, even if they were in the face of so much that was more difficult and ambiguous.

Logistically, there was also work to be done. Maria de la Luz's counselor (who was bilingual and had been hired in part for her capability to communicate with parents at a school with a high Latinx enrollment) assembled Maria de la Luz's transcripts, met with her mother, and shared a letter co-written with the professor that included the names of two professors in Puebla (the state where the family was relocating). One of the professors worked in Puebla permanently and one was there on a Fulbright. That step proved serendipitous, as the permanently-in-Mexico professor helped Maria de la Luz's mother when she encountered resistance to enrolling Maria de la Luz in her new community's school two months before the school year ended.

Given the suddenness of the relocation, it was not yet clear when the Nebraska counselor met with Maria de la Luz's mother where specifically the family would end up. They knew which larger community, but not which particular school catchment zones, so creating means for continued email communication was important. Maria de la Luz's mother brought Nebraska school records with her to Mexico for both Norberto and Maria de la Luz, but once in Mexico she could still reach out to the counselor in Nebraska to obtain additional information and forms, if needed. It was fortunate that Maria de la Luz's school had a counselor who could communicate with Maria de la Luz's mother and who could remain reachable (through email), even after the family's forced relocation.

TEACHING NOTES

The task of how to respond with a week's notice is not the only way to think about Maria de la Luz's and Norberto's challenges. Given the prospect of some students' international dislocation for reasons like those encountered by Maria de la Luz and Norberto, or for other reasons (see Hamann & Zúñiga, 2011), schools need mechanisms to communicate with parents in parents' home language(s) and to be reachable in an uncomplicated way even after students have left that system for another one. While knowing a professor with ties in Mexico was useful in this instance, that does not seem like a coincidence that should be expected. But planning for the prospect of working with about-to-be-dislocated students and their parent(s) can and should be undertaken.

U.S. schools need to plan for more than what to do during a crisis. This country has long thought of itself as "a nation of immigrants" and for almost as long thought of its schools as vehicles for helping students and ultimately their families find a footing to integrate into the larger society (Dewey, 1902; Proefriedt, 2008). While taking on this role of immigrant integration has always been more fraught and complicated than the rhetoric supporting it would suggest, the truism of schooling as a key mediating site where newcomers and established residents come into contact remains very true (Goode, Schneider, & Blanc, 1992), although that mediation is more complicated than is typically recognized.

Schools' tasks are not just to help students and families live here, in this country, with its dominant language and culture. Instead, students increasingly need to be helped to be ready to negotiate multiple possible geographies and languages, because the contemporary globalized economy (which moves both goods and people) and contemporary contestation of immigrant rights and statuses together make the likelihood of binational or multinational lives higher. Thinking of Maria de la Luz and Norberto as "immigrants" or "'English Learners" is not pejorative (although it would ignore their birthplaces), but it does steer away from helping students develop and maintain some of the identities and skills they may need if their schooling and lives are to be enduringly multinational. Even though they were U.S.-born and U.S. citizens, both Maria de la Luz and Norberto were more than just Nebraskans and more than just Americans. Pretending otherwise did not protect them from the shock that came from their family's forced relocation; nor did it position them well for success in Mexican schools. They needed skills in Spanish and an understanding of Mexican culture. Promoting the students' heritage language (in this case Spanish) would likely have illuminated its relevance and thus supported their maintenance of that language and confidence with it (Hornberger, 2005; Valdés, 2005). Valuing Spanish and other culture/heritage features would also have reinforced students' identity development through the continued ability to connect with community (Leeman, Rabín, & Román-Mendoza, 2011). This may well have aided both children in their transition into an educational setting of a different, yet recognizable, language and culture.

Some may protest that it is not the job of U.S. schools to teach Spanish. Perhaps not, but not having the choice to study or use their home language(s) at school makes students like Maria de la Luz and her brother vulnerable in predictable and avoidable ways. If they had been encouraged to develop their heritage language as well as learning English, they would have been less vulnerable to their sudden move. Moreover, there is evidence that supporting students' academic development in their heritage language along with English improves educational outcomes (Yanguas, 2010). (So even if Maria de la Luz and Norberto had never moved, their cultivated multilingualism would have been a useful asset.)

Both children could have also gained from overt metalinguistics instruction (e.g., attention to details like word order conventions and grammar varying by language, and recognition that language is used differently in various content areas). There is good evidence from the U.S. that older English Learners with school experience elsewhere use their literacy skills in a native language to learn English (Meltzer & Hamann, 2004, 2005). There is no reason why this logic could not be reversed, with knowledge about language derived from studying English in U.S. schools being used as a resource for studying in Spanish in Mexico. Metalinguistic awareness includes knowing that content areas have particular vocabularies, text structures, and discourses, that informal oral registers and academic ones differ, that there are appropriate places for each, and that language indexes what a society pays attention to. Knowing each of these things can give a student starting points for how to learn Spanish (or any other language), but that only works if the metalinguistic instruction is intentional. While this is useful for a student who may be mobile, it is also useful for geographically stable students who have to negotiate the coming and going of some peers and who live in an increasingly transnational world.

Schools are not usually organized to expect mobility, even though mobility (across town, across country, and/or across national borders) is a factor in practically every school. While Maria de la Luz and Norberto's district mobility rate only barely exceeded the Nebraska average (of approximately 11% changing schools in a given year), the mobility rate at Maria de la Luz's school was more than one in six and at Norberto's almost one in four. Given those ratios, it behooves such schools to step outside the traditional paradigm of preparing students to come of age locally. Phrased more bluntly, if it is predictable that many students will move, then it is a school's responsibility to help that movement occur as successfully as possible.

Focusing on the week between learning about their pending dislocation and their departure, Maria de la Luz's school did several things right. It was flexible in terms of when it met with Maria de la Luz's mother, whose life was clearly more upended by what was transpiring than were teachers and staff, allowing her to juggle getting information from both of her children's schools while attending to myriad other details. It indicated that the school cared what happened to Maria de la Luz and her family after their departure. It recognized the ambiguity entailed by starting a new life in Mexico after more than a decade away and emphasized a willingness to continue being "reachable" from afar. This proved valuable when the mother met resistance to enrolling Maria de la Luz and Norberto in Mexican schools and could appeal back to the counselor for support. It gave Maria de la Luz some space to consider and strategize about her pending changes. While the chance to meet grandparents she knew only by telephone and WhatsApp did not undo the shock of what she was negotiating, it did put something favorable on the ledger with all of the more challenging and difficult parts of uprooting. The act of naming her concerns—like how she would sustain her English—may have also contributed to her developing intentionality and plans to problem-solve once she got to Mexico.

In summary, schools like those attended by Maria de la Luz and Norberto in Nebraska need to think about and plan for how to help children negotiate both *here* and *somewhere else*, attending to the likely patterns regarding where students can be dislocated to and under what circumstances. Understanding and working to educate children beyond borders will allow for a system that thinks and acts critically to address the needs of a changing global population through attending to individual student stories, understanding and preparing for patterns of migration common to their communities, and forming partnerships that allow for the broader support of students' futures. Moreover, if we know that children who feel safe and welcomed are better positioned to focus on academics than those who are scared and stressed (Erickson, 1987), then we can see how helping Maria de la Luz and Norberto appraise a situation, make new friends, and develop a reputation with teachers as respectful could support their transition. These are skills worth helping students develop anyway, but they become more salient and pressing for students who are or could be mobile.

TEACHING ACTIVITIES

1. Retrace the steps taken by Maria's school. Create a visual flow chart for actions taken to support both the student and the family as they navigated the transition. What was done before they moved, what was done after?
2. Discuss how schools can anticipate and position students for success in their mobile and global geographies. In what ways can schools in the U.S. help a student continue to be successful if/when that student moves to Mexico? Are there other countries that students might move to?

   a. Who are the key actors in helping students negotiate both the here and somewhere else of their possible biographies?
   b. What are the essential tasks of the key actors in both the short term and the long term in supporting students that are (or are potentially) mobile?
   c. What are pathways to continued and uncomplicated communication with families after they have transitioned somewhere else?
3. How can schools in the U.S. support the maintenance of students' heritage languages (e.g., Spanish) and other resources (e.g., pride in family and culture) that can be useful in the event of a move and/or for communication with international family members?
4. This chapter recommends explicit attention to metalinguistics. How can metalinguistic awareness be incorporated in student learning inside the classroom throughout the school day? How is metalinguistic awareness beneficial to the learning of any student (mobile or not)? How might it specifically help a student negotiating schooling in a new country that uses a different primary language? (See Chapter 5 on translanguaging for some ideas.)

REFERENCES

Dewey, J. (1902). Address to the National Council of Education. The school as social center. *Elementary School Teacher*, *3*(2), 73–85.

Erickson, E. (1987). Transformation and school success: The politics and culture of educational achievement. *Anthropology & Education Quarterly*, *18*(4), 335–356.

Goode, J. G., Schneider, J. A., & Blanc, S. (1992). Transcending boundaries and closing ranks: How schools shape inter-relations. In L. Lamphere (Ed.), *Structuring diversity: Ethnographic perspectives on the new immigration* (pp. 173–213). Chicago, IL: University of Chicago Press.

Hamann, E. T., & Zúñiga, V. (2011). Schooling and the everyday ruptures transnational children encounter in the United States and Mexico. In C. Coe, R. Reynolds, D. Boehm, J. M. Hess, & H. Rae-Espinoza (Eds.), *Everyday ruptures: Children and migration in global perspective* (pp. 141–160). Nashville, TN: Vanderbilt University Press. http://digitalcommons.unl.edu/teachlearnfacpub/100/

Hornberger, N. H. (2005). Opening and filling up implementational spaces in heritage language education. *Modern Language Journal*, *89*(4), 605–609.

Leeman, J., Rabín, L., & Román-Mendoza, E. (2011). Identity and activism in heritage language education. *Modern Language Journal*, *95*(4), 481–495.

Meltzer, J., & Hamann, E. T. (2004). Meeting the needs of adolescent English language learners for literacy development and content area learning – part one: Focus on motivation and engagement. Education Alliance. Providence, RI: Brown University. http://digitalcommons.unl.edu/teachlearnfacpub/51/

Meltzer, J., & Hamann, E. T. (2005). Meeting the needs of adolescent English language learners for literacy development and content area learning – part two: Focus on classroom teaching and learning strategies. Education Alliance. Providence, RI: Brown University. http://digitalcommons.unl.edu/teachlearnfacpub/53/

Pipher, M. (2003). *The middle of everywhere: Helping refugees enter the American community*. Boston, MA: Mariner Books.

Proefriedt, W. (2008). *High expectations: The cultural roots of standards reform in American education*. New York: Teachers College Press.

Suro, R., & Suárez-Orozco, M. M. (2015). Think of undocumented immigrants as parents, not problems. *New York Times* (April 27). Retrieved from http://nyti.ms/1A4hBqr

Tileva, A. (2018). "Making it" in the United States. Anthropology News website, May 23, 2018. doi:10.1111/AN.877

Valdés, G. (2005). Bilingualism, heritage language learners, and SLA research: Opportunities lost or seized? *Modern Language Journal*, *89*(3), 410–426.

Yanguas, I. (2010). A quantitative approach to investigating Spanish HL speakers' characteristics and motivation: A preliminary study. *Hispania*, *93*(4), 650–670.

Zúñiga, V., & Hamann, E. T. (2015). Going to a home you have never been to: The return migration of Mexican and American-Mexican children. *Children's Geographies*, *13*(6), 643–655.

Section I Resources

ORGANIZATIONS—REPOSITORIES OF RESEARCH AND POLICIES

Bridging Refugee Youth and Children's Services: www.brycs.org/
Center for Applied Linguistics: www.cal.org/
Colorín Colorado (a bilingual website for educators and families of ELs, supported by Washington, DC's PBS affiliate):

- New Immigrant Communities in the Heartland: www.colorin colorado.org/article/new-immigrant-communities- heartland-interview-dr-ted-hamann
- How to Support Immigrant Students and Families: Strategies for Schools and Early Childhood Programs: www.colorincolorado.org/immigration/guide#topics

Cultural Orientation Resource Center: www.culturalorientation.net/library/publications
Great Lakes Equity Center: https://greatlakesequity.org/
Teacher Perspectives on Equitable Education for Immigrant Students: https://greatlakesequity.org/resource/teacher-perspectives-equitable-education-immigrant-students

- U.S. Teachers' Responsibilities Given That Some of Their Students Will Later Go to School in Mexico: https://greatlakesequity.org/resource/students-we-share-us-teachers-responsibilities-given-some-their-students-will-later-go

Institute for Immigration, Globalization, and Education: http://ige.gseis.ucla.edu/

Migration Policy Institute. Analysis of Unauthorized Immigrants in the U.S. by Country and Region of Birth: www.migrationpolicy.org/research/analysis-unauthorized-immigrants-united-states-country-and-region-birth

National School Boards Association. Legal Guide to Serving Undocumented Students in Public Schools: www.nsba.org/lifting-lamp-beside-schoolhouse-door-legal-guide-serving-undocumented-students-public-schools

U.S. Department of Education. Schools' Civil Rights Obligations to English Learner Students and Limited English Proficient Parents: https://www2.ed.gov/about/offices/list/ocr/ellresources.html

U.S. Department of Justice, fact sheets:

- www.justice.gov/sites/default/files/crt/legacy/2014/05/08/plylerfact.pdf
- www.justice.gov/sites/default/files/crt/legacy/2014/05/08/plylerletter.pdf

ILLUSTRATIONS—RESOURCES FOR LEARNING AND LESSONS

Student-Driven Research, by Makeba Jones and Susan Yonezawa: www.ascd.org/publications/educational_leadership/dec08/vol66/num04/Student-Driven_Research.aspx

Youth-Led Participatory Action Research, website that curates student research and offers lesson plans: yparhub.berkeley.edu

Being a Young Translator, video by kids: https://youtu.be/OvljhyuM4Us

Child Language Brokering: https://languagebrokeringidentities.com/

Child Language Brokering in School: http://child-language-brokering.weebly.com/

Translation as a Generative Construct for Lesson Ideas: https://cxarchive.gseis.ucla.edu/xchange/repertoires-of-linguistic-practice/suppliment-to-lesson-plan

Civic Online Reasoning (Stanford History Education Group): https://sheg.stanford.edu/civic-online-reasoning

Translanguaging guides and videos: www.cuny-nysieb.org

SECTION II

COMMUNITY LEADERSHIP

Chapter 11

Balancing School Priorities on the Border

A Case of School Leadership in Immigrant Communities

David DeMatthews and Guadalupe Vela

CONTEXT

Border City Independent School District (BCISD) is an urban school district on the U.S.–Mexico border. BCISD has more than 45,000 students and serves a majority Mexican-American community. The student population is approximately 85% Latinx, 27% English Language Learners (ELLs), and almost 75% economically disadvantaged.[1] Like many districts along the border, BCISD has a long history of racial segregation and underserving Mexican-American students. In the 1970s, a federal court found BCISD was operating segregated and underfunded schools for Mexican-American students. In the 2000s and 2010s, several cheating scandals revealed how the district's administration viewed Mexican-American students as testing liabilities and forced them to drop out to improve average test scores. Ciudad Juárez, México, a nearby city, has also been immersed in a violent drug war for the last decade. Many children who now attend BCISD schools have witnessed or lost loved ones to violence and have sought asylum in El Paso for protection.

Tays Elementary School (ES) serves a low socioeconomic community located near the border and enrolls 578 students from pre-kinder to fifth grade. The student population is predominantly Latinx (93%; White, 3%; American Indian, 2%). Most students are considered economically disadvantaged (97%) and ELLs (80%). Students frequently move in and out of the area, which is reflected in Tays' annual mobility rate of 21%. The surrounding neighborhoods have some of the highest indicators of community needs in the city. Thereby, Tays ES participates in a Community Schools program that facilitates partnerships between the school and community organizations. The program ensures a focus on academics, health and social services, and youth and community development.

Principal Ruiz is a Mexican-American woman who has worked in BCISD and surrounding districts for the past 20 years, including as a bilingual education teacher, instructional coach, and assistant principal. She has been principal at Tays ES for four years. She was interested in closing achievement gaps and raising student achievement, but also cares about students' social and emotional needs. The Tays community has many families who are homeless and struggling to access basic necessities. Many students cross the border to attend school. Every morning, many students wait in line to cross at the U.S. Port of Entry and meet with their family members on the other side to attend their designated school. Students often have parents who do not have U.S. citizenship and who rely on other trusted individuals like aunts, uncles, cousins, and family friends to help their children commute safely (see Deruy, 2016). Principal Ruiz has recognized that in some cases poverty and the commute back and forth over the border are taxing on families: "Some of our students are getting up at 5am or earlier to get here on time each day. It can be difficult for them." At the same time, Principal Ruiz knows that many students come to school with amazing energy despite their life circumstances.

To support students, Principal Ruiz works to facilitate partnerships and collect donations. One community partnership regularly provides clothing, including jeans, uniform pants, shirts, t-shirts, underwear, socks, jackets, shoes, and hygiene items. Another local organization associated with a nearby high school facilitates family–community events, makes holiday food baskets, and leads clothing drives. Tays ES also partners with a non-profit to facilitate additional partnerships to provide dental and medical services, help families with filing taxes and government documents, and create extracurricular activities. These partnerships have created a strong connection between the school and community.

CASE NARRATIVE

The El Paso-Juárez border community has a long history of families dealing with immigration policies and historically has found ways to build partnerships to address concerns. However, since the election of President Donald Trump, many teachers report to Principal Ruiz a growing fear. One teacher in a faculty meeting noted, "More students are afraid their parents are going to be deported and that they will be separated from their family." Other teachers reflected that many students do not fully understand the meaning of immigration status or know their status but have a sense that they will be forced to leave their school and community as a result of a family member's deportation. Teachers began venting their frustration with Principal Ruiz and stated that the school needed to do more to help families. Principal Ruiz promised to follow up with a plan of action.

Principal Ruiz knew she could not ignore that some families and students were facing more severe needs. Students who are undocumented or whose families are undocumented confronted an additional set of challenges that made them vulnerable, which also could impede their academic progress. Principal Ruiz noted that when families struggled with the harmful effects of immigration policy, students could not learn. She communicated with teachers the importance of recognizing the challenges confronted by students. She told teachers that many students "just don't feel safe, because they are worried about their parents. They are worried about whether they are going to be separated from their family." Two cases were especially challenging for the school.

Rosio Talamantes, 47, was facing deportation for the third time within a two-year frame. Talamantes first sought asylum in the United States in 2015. She was impacted by the violence in Mexico and she feared for the safety of her children. A year later, immigration officials denied her request and, at that time, her daughter Sofia, 11, became ill. Talamantes submitted a permit to stay in the country while Sofia was undergoing cancer treatment. A six-month extension was granted. The mother of two received a second permit in 2016. However, under the Trump administration, Talamantes was denied her third petition. Religious leaders intervened on her behalf to delay her deportation. Meanwhile, Talamantes's younger son Jacob, 9, attends Tays Elementary and is constantly referred to the office for insubordination and extreme disruptive behavior. Jacob's teachers reported, "Jacob probably isn't getting enough attention, because his mother is focused on her daughter's health and maintaining her legal status." Talamantes can easily be reached via telephone when teachers want to contact her. Sofia and Jacob have a basic understanding that they may be separated from their mother after her permit expires.

Eduardo Esparza, a father of two, had been living in the U.S for two decades. He had an upcoming meeting to discuss his application for asylum. His older daughter Erica, 22, had arranged to accompany her father that day. Eduardo was detained upon arrival. Erica initially thought it was a normal procedure. After all, it had been a lengthy process to resolve her father's situation. After several hours of waiting, Erica was finally informed he was going to be deported. Erica and her father did not have any other family members in the U.S. She had assumed the role of her deceased mother and took care of her sister while her father worked. She had graduated from high school and was completing her second year in college. Eduardo's youngest daughter Daisy, 6, attended Tays ES and struggled to socialize with her peers. She had several referrals for being defiant with teachers. Daisy's teacher reported that she "was not on grade level" and "did not have a good relationship with her peers." One teacher said, "On some days, she just gets triggered and it throws her off track for part or all of the day." Erica and her father knew the situation would greatly affect Daisy's emotional stability and impact her ability to be successful.

A School Community Meeting

Principal Ruiz recognized her school was not doing enough to help undocumented families. She concluded, "The education we provide will never be enough if we don't address the social and emotional needs." She met with her leadership team, which consisted of her assistant principal, counselor, instructional coaches, family intervention specialist, and faculty representatives. The team met and discussed the two students. Principal Ruiz asked, "What actions have we been taking, and what can we do to help more?" The group agreed to provide additional support to the students, but overall felt a sense of powerlessness. One team member said, "It all just feels like it's so out of our control. The government will make its decision and what will happen will happen." As Principal Ruiz listened to the discussion, she felt a need to do something but she did not know what to say or do.

Principal Ruiz called her mentor and other principals for advice. She wondered if she should call a faculty meeting to discuss the challenges confronted by students and families. However, she had a sense of fear in having a public conversation. Perhaps she would be jeopardizing the privacy of her parents by raising these issues. She also worried about her own legitimacy. She thought, "What if I cannot answer all of my teachers' questions?" Her mentor warned her that the current political context in the state of Texas was one of "insecurity." The governor signed anti-sanctuary city legislation. Public advocacy for or attention to helping undocumented families could put a principal's job at risk. Her mentor said, "What if someone recorded the conversation you had with teachers about helping undocumented families? It could be on Fox News tonight." A district administrator who had been friends with Principal Ruiz recommended she focus on these issues on a case-by-case basis because each family's circumstance was different and because it allowed the school to maintain a "lower profile." The administrator said, "Not all battles can be fought publicly; sometimes, you have to lay low and not bring much attention to the issue you want to address."

Principal Ruiz recalled that over her 20-year career she had never had a principal or district administrator publicly talk about helping undocumented families at a school or district-wide level. She understood the politics of taking such a public stance, but she also felt she needed to act or else more students would languish academically and live in fear. She felt her values and why she became a principal were threatened. She knew meaningful action was necessary, but did not know what to do next.

TEACHING NOTES

Principals engage in several key leadership practices to create high quality schools, such as building a vision and setting directions, understanding and developing people, redesigning the school's organizational conditions, and managing the teaching and learning program (Leithwood, Harris, & Hopkins, 2008). However, leadership cannot be standardized, but instead needs to be responsive to school and community context. When students are vulnerable and struggling with the effects of problematic social policies, principals need to draw upon their repertoire of leadership skills to facilitate change. Principals can lead in ways that help teachers and staff develop a sense of agency to facilitate student learning for vulnerable populations (Dell'Angelo, 2016). They can also broaden their focus beyond instruction to think more holistically and develop systems and supports that help Latinx immigrant communities (Gonzalez, Borders, Hines, Villalba, & Henderson, 2017).

Some policymakers, administrators, and preparation instructors disagree with principals prioritizing family and community engagement over a narrower focus on curriculum and student achievement. However, challenges confronting Latinx immigrant communities cannot be ignored by principals, because students need to feel safe and secure to be successful. Principals must remember:

- A lack of access to housing, healthcare, and healthy food are detrimental to student success (Rothstein, 2004).
- Students are more likely to underachieve when they feel unsafe, insecure, or uncertain about their future (Suldo, Gormley, DuPaul, & Anderson-Butcher, 2014).
- Latinx immigrant students are likely to experience academic success when they feel safe and certain about their futures (Perez, Espinoza, Ramos, Coronado, & Cortes, 2009).

Thus, Principal Ruiz and leaders in similar contexts must orient their leadership toward supporting Latinx immigrant families and students.

Principals who are responsive to context and think critically about the diverse needs in their schools and communities can have a powerful impact on their teachers and students. Some scholars have called such responsive and critical approaches "social justice leadership" because of a focus on identifying and engaging in efforts to alter inequitable arrangements that exist within society and in schools (Dantley, Beachum, & McCray, 2009; Furman, 2012; Murtadha & Watts, 2005; Theoharis, 2007). DeMatthews (2018) put forth a community engaged leadership framework focused on catalyzing and meaningfully engaging teachers, students, families, and communities in transformational change in marginalized communities. The framework emphasizes several elements: *personal experiences and commitments*, *situational awareness*, *advocacy*, *critical reflection*, and *technical expertise*.

The *personal and professional experiences* of principals are integral to the ways they engage in leadership. Their lived experiences coupled with ongoing daily leadership practice support the development of a *situational awareness*, which allows principals to acknowledge community assets, recognize the political nature of challenging the status quo, and foresee future challenges to social justice agendas. Understanding the school, community, and district landscapes allows principals to engage as advocates for students and families. However, *advocacy* is strategic and not always a public and head-on activity. Principals may need to be "tempered radicals" (Alston, 2005) who consider unequal power dynamics and collaborate with others to identify the best courses of action. Being "tempered" reflects an understanding that advocacy does not always allow for using the power of their own voice publicly.

Principals need to consider their ethical and moral obligations to the communities they serve. Sergiovanni (1996) called for leadership that was "responsive to the norms, values, and beliefs that define the standard for living together as a group" (p. 14). This call to leadership requires principals to develop a school community where "everyone watches out for the ones carrying the heaviest burdens" (Starratt, 2004) and acts in ways that support all community members. A broad-based coalition and other leaders are necessary to advocate for schools and communities. As Crawford (2017) noted, "effective leaders are to act as public advocates for students and their families as well as the community" (p. 171). Such leadership requires consistent *critical reflection* to understand the ways in which one might not only disrupt but also inadvertently contribute to the status quo. Principals cannot assume they have all the answers, be seduced by heroic narratives, or try to do everything at once.

Finally, principals need school leadership *technical expertise* including knowledge of law and policy, school budgeting, high-quality curriculum and instruction, and how to develop school-wide systems that support all students. Without such knowledge, principals struggle to utilize resources and find innovative ways to meet multiple demands of districts, teachers, families, students, and communities. Relatedly, principals working in Latinx immigrant communities and with undocumented immigrant students can utilize resources to create systems of support (Crawford, 2017; Crawford, Walker, & Valle, 2018; DeMatthews & Izquierdo, 2018). (See Chapter 7 for an overview of legal definitions and court cases impacting immigrant students in schools.)

TEACHING ACTIVITIES

1. Legal Knowledge and Training

In 1975, the Texas legislature passed a law authorizing school districts to deny enrollment to children who had not been "legally admitted" into the United States. According to the law, districts could bar undocumented children or charge them tuition. In 1982, the U.S. Supreme Court ruled in *Plyler v. Doe* that the Texas law violated the Equal Protection Clause of the 14th Amendment. States cannot discriminate against undocumented children on the basis of immigration status or deny them access to public education. The Supreme Court highlighted the pivotal role of education in the life of children and society. The decision reinforced the prevailing notion that schools provide the primary means of preparing children to contribute to social, political, and economic life.

Principals need to be knowledgeable about the implications of the Plyler decision. Working individually or in small groups, consider the following tasks. Take the position of a local school principal, and develop one of the following:

- Write up a statement for a local district that articulates and defines support for undocumented students, defining the responsibilities of principals, teachers, and schools in this work.
- Create a parent or teacher professional development session to provide knowledge to support, advocate for, and protect undocumented students and their families. Consider how to provide these sessions in multiple languages and spaces.
- Make a list of community organizations that provide support, counseling, and mental health services for undocumented students and families. Write an action plan for working with one.
- Affirm that undocumented students can go to college, but may require additional research and support given the vulnerability

and changing circumstances of policies like the Deferred Action for Childhood Arrivals (www.nilc.org/issues/daca/status-current-daca-litigation).

- Designate and support an undocumented student specialist who can help students and families investigate school and career options, provide student mentoring, and make connections between different community organizations based on individual needs and circumstances.
- Collect and make a plan to distribute information about community programs and events that address the needs of immigrant communities and ensure school personnel are in attendance as a sign of solidarity. Consider how to provide this information in multiple languages and spaces.

2. Identifying Community-Based Resources

Community-based equity audits (CBEAs) are an "instrument, strategy, process, and approach to guide educational leaders in supporting equitable school outcomes" (Green, 2017, p. 5). CBEAs start with the development of a team of stakeholders that work to define and discuss current practices and approaches. Then, this team works to understand the assets of families and communities. Next, the team assesses the effectiveness of current school–community practices and engages in local asset mapping. They identify non-profits, places of worship, businesses, universities, and other organizations that can potentially partner to support families. Finally, the team and its partners gather data, learn more about challenging issues, and produce new ideas and processes that promote school–community change.

- In small groups, consider the immigrant communities served by your local school(s). Develop a CBEA to focus specifically on issues and challenges impacting undocumented families and students. As part of this work, pay special attention to indigenous resources. If there is time, invite immigrant advocacy organizations or take field trips to non-profits serving immigrants and refugees to help with mapping community assets. Examples of relevant community organizations are listed in Section II Resources.

NOTE

1 "Economically disadvantaged" is a term used by the Texas Education Agency based on state criteria.

REFERENCES

Alston, J. A. (2005). Tempered radicals and servant leaders: Black females persevering in the superintendency. *Educational Administration Quarterly*, *41*(4), 675–688.

Crawford, E. R. (2017). The ethic of community and incorporating undocumented immigrant concerns into ethical school leadership. *Educational Administration Quarterly*, *53*(2), 147–179.

Crawford, E. R., Walker, D., & Valle, F. (2018). Leading for change: School leader advocacy for undocumented immigrant students. *Equity & Excellence in Education*, *51*(1), 62–77.

Dantley, M., Beachum, F., & McCray, C. (2009). Exploring the intersectionality of multiple centers within notions of social justice. *Journal of School Leadership*, *18*(2), 124–133.

Dell'Angelo, T. (2016). The power of perception: Mediating the impact of poverty on student achievement. *Education and Urban Society*, *48*(3), 245–261.

DeMatthews, D. E. (2018). *Community engaged leadership for social justice: A critical approach in urban schools*. New York: Routledge.

DeMatthews, D. E., & Izquierdo, E. (2018). Supporting Mexican American immigrant students on the border: A case study of culturally responsive leadership in a dual language elementary school. *Urban Education*. https://doi.org/10.1177/0042085918756715.

DeRuy, E. (2016, November 3). Crossing the border for school: Some children commute from Mexico to the U.S. on a daily basis, a process that Donald Trump's candidacy complicates. *The Atlantic*. Retrieved from www.theatlantic.com/education/archive/2016/11/crossing-the-border-for-school/506342/

Furman, G. (2012). Social justice leadership as praxis: Developing capacities through preparation programs. *Educational Administration Quarterly*, *48*(2), 191–229.

Gonzalez, L. M., Borders, L. D., Hines, E. M., Villalba, J. A., & Henderson, A. (2017). Parental involvement in children's education: Considerations for school counselors working with Latino immigrant families. *Professional School Counseling*, *16*(3), 185–193.

Green, T. L. (2017). Community-based equity audits: A practical approach for educational leaders to support equitable community–school improvements. *Educational Administration Quarterly*, *53*(1), 3–39.

Leithwood, K., Harris, A., & Hopkins, D. (2008). Seven strong claims about successful school leadership. *School Leadership and Management*, *28*(1), 27–42.

Murtadha, K., & Watts, D. M. (2005). Linking the struggle for education and social justice: Historical perspectives of African American leadership in schools. *Educational Administration Quarterly*, *41*(4), 591–608.

Perez, W., Espinoza, R., Ramos, K., Coronado, H. M., & Cortes, R. (2009). Academic resilience among undocumented Latino students. *Hispanic Journal of Behavioral Sciences*, *31*(2), 149–181.

Rothstein, R. (2004). *Class and schools*. Washington, DC: Economic Policy Institute.

Sergiovanni, T. J. (1996). *Leadership for the schoolhouse: How is it different? Why is it important?* San Francisco, CA: Jossey-Bass.

Starratt, R. J. (2004). *Ethical leadership*. San Francisco, CA: Jossey-Bass.

Suldo, S. M., Gormley, M. J., DuPaul, G. J., & Anderson-Butcher, D. (2014). The impact of school mental health on student and school-level academic outcomes: Current status of the research and future directions. *School Mental Health*, *6*(2), 84–98.

Theoharis, G. (2007). Social justice educational leaders and resistance: Toward a theory of social justice leadership. *Educational Administration Quarterly*, *43*(2), 221–258.

Chapter 12

How School Leadership Influences (and Is Influenced by) Immigration

St. Claire Adriaan, Anthony H. Normore, and Jeffrey S. Brooks

CONTEXT

Middle school principal St. Claire Adriaan woke up on the morning of November 9, 2016, to the announcement of the American presidential election result. The first thought that came to his mind was, "What do I tell my students today?" Academia Avance Charter School is located in Highland Park, a Los Angeles neighborhood school that serves a Latino population with sons and daughters of immigrants. During the run-up to the election, principal Adriaan overheard many of the students' conversations about fears of what would happen if Donald Trump won the election. This was all in the context of the unprecedented negative rhetoric then-candidate Trump voiced about Mexicans.

Principal Adriaan was a recently trained Restorative Justice facilitator through the International Institute of Restorative Practices (IIRP) and felt the most effective way to start the school day was to implement a process called restorative circles. Restorative circles allow for student voice within an inclusive space. He immediately sent an email to all teachers asking them to have circles with their student advisories and instructed them to ask two questions:

1. How are you feeling?

2. What are your concerns?

Principal Adriaan went to school and moved from class to class listening to his eighth-grade students share their feelings. He realized they were shaken, scared, and worried. He felt that things had quickly changed and that the change would demand a change within the school and his leadership. He reflected on Maslow's Hierarchy of Needs and how feeling "safe and secure" is a basic human need. What he heard from his students that morning was clear; they did not feel safe and were afraid for themselves, their families, and the immigrant community. Principal Adriaan learned long ago that any student who sits in class feeling afraid is not capable of learning, or actualizing their full potential.

On that November morning, principal Adriaan facilitated a restorative circle with faculty and staff. He felt it was important to "take the temperature" and gauge where the staff were emotionally, too. Most of the staff were Latino, and some were recipients of the Deferred Action for Childhood Arrivals (DACA), which gave them legal documentation to work in the U.S. but not a path to citizenship (see Chapter 7).

For Principal Adriaan, it was important that the school empower the faculty and staff to adapt to the changes and provide them with strategies to help the students. In the restorative circle for the faculty and staff, two questions were posed:

1. How are you feeling?

2. How do we best serve our students during this trying time?

After the circle, Principal Adriaan broke the faculty and staff into collaborative groups where teachers discussed the current political climate, how it affected the students, and how they could help the students. Groups then reported to the larger group and a discussion ensued based on the following outcomes:

1. Students are afraid.
2. Teaching and learning must be culturally relevant and adaptable to serve the needs of students and the community.
3. Faculty and staff will have to be empathetic and check in regularly with students.
4. Restorative circles will be key during student advisories to check in with students often.
5. Teachers and administrators will create opportunities for students to express themselves orally and through visual and performing arts.

CASE NARRATIVE

The eighth graders were reading *The Diary of Anne Frank* in Mr. Webb's English class. Principal Adriaan was often impressed with the level of questions asked by students, and how they were able to draw comparisons between the novel and modern-day America. The students were excited because, as they neared the end of the novel, they would go on a field trip to the Simon Wiesenthal Museum of Tolerance (MOT). The museum is world renowned for delving into the dark issues of oppression, anti-Semitism, racism, and prejudice, highlighting the Holocaust as the extreme example of inhumanity. Interactive exhibits, two theaters, a research floor, and gallery for special exhibitions within the Simon Wiesenthal Center are just part of the experience found there.

On the morning of February 28, 2017, Principal Adriaan greeted his students as they arrived to school. He greeted every student by hand every morning as a means to check in with each student, to look him or her directly in the eyes. After having a quick school assembly with the students to remind them of the expectations for the day, they were ready to leave for MOT. However, a student then approached Principal Adriaan and asked if it was possible to delay the departure because Fatima, an eighth-grade student, was involved in a situation and should be arriving soon. Principal Adriaan had no idea what the situation was with Fatima and said that they could wait a few minutes. He was still waiting to greet students when Fatima arrived at school. She was visibly shaken, upset, and in tears. He took her into the principal's office and asked her what was wrong. Tearfully, she explained that after her dad, Romulo Avelica, had dropped her younger sister off at the nearby elementary school and was on his way to drop off Fatima, U.S. Immigration and Customs Enforcement (ICE) stopped them. ICE arrested her dad in front of her and her mom. Fatima had no idea if she was ever going to see him again, or what was going to happen. Fatima was scared, uncertain, and worried. Her principal did not know what to say, and did not want to make false promises.

Principal Adriaan felt Fatima's pain and wanted to cry with her but kept his composure until she calmed down. During this time, he relived many of the atrocities he experienced as a child growing up in Apartheid South Africa. He knew that no child, no matter what race, religion, ethnicity, or immigrant status, should experience what Fatima just experienced. His mantra was: "We simply do not do this to children." He felt that this dramatic event would haunt Fatima for the rest of her life. When Fatima had calmed down, he reminded her of the field trip for the day and gave her the option to go home and be with her family. Courageously, she decided to participate in the field trip to MOT. Principal Adriaan thought to himself how difficult this MOT experience might be for Fatima, and for the other students too, given what had just occurred.

Principal Adriaan knew it had been widely stated in recent months that the new government was going to crack down on "illegal immigrants," and that deportation was going to be "the order of the day." Romulo Avelica was an undocumented father of four U.S.-born children, two of whom were students in the middle school. Romulo, originally from Nyarit, Mexico, had lived in the U.S. for over 20 years. While raising his four daughters, he also acted as a surrogate father figure to his four nieces and nephews, some of whom were also enrolled in the school. The primary breadwinner of the family, Romulo worked as a food preparer at one of the local Mexican restaurants. He had two misdemeanor criminal convictions which ICE used to justify what later became his deportation.

After they boarded the school bus, Principal Adriaan kept an eye on Fatima to make sure that she was okay. At one point, he saw her near tears. He spoke with her. She indicated she had recorded the arrest of her father. After obtaining permission from Fatima, he watched the video on her phone, as she continued to sob about her father's arrest. Principal Adriaan knew he needed to protect his students, and quickly jumped into activist mode. He felt that no child should experience the trauma he just witnessed on the video. He contacted his Executive Director and informed him there was a video recording of the event that had just happened. The Executive Director immediately reached out to the family and sent a team member to pick up the phone from Principal Adriaan at the Museum of Tolerance. The school then jumped into action to see what would happen, and to determine how to assist the family.

By 3pm that afternoon, the Highland Park community came together for an assembly at the school: all students, families, community organizations, including the National Day Laborers Organizing Network who became a strong ally in the fight for the release of Romulo Avelica. Different religious clergy were there to support the family and the school. During this time, members of the school team were working the phones in efforts to contact the ICE office, the mayor's office, and any other organizations that they felt could assist. Shortly after the conclusion of the school assembly, an announcement was made that Romulo would be deported to Mexico at 5pm from the ICE office in downtown Los Angeles. After a short meeting to design a plan of action, Principal Adriaan had to quickly decide what his role as school leader required from him at this time. He felt he had no choice. He had to be an advocate and an activist.

Advocacy and Activist Leadership

Principal Adriaan joined the group heading to the ICE office to form a human chain to prevent the van from leaving the downtown Los Angeles office. Shortly prior to the scheduled van departure from the office, a "stay" was granted, and Romulo was removed from the van. Principal Adriaan would always remember the look in Fatima's eyes that evening when they parted. There was pain there, uncertainty, fear, and tears. As she got inside the family car, she looked at him and expressed deep gratitude for what he had helped do. From that point, Principal Adriaan knew that his leadership was about to change dramatically.

The video that Fatima had sobbingly recorded of her dad's arrest was aired on local television. Within days, it went viral throughout the country and worldwide. This led to media interest from around the world, and while it was important to get the story out to the world, it was also important to have as little disruption as possible to the school. The fact that one of the students had her family torn apart also brought fear and anxiety to the student body and to the Highland Park community. This demanded that Principal Adriaan carefully rethink his leadership to ensure the world heard Fatima's story by allowing reporters, news cameras, politicians, and civic organizations on campus. At the same time, he needed to make sure there was as little disruption as possible to the academic program. Likewise, it was important to empower students and families with knowledge about their rights, ease their fears, and provide counselling.

The school campus welcomed television stations from across the United States as well as the BBC, Sky News, Belgian Television, Dutch Television, Japan Television, Univision, and many more. At the time the video and Fatima's story hit the viral airwaves, Romulo was being held in an immigration detention center. While the attorneys were working on getting Romulo released from immigration detention, Principal Adriaan had to adjust some policies at school to help students get through this difficult time. Nobody ever asked about the immigration status of parents when children registered for school. In fact, many students would likely not know the status of their parents. However, given the recent circumstances, Principal Adriaan felt it was time for students to have these difficult conversations with their parents in order to be prepared in the event that any of them were affected by deportations. He led a family information night where attorneys and civic organizations shared knowledge of immigrant rights and provided information on how families can assign legal guardianship to a family member or friend to prevent students from ending up in foster care in the event of an arrest or deportation.

In the meantime, Principal Adriaan attended "Free Romulo" rallies and fundraisers to help the family keep food on the table. Fatima and her sister, Yuleni, completed the LA marathon without their dad present. He was their training coach and their biggest cheerleader. Principal Adriaan attended Rapid Response Training in order to be available when needed and to learn what lawful action could be taken by the school.

Because the school was affiliated with UnidosUS, and because both the Executive Director and Principal Adriaan were members of the National Institute for Latino School Leaders with UnidosUS, they were given access to training on advocacy. This training on both local and national levels proved a great asset in their efforts to assist the Avalica family. Through their affiliation they were able to facilitate a media event on March 28, 2017, at the Capitol in Washington, DC. There, Civil Rights activist and president and CEO of UnidosUS Janet Murgia, along with United States Senator Chuck Schumer and United States Representative Nancy Pelosi, joined the Avelica students as they told their story.

On June 2, 2017, there was a press conference prior to a court hearing on Post-Conviction-Relief. At this stage the mayor, 11 members of the City Council, three county supervisors, the president of the Los Angeles Unified School District's Board of Directors, the leadership of the California Caucus in Sacramento, many religious leaders, and countless community members had all urged that Romulo not be deported. There were many requests to the city attorney for relief for Romulo. With 100% of parents signing permission slips for students to attend the press conference, Principal Adriaan filled the school bus and drove to the courthouse where the students repeated the daily pledge and some of their affirmations as college-bound students.

In the meantime, through a Diego Rivera Art Project, students were encouraged to reflect on their current situation and express their feelings through art. They focused on social inequality, technology, and the ecosystem. Through collaboration, student projects mostly focused on immigration and deportation issues. Their fear and anger were real. In June 2017, Fatima culminated from eighth grade without her dad present at the ceremony. At the culmination ceremony, both Fatima and Principal Adriaan were recognized by the city of Los Angeles with Certificates of Recognition from Gilbert A. Cedillo, council member of the 1st District.

To conclude, the Academia Avance Charter School is committed to serve all students, and to stand by immigrant families and DACA students. Executive Director Mireles is considered a role model to school leaders across the country. In Fatima's first television interview following her father's arrest she said, "I knew if I went to school, they would help me." Principal Adriaan is thrilled his school system did not let her down.

TEACHING NOTES

The issue of undocumented immigration has grown in importance during the past two decades, as the number of such immigrants has increased significantly and as immigrants have arrived to many new destinations in the

United States. These trends have prompted calls for greater immigration enforcement and reform (Lozano & Sorensen, 2011), but also for an eventual path to legalization for those who have lived and worked in the United States for many years (see Chapter 7).

It is critical to explore how leaders throughout the educational system can use their influence and agency to help create and honor spaces where conflict and cohesion can both happen, but in a manner so that they are productive and positive in terms of their educational value (Jaenee-Fraise & Brooks, 2015). Culturally relevant leadership literature indicates that U.S. school cultures have traditionally led to inequitable dynamics that privilege an abstract dominant culture while marginalizing others (Brooks & Miles, 2010). In reality, several cultures and subcultures flow into and out of schools at all times (Brooks & Normore, 2010). Given such conditions, educators must seek to "build bridges and cross borders so that the multiple cultures in the school-community can have empathy and define their own values instead of having this done by someone else" (Jaenee-Fraise & Brooks, 2015, p. 7). Not only are self-defining values imperative, but from an ethical lens it is the "right thing to do" and a support for restorative processes.

The principal aim of restorative processes in schools is to repair the harm that has been caused by incidents through the active involvement of all stakeholders. Beyond the significant shift required of the schools and community to effectively curb fear and achieve justice within a restorative response, there is the impact that this has for altering the leadership role at the school level and throughout the community (Van Ness & Strong, 2010). Social and restorative justice leaders engage with the communities. They feel a moral obligation to work with those they serve, including students, teachers, families, partners, and other entities in the communities, to understand the problem and then to seek positive solutions to trauma as a whole community.

From a trauma-informed orientation, we are witnessing increasingly high numbers of research papers that highlight the impact that toxic stress and trauma have on the developing brain (see Chapter 8). Educators may well be misdiagnosing many students, including students from immigrant families, due to the lack of understanding of how trauma is manifested in the developing brain. As asserted in brain research (Newton, 2015), brains in pain will not learn the same way as pain-free brains, and culturally relevant leaders must take such conditions into account within their schools.

DISCUSSION QUESTIONS

1. What are the pros and cons of responding to the situation in the manner undertaken by the Executive Director? Principal? Community? Students?

2. How do educational leaders utilize relationships with other educational stakeholders and community/government services to support undocumented immigrant students and families?
3. How do schools ensure that immigrant student populations are protected in their learning environments?

TEACHING ACTIVITIES

Immigration in Global–Local Perspective

This activity can be conducted in either a school or university setting. The activity is designed to deepen participants' understanding of issues related to immigration and education.

Step 1: Initial Discussion. Use the following prompts to have an initial discussion about the issue: (a) How are you feeling about immigration in school, community, and society? (b) What are your concerns about immigration for yourself, the organization, and the community? Based on this discussion, collectively identify three to five significant issues related to immigration and education that are most important to the group.

Step 2: Researching Immigration, from Global to Local. Assign participants to teams focused on the issues identified at the end of Step 1. Each team should endeavor to understand their issue at the global, national, regional, local, community, and organizational levels. This means looking for pertinent statistics, reviewing policies related to immigration, reading peer-reviewed research, and identifying important facts, figures, and concepts that help deepen the group's understanding of their issue at multiple levels—and also considering the ways that the different levels are well or poorly aligned.

Step 3: Interviews in Organization and Community. Each team member should commit to interviewing at least one other person in the organization and one person from the community on their issue. These interviews should preferably take place with people the interviewer does not know well, so they can hear a new perspective. Interview prompts may include questions like: (a) What is your personal experience with immigration? (b) What is the state of immigration, both globally and in the local community? (c) How does immigration influence people's education? (d) Does immigration change or maintain the purposes of education?

Step 4: Presentation and Intention. Teams present the findings of their research and interviews (steps 2 and 3) to each other. Given any new information or insights into immigration and education, they should discuss their intentions to both change and maintain current practices in the organization. This may mean revisiting or creating policies, changing practices, connecting more with the community, a whole-school book reading, etc. In keeping with best practice in educational leadership, this course of action should be evidence-based, inclusive, and co-designed with leaders and followers (Brooks & Normore, 2017).

REFERENCES

Brooks, J. S., & Miles, M. T. (2010). The social and cultural dynamics of school leadership: Classic concepts and cutting-edge possibilities. In S. D. Horsford (Ed.), *New perspectives in educational leadership: Exploring social, political, and community contexts and meaning* (pp. 7–28). New York: Peter Lang Publishing.

Brooks, J. S., & Normore, A. H. (2010). Educational leadership and globalization: Toward a global perspective. *Educational Policy*, *24*(1), 52–82.

Brooks, J. S., & Normore, A. H. (2017). *Foundations of educational leadership: Developing excellent and equitable schools*. Routledge: New York.

Jaenee-Fraise, N., & Brooks, J. S. (2015). Toward a theory of culturally relevant leadership for school-community culture. *International Journal of Multicultural Education*, *17*(1), 6–21.

Lozano, F., & Sorensen, T. (2011). The labor market effects of immigration reform. *Policy Matters*, *4*(3), 1–12.

Newton, P. M. (2015). The learning styles myth is thriving in higher education. *Frontiers in Psychology*, *6*, 1908.

Van Ness, D., & Strong, K. (2010). *Restoring justice: An introduction to restorative justice*. Cincinnati, OH: Anderson Publishing.

Chapter 13

A Principal's Mission to Create Space and Inclusivity for Immigrant Students in a Predominantly Latinx Charter School

Uzziel H. Pecina and Dea Marx

CONTEXT

Across the nation, many immigrant families choose to settle in urban centers, often due to consanguinity with community or family members residing in the same location. These valued connections and relationships provide a sense of welcoming and belongingness. Services such as transportation, affordable housing, and culturally sustaining educational opportunities also weigh into the decisions to move to urban locations (Lopez, 2015). Such is the context of this case which focuses on one Midwestern urban public school district with a history of over 100 years of immigration from Mexico. Between 2007 and 2017, the number of students receiving "English Learner" (EL) services increased from 3,978 to 5,710. In 2017, demographic data reported district students as Black 57%, Latinx 27%, White 10%, and other or undeclared groups 6%. In addition, poverty levels, as measured by free and reduced lunch status (86%), reflected a student population with concentrated needs.

Historically, racial and political agendas among the public-school district board members of Midwest City focused on binary Black/White racial issues and left no place for Latinx students. Desegregation and magnet school initiatives resulted in multiple neighborhood school closures. This left many Latinx families searching for high quality educational opportunities. In 1990, Caridad Community Center[1] founded César Chávez Charter High School (CCCHS) in response to this upheaval in the public school district. Caridad Community Center is a century-old social service organization that served the local Latinx community through wraparound and holistic approaches. Caridad continues its commitment to CCCHS, providing myriad community services to support newly immigrated families.

CCCHS reports that its student population is over 90% Latinx. Such data, however, disguise the mosaic of students designated by this demographic category. Under the Latinx umbrella, some students at CCCHS are U.S.-born, speak only English, and identify as first-, second-, or third-generation Mexican-Americans. Others identify as new immigrants, are fluent only in their native language, and may have entered the U.S. to escape traumatic social, economic, or political experiences in their home countries of Guatemala, Nicaragua, Cuba, and El Salvador. Immigration experiences range from professional visas (i.e., H-1B, specialized occupations) to undocumented families. In short, students and their families represent an array of languages, cultural identities, customs, educational experiences, and traditions.

Mr. José Ortega began as a History teacher at CCCHS in 1999 and became principal in 2006. Under his leadership, CCCHS now serves over 330 students with an annual wait-list of 100 potential applicants. Over the last 29 years, CCCHS has outgrown several buildings, finally settling on the east side of Midwest City, commonly referred to as the "New American" community. The teaching staff has grown over the years, though most are still White and monolingual. Local immigration resettlement centers assist newly arrived immigrants in finding neighborhoods with similar nationalities, cultures, and languages. CCCHS, however, did not foresee the influx of international immigrant communities that had heard about the welcoming and inclusive charter school.

CASE NARRATIVE

It was a bright, sunny spring day at César Chávez Charter High School (CCCHS), and Mr. Ortega welcomed students at the front steps of the school. Giving "high-fives" and "fist-bumps," and saying "Buenos días" and "welcome," reassured students at CCCHS they were members of one big family.

Mr. Ortega is a first-generation Mexican-American with roots in Monterrey, Mexico, where his parents were born. He is bicultural and bilingual in Spanish/English and grew up in a neighborhood across the river from CCCHS. Mr. Ortega's neighborhood mirrors that of much of the CCCHS community, which he believes allows him to relate to diverse students and their families. Over time, Mr. Ortega has learned to engage the ever-changing student population of the city's east side, where more affordable housing and resettlement centers exist. Parents from the multigenerational Latinx and Black communities enrolled their children in CCCHS to capitalize on its safe and welcoming academic environment. With a significantly increased enrollment of new immigrant families from Cuba, Central America, and Mexico, the breadth of diversity under the Latinx umbrella created new challenges to the established school culture. Specifically, multiple dialects, differing customs, and unfamiliar indigenous languages presented concerns, yet also new opportunities, to the school.

During these unprecedented demographic changes, Mr. Ortega began to recognize cultural dissonance and teacher biases at CCCHS. Signs of cultural dissonance were reflected in a significant increase in discipline referrals, teacher comments expressing an "us versus them" attitude, and resistance to cultural competency professional development. Recognizing the situation's urgency, Mr. Ortega did a critical analysis of teacher and family engagement in order to identify ways to create a more culturally responsive school climate. Mr. Ortega gathered data from teacher feedback forms, observations, and information from teachers, families, and students.

Key themes from the data Mr. Ortega collected included teacher/community disconnect, new immigrant needs, and teacher requests for support. Each theme reflected an unmet need within the school community. For example, within teacher/community disconnect, one Spanish-speaking parent reported, "I wish we had better communication with our teachers," while a Black parent wanted to see "more culturally relevant material related to our community." Within teacher requests for support, a monolingual teacher said to a staff member, "I need help communicating with our Spanish-speaking parents to keep them informed!" Another teacher made the following culturally insensitive statement, "They [the ELLs] don't speak English! I don't know what to do with them so they shouldn't be in my class." Quotes such as these provided guidance as Mr. Ortega weighed multiple options for meeting immediate needs with significant impact on the school's culture and climate. In consultation with his leadership team, Mr. Ortega selected two initiatives for the next school year: home visits and wraparound family social services.

Home Visits

Mr. Ortega identified foundational issues stemming from implicit cultural biases among his predominantly White teaching staff, such as new teachers' lack of awareness of cultural community assets or the economic impact of assignments for some new immigrant students (e.g., homework assignments that required computers and/or internet access). Mr. Ortega required that teachers visit students' homes at the beginning of the year to acquaint themselves with neighborhoods and families. He stated, "We want teachers to know the neighborhoods our students are coming from," and to hear from parents "what their dreams and aspirations are for their children."

To prepare for the home visits, Mr. Ortega arranged a day of professional development that included touring local neighborhoods. As a bus took the staff through students' neighborhoods, a local community expert gave the historical context of community growth and development. Community members engaged with staff, sharing both family stories and experiences, and answering questions. Mr. Ortega guided staff members through professional development that unpacked the community visit experience, learned about cultural and familial expectations, acknowledged biases, and planned how this new learning could increase student and family engagement.

Later, teachers and staff collectively planned home visits that included visiting families in pairs throughout the school year. In some cases, translators were requested. Not all teacher visits were made directly to homes; to respect families' desires or comfort level with this project, the CCCHS leadership also recommended that teachers offer to meet in spaces like local libraries, community centers, or churches.

Wraparound Services

Without acknowledging the dreams and aspirations of parents and families as a vital part of CCCHS's culture, Mr. Ortega realized students' success would not be fully actualized. Data reflected newly immigrated parents needed support finding employment, accessing medical and health services, and understanding the educational system. As the number of immigrant students continued to increase, Mr. Ortega enlisted the community to provide full services to both students and families. Immigrant families were provided wraparound social services from Caridad Community Center, the sponsoring community agency, in concert with local city and government social agencies. Services included housing and utility assistance, family and substance addiction counseling, a culinary arts preparation program, elderly day care, "meals on wheels" for homebound elders, and a community and employee childcare center. Mr. Ortega asked Ms. Martinez to act as a designated CCCHS liaison for immigrant families. Ms. Martinez contacted families and connected them with the community organizations, local government agencies, or programs that could best assist them.

To provide academic support, Mr. Ortega annually invited parents and families to information sessions regarding academic opportunities specific to immigrant students. For example, immigrant parents were introduced to a list of opportunities for students. Mr. Ortega firmly believed in national and local partnerships, such as agreements with the local public school that offered technical programs, the local community college, and a mutual understanding with the local public university to offer college credit.

TEACHING NOTES

In this case study, Mr. Ortega recognized that incoming immigrant students had unmet needs within the current school culture. Student enrollment shifted from predominantly bilingual multigenerational Latinx to an increasingly diverse student population that included multiple immigrant communities with a variety of languages, cultures, and traditions. Despite being a charter school founded with a culturally sustaining vision, CCCHS still had to adapt and learn how to serve new communities.

Like CCCHS, many public and charter schools across the nation are experiencing an increase in ethnic and racial diversity (Hussar & Bailey, 2014; Musu-Gillette et al., 2016). While all PK-12 public schools include 51% students of color (Hussar & Bailey, 2014), 80% of teachers are still White, middle-class, and prepared by educator preparation programs based on predominantly White values and practices (Howard, 2016). Paris and Alim (2017) highlight the nationwide need to increase the racial and ethnic diversity of teachers and for teacher preparation programs to address culturally sustaining practices for a diverse classroom in an increasingly pluralistic and global society (Marx & Pecina, 2016). This Teaching Notes section reviews background research on charter schools as well as culturally sustaining practices important for all schools.

Charter Schools

Minnesota passed the nation's first charter law in 1991. Soon after, 28 states legislated charter school laws (Manno, Finn, Bierlein, & Vanourek, 1998). Charter schools currently serve 6% of all students nationwide (Cordes, 2018) and provide a public education paid for by tax dollars. These schools are accountable to the same standards for learning outcomes, basic health, safety, and non-discrimination requirements as district public schools, but may be developed by parents, teachers, or community organizations (Manno et al., 1998). Recent studies indicate charter schools and district public schools have a similar impact on student achievement (Cohodes, 2018; Sahin, Wilson, & Capraro, 2018) and may be especially effective for students of color in urban areas (CREDO, 2015).

School choice for immigrant parents. While research is limited on how many charter school students are immigrants, statistics on "English Learners" suggest that many immigrant families choose charter schools. While some charters in certain contexts may "under-enroll" historically underserved communities (see Chapter 14), national data collected by the Office of English Language Acquisition (OELA, 2017) revealed 10% of students in charter schools were designated as English Learners (ELs) in 2013, a percentage equivalent to that for ELs attending district public schools nationwide (National Center for Education Statistics, 2018).

Some immigrant parents turn to charter schools, when available, to meet students' academic needs and "honor their cultural heritage" (Jackson, 2010, p. 23). The focus of some charter schools is to support students as they build proficiency in English at the same time as they learn grade-appropriate content (Mavrogordato & Stein, 2016). As immigrant parents share information and their children's success in charter schools, other parents bring their own children there in search of this same success (Mavrogordato & Stein, 2016).

The role of the principal in charter schools. As the primary leader, the principal is responsible for establishing a charter school's mission and values, determining the academic and cultural climate, and setting expectations for effective teaching and learning (Howard, 2016). Stable and consistent school leadership often drives the academic achievement of students, effectiveness of teachers, and engagement of parents. Charter school principals share many similarities with public school principals, yet charter principals' roles may include myriad additional responsibilities (Klocko, Jankens, & Evans, 2018). They may serve as superintendents, be responsible for state and national standards, manage facilities, recruit both staff and students, and collaborate with their governing board and local community organizations (Garcia & Salinas, 2018; Klocko et al., 2018). At the same time, charter principals may have greater autonomy, independence, and flexibility (Garcia & Salinas, 2018).

To effectively and ethically serve immigrant students, charter school principals must provide leadership and engage in the planning of professional development for teachers (Garcia & Salinas, 2018). Principals must take conscious action to build inclusive school cultures by engaging their teaching staff in immersive activities, such as home visits or neighborhood walks (Marx & Pecina, 2016). Among other activities, professional development opportunities include immersion in cultures other than their own (Richly & Graves, 2012) and increasing awareness of unconscious biases (Torino, 2018).

Culturally Sustaining Practices

Home visits. Home visits are not a new concept for either public or charter schools. Reasons for home visits can include: attendance issues, unattended parent–teacher conferences, academic concerns, or just an opportunity to get to know and learn more about families. Community organizations can support home-visit projects, with some recommending the following: 1) teacher preparation is essential; 2) staff should not visit alone but rather in pairs; 3) family–school collaboration should continue in other ways beyond the home visit (see teacherhomevisit.org).

Henke (2011) provides an overview of one "Teacher Home Visit Program" in which school personnel saw positive results. For example, teachers found that home visits transformed their teaching and resulted in greater efficiencies to support student success. Home visits are also a great way to learn about culturally and linguistically diverse families and how their valuable funds of knowledge can support their students' school life; visiting breaks down stereotypes, as teachers can learn that their immigrant families are affluent and/or have highly educated parents (El Yaafouri-Kreuzer, 2017). Respecting family spaces assists in building school and family relationships that may often last the high school career (Henke, 2011).

Wraparound services as community support. Charter and public schools, including CCCHS, have engaged community organizations as vital supports for students and families (Garrett, 2012). According to Garrett (2012), school–community partnerships have positive effects on many school issues related to dropout rates, school attendance, discipline, student attitudes, and academic success. Districts also embrace the concept of wraparound services so students and families can gain access to health and mental wellness, social welfare, and after-school programming. Dryfoos (1994) suggested that coordinating with community organizations and social service systems provides a broader support system. Schools that keep students and their families at the forefront of policy development and practices provide a climate and culture of trust between students, parents, and teachers that fosters collaborative partnerships. Parent involvement in education is vital, but remains weak in many schools. Relationships across not only families but also communities are the key to student success (El Yaafouri-Kreuzer, 2017; Henke, 2011; Kronholz, 2016). Wraparound services that include bilingual support for parents may increase parental involvement, providing inclusive benefits for the entire community (Warren, Hong, Rubin, & Uy, 2009).

TEACHING ACTIVITIES

1. Community Walk/Ride

Make small groups (four or five individuals). Have each group design a community walk or ride and research the historical development and demographic changes of your school's neighborhood. Provide the following prompts to begin brainstorming, but leave the activity open-ended:

1. What parts of the current neighboring community are most representative of your student population?
2. What is unique about the surrounding community, both currently and historically?
3. How would a walk/ride through the community increase understanding of students' culture, customs, and traditional ways of understanding the world?
4. Identify the "unseen" and "unknowns" that only those who are considered "insiders" would be aware of (i.e., mortgage companies' policies that denied loan approvals in certain neighborhoods based on hyper-racialization).

After designing the community walk, have one or two group members present a brief overview of where faculty/staff would go and what they would see if they went on the walk in real life. Follow up the presentations with these discussion questions:

1. Who should participate in this activity and how often?
2. Who should conduct the walk/drive and why?
3. How do you ensure information presented during the walk/drive is authentic?
4. What processes or measures should a principal take to ensure this activity is not presented from a dominant culture reference perspective (e.g., White, middle class, suburbanite)?

2. Wraparound Services

Assume you are currently the principal of a Latinx-serving charter school and are dedicated to supporting new immigrants as they choose to come to your school. Identify the unique needs of both students and their families and the services they may require to successfully engage in the school community. Create a list of local community services that may benefit your students and their families.

1. What supports are needed and where are they available to support a student who is proficient in a language that no one in the school currently speaks?
2. What new knowledge will your teachers need in order to sustain new immigrant students' heritage cultures, while offering access to U.S. cultural ways of being and understanding the world?

3. What community resources can aid teaching staff, students, and the students' families (e.g., utility assistance, psychological services, employment assistance/training, social welfare organizations, etc.)?
4. How might engaging the family be helpful? What obstacles do you anticipate, and how can the obstacles be overcome?
5. What new ways of communication need to be considered in welcoming and involving immigrant parents to your school?

NOTE

1 Pseudonyms are used throughout this chapter.

REFERENCES

Cohodes, S. (2018). Charter schools and the achievement gap. The Future of Children. Retrieved from https://futureofchildren.princeton.edu/sites/futureofchildren/files/resource-links/charter_schools_compiled.pdf

Cordes, S. A. (2018). Charters and the common good: The spillover effects of charter schools in New York City. *Education Next*, *18*(2), 60.

CREDO. (2015). Urban charter school study: Report on 41 regions. Center for Research on Educational Outcomes. Stanford, CA: Stanford University. http://urbancharters.stanford.edu/download/Urban%20Charter%20School%20Study%20Report%20on%2041%20Regions.pdf

Dryfoos, J. G. (1994). *Full service schools: A revolution in health and social services for children, youth, and families* (pp. 123–137). San Francisco, CA: Jossey-Bass.

El Yaafouri-Kreuzer, L. (2017). How home visits transformed my teaching. *Educational Leadership*, *75*(1), 20–25.

Garcia, A., & Salinas, M. H. (2018). Best leadership practices from an exemplary charter school district in South Texas. *Charter Schools Resource Journal*, *12*(2), 3–37.

Garrett, K. (2012). Community schools: It takes a village. *Education Digest*, *78*(3), 14–20.

Henke, L. (2011). Connecting with parents at home. *Educational leadership*, *68*(8), 38–41.

Howard, G. R. (2016). *We can't teach what we don't know: White teachers, multiracial schools*. New York: Teachers College Press.

Hussar, W. J., & Bailey, T. M. (2014). Projections of education statistics to 2022. National Center for Education Statistics. Washington, DC: U.S. Government Printing Office. https://nces.ed.gov/pubs2014/2014051.pdf

Jackson, C. (2010). *Immigrant charter schools: A better choice?* Montgomery, AL: Southern Poverty Law Center.

Klocko, B. A., Jankens, B. P., & Evans, L. M. (2018). The charter school principal: Foundations for leadership preparation and practice. *Charter Schools Resource Journal*, *12*(2), 82–102.

Kronholz, J. (2016). Teacher home visits: School–family partnerships foster student success. *Education Next*, *16*(3), 1–7.

Lopez, A. E. (2015). Navigating cultural borders in diverse contexts: Building capacity through culturally responsive leadership and critical praxis. *Multicultural Education Review*, *7*(3), 171–184.

Manno, B. V., Finn Jr, C. E., Bierlein, L. A., & Vanourek, G. (1998). How charter schools are different: Lessons and implications from a national study. *Phi Delta Kappan*, *79*(7), 489–498.

Marx, D., & Pecina, U. (2016). Community: The missing piece in preparing teacher candidates for future urban classrooms. *Action in Teacher Education*, *38*(4), 344–357.

Mavrogordato, M., & Stein, M. (2016). Accessing choice: A mixed-methods examination of how Latino parents engage in the educational marketplace. *Urban Education*, *51*(9), 1031–1064.

Musu-Gillette, L., Robinson, J., McFarland, J., KewalRamani, A., Zhang, A., & Wilkinson-Flicker, S. (2016). Status and trends in the education of racial and ethnic groups 2016. NCES 2016-007. *National Center for Education Statistics*.

National Center for Education Statistics (NCES). (2018). English Language Learners in Public Schools, (2018–144). Retrieved from https://nces.ed.gov/programs/coe/indicator_cgf.asp

OELA. (2017). English Learners (ELs) and charter schools. Office of English Language Acquisition. Retrieved from: https://ncela.ed.gov/files/fast_facts/05-19-2017/ELs_andCharterSchools_FastFacts.pdf

Paris, D., & Alim, H. S. (Eds.). (2017). *Culturally sustaining pedagogies: Teaching and learning for justice in a changing world*. New York: Teachers College Press.

Richly, L., & Graves, E. (2012). Teacher characteristics for culturally responsive pedagogy. *Multicultural Perspectives*, *14*(1), 44–49. doi:10.1080/15210960.2012.646853

Sahin, A., Wilson, V., & Capraro, R. (2018). Charter school achievements in Texas: Public versus charter schools. *International Journal of Educational Reform*. *27*(1), 46–62.

Torino, G. C. (2018). Examining biases and white privilege: Classroom teaching strategies that promote cultural competence. In A. L. Dottolo and Ellyn Kaschak (Eds.), *Whiteness and white privilege in psychotherapy* (pp. 129–141). London: Routledge.

Warren, M. R., Hong, S., Rubin, C. L., & Uy, P. S. (2009). Beyond the bake sale: A community-based relational approach to parent engagement in schools. *Teachers College Record*, *11*(9), 2209–2254.

Chapter **14**

School Choice and Immigrants

Do Families Choose or Do Schools Choose?

Stephen Kotok and Elizabeth Gil

CONTEXT

Although many academically successful charter schools have been accused of cream-skimming their students (e.g., targeted marketing to higher-income students, counseling out difficult students), Empire State Charter School (ESCS) had a reputation for being welcoming and inclusive regardless of the students' academic ability or socioeconomic background. ESCS is a community-run K-8 charter school located in Brooklyn, New York, that currently serves approximately 400 students. The school, which opened in 2007, has been celebrated for its students' academic performances as well as its service learning component. Yet, ESCS has failed to reflect the neighborhood in one key way. Over a quarter of the families in its census tract are immigrants, and many of the children in these families are designated as English Language Learners (ELLs). However, ESCS served very few immigrant families and virtually no ELLs during its first years of operation. Moreover, the few ELLs enrolled in the school were not very satisfied with its services.

Although charters across the U.S. serve, on average, the same percentage of ELLs as district public schools (Office of English Language Acquisition [OELA], 2017), charter schools have been found to under-enroll ELLs in many jurisdictions (Buckley & Sattin-Bajaj, 2011). This case explores how even a diverse, civically engaged school struggled to enroll immigrant families and how the school ultimately found strategies to attract and retain more immigrant students.

Empire State Charter School was located in an old immigrant neighborhood in outer Brooklyn. Increasingly, the neighborhood had been gentrified with a Whole Foods and a few cafés displacing some of the neighborhood businesses, but the main commercial areas were still mostly lined with smaller immigrant-owned businesses and a number of community organizations, old churches, a synagogue, and two mosques. Moreover, the majority of families living in the area were working or middle class. According to New York City Department of Education data, around 25% of public-school students in the area are African-American, 25% White, 30% Latino, and 20% Asian (mostly Chinese and Indian), with 20% labeled ELLs. Incomes are mixed, with almost two-thirds of students receiving free/reduced lunch, so ESCS's population is poorer than that of the surrounding neighborhood itself. This income disparity was a function of high private school enrollment in the area.

CASE NARRATIVE

In 2006, Sharita Harris, a community activist and former public-school English teacher, led a racially diverse coalition to start a charter school in the neighborhood that provided students and their families an opportunity to learn through service and civic engagement. After the state authorized the charter the following year, Harris assumed the job of principal. She and her staff worked hard to deliberately recruit what they saw as a student population that represented the local area. However, ESCS, similar to many charter schools, failed when it came to linguistic diversity (Winters, 2014). At one meeting soon after the school's opening, Harris and other ESCS founders acknowledged that neighboring schools enrolled far more ELL students: "It's not really an issue, though," Harris reported. "The district, the school community, our authorizer really have not said anything about this. We're new, we have limited resources and we want to be sure they are going toward supporting our mission. Really, the district is more equipped to provide services for ELLs." Harris's perspective was not challenged by anyone present, as parents and staff nodded their heads in agreement.

Nonetheless, there were some ELLs at the school, but few institutionalized resources for them. One of the science teachers had TESOL certification and tried to help out with curricular needs, but she was mainly focused on her science teaching duties. The Spanish teacher, Señora Sherman, was often asked to serve as a translator during conferences or Individualized Education Program (IEP) meetings for the Spanish-speaking students, but this drew her away from her teaching responsibilities.

Although this ad hoc approach was helpful for some Latino students, the neighborhood was home to many other immigrant groups with substantial enclaves of Creole-speaking Haitian-Americans, Mandarin-speaking Chinese-Americans, and South Asian immigrants who mainly spoke Urdu or Hindi. Given their experiences of having few teachers and staff who spoke languages other than English, and communications home often not translated into families' native languages, the few ELL families at ESCS generally self-selected out after they realized they did not get the same services they could receive at the neighborhood public school. Most recently, a Haitian-American parent was heard exclaiming that the school was definitely not delivering on its mission of service. As she walked out of the school office, the frustrated mother told her daughter to translate: "They say service learning is good for students. What about serving the families that are right here? I care about my children's learning—but I cannot do more if I can't understand all these letters coming home." Harris explained to the student and her mom, "We're doing our best. We are a small school." Harris was conflicted, but she and her leadership team justified that "school choice" meant each school was unique, and other schools would hopefully step up to fill the need for ELL families.

Yet, over time, the New York State Legislature increasingly viewed enrollment and retention of ELLs as the responsibility of all schools, including charters. Following the initial passing of such laws in New York in 2010 (and again in 2014), the ESCS school board and administration proposed some minor changes to conform to the law. Assistant Principal Rosen reassured Harris. "Don't worry. We just need to let the families know about our test scores and programs. They'll come." Harris responded, "Yes. Let's pass out flyers this weekend at the community arts festival. Maybe some other events." However, this type of outreach had not been very successful, especially with non-Spanish speaking ELLs. In speaking with some of the ELL parents, it was evident that most immigrant families still viewed the school as inadequate for their needs. The parents did not feel a connection with the teachers and administrators, whom they saw as caring more about academics than about the overall well-being of their children and community needs.

In 2015, the school finally hired a full-time ELL teacher. Harris and the staff wanted to do more to attract immigrant families, but they also felt overwhelmed by other concerns and regulations related to academic measures, such as getting eighth graders ready for high school, retaining teachers, and expanding extra-curricular activities. Many of the teachers who started with the school had since left, and the administration had devoted a great amount of time to interviewing teachers and bringing them in to perform mock lessons related to their service-learning mission. Although the school had a charitable foundation that typically raised over $30,000 a year, there had been pressure to use this money toward the service-learning projects proposed by classes. Thus, conflicting goals continued to create a tension when it came to resources and priorities.

In the fall of 2016, a prominent New York City newspaper ran a scathing exposé about how schools such as ESCS were still underserving ELLs and immigrant populations compared to district-run schools. Harris held an emergency meeting, but the staff presented more of the same ineffective ideas such as another postcard mailing. Harris began to realize that a solution was unlikely to come from within and that the school needed to seek help. One day, walking in the neighborhood, Harris saw several families entering the Boys and Girls Club and had an epiphany:

> We've been going at this all wrong. We've been trying to do everything ourselves when we already have a network of community organizations we've built relationships with all these years! What we need to do is invite our partners to our next meeting and ask them for their ideas for engaging our immigrant families. Translation, outreach—we can ask them for help with those efforts, too. They work with the same families we have in our school.

Harris immediately called a meeting with the school's partner organizations where she briefly shared her revelation to seek their help. She also shared the data she had regarding staffing, resources, and the enrollment and mobility trends of immigrant students that so concerned the school.

> We really do want to do right by our students and their families and when they leave the school, it means something is not working for them. I want to take more time to listen to your ideas rather than to say a lot more. Here are some documents that might help as some background. We need your help because there is something we are just not understanding.

She paused, "…and we really do want to." Several of those present seemed surprised. Until now, the school seemed to be positioned to have the answers. While organization partners had been a part of projects with the school, this deeper discussion about needs in the community had not been the center of many conversations. After what felt like a long silence to Harris, Camila González from La Comunidad Unida (LCU) spoke.

> Honestly, this is a first. You've never asked before. We've tried to touch on this in the projects you've done with LCU, but it seemed like you did not quite get it. We can share some of what we do and maybe this will help. Inclusion and awareness of our constituents' needs are part of our mission and culture in word and in action.

As the meeting went on, one organizational partner after another shared strategies with the principal. It was overwhelming at moments, but also enlightening, and made Harris feel that there were tangible steps she and her staff could take to reduce the number of immigrant and ELL students leaving the school.

Refugee Inc., a local community organization that mostly provided legal assistance to refugees, saw Harris's invitation as a golden opportunity. The group assisted families from places such as Syria, Sudan, and Afghanistan to settle in the New York area, and finding a school that felt welcoming to these students and their families often proved difficult. With its deep awareness of the needs of these community members and by coordinating with ESCS, Refugee Inc. worked closely with the school and helped the school promote an inclusive environment. After classroom visits from Ms. Omer and Mr. Khan, to teach Mr. Simmons's seventh-grade class about the local refugee community, the class modified its initial idea to have a winter holiday charity drive. Instead, after learning from the Refugee Inc. representatives, the class decided that they would focus on helping Syrian refugees through a letter-writing campaign to lawmakers in order to increase the number of Syrians allowed to come to the U.S. The service-learning project alone did not greatly increase the immigrant population of the school, but it served as a powerful example of how the school community could show their commitment to immigrant populations.

At the beginning of the 2017 school year—after intensive community outreach—ESCS still slightly under-enrolled in terms of ELLs, but the proportion at the school greatly increased and the school was no longer struggling to retain ELLs. Anecdotally, many immigrant families shared with the staff that they felt more welcome and that they were encouraging their friends to apply. Despite not reaching their goal, ESCS was being touted as a model for how a charter school could better serve the community. Although there was some minor push-back from a few teachers and parents regarding the resources allocated to serving ELLs, most saw the effort as consistent with the school's mission and felt the diversity of students provided constant learning opportunities. These opportunities culminated in a new annual heritage festival where students and their families showcased different music, dancing, crafts, and history from around the world and families were invited to bring a homemade food dish. The school also invited families to share stories and activities from their native cultures, further illustrating to all segments of the school community that the school's diverse families were welcome and valued.

TEACHING NOTES

The dilemma faced by Principal Harris and ESCS illuminates both the legal and ethical obligations of schools to serve ELLs, as well as practical challenges in implementing changes. Thus, we have divided the Teaching Notes into a section on legal background and a section on strategies for creating a school community that attracts immigrants and ELLs.

Federal and State Laws

When it comes to serving ELLs, charter schools like all public schools must follow certain federal and state laws. Specifically, Title VI of the Civil Rights Act of 1964 forbids federal financial assistance to any entity engaging in discrimination based on race/ethnicity or national origin. In 1970, the Office of Civil Rights (OCR) issued an elaboration of Title VI in order to ensure reasonable access for non-English speakers in schools (United States Department of Education, n.d.). The Supreme Court upheld the interpretation of Title VI in *Lau v. Nichols* (1974) and has continued to add further guidance for school districts in recent years. These resources can be found at the Office of Civil Rights website under "Programs for English Language Learners" (United States Department of Education, n.d.). Since almost all charter schools receive federal funds through programs such as the school lunch program, Title I funds (money allocated to schools with at least 40% free or reduced lunch), or Individuals with Disabilities Education Act (IDEA), they certainly fall under the Title VI guidance.

Unfortunately, some charter schools evade their legal responsibility through restrictive recruitment of students or simply by not providing services under the guise of being a small school with limited resources (Green, Baker, & Oluwole, 2013). Although legally charters are independent Learning Education Agencies (LEAs) in most states, some charter school leaders may feel that they do not have the same legal responsibility as districts do.

Some states have started to add additional legislation to ensure charter schools comply with the spirit of these laws. The National Charter School Resource Center (2014) summarizes the various state laws regarding charter schools and ELLs. Both New York and Massachusetts have passed regulations to ensure charter schools recruit, enroll, and retain ELLs "at rates comparable to the district." In 2010, New York first passed such legislation requiring charter schools to recruit and retain ELLs. Following the passing in 2014 of another state law, charter schools in New York must work toward specific enrollment targets as well as make certain services such as translation available to all parents (New York State Education Department, n.d.). Although most charters use blind lotteries, states such as New York and Utah actually allow schools to accept some ELLs prior to the lottery to ensure the school enrollment reflects local demographics. Still, states such as Texas, Arizona,

Nevada, and New Mexico focus laws on accountability for serving ELLs once they enroll in charter schools rather than ensuring access in enrollment. Notably, the legal authority governing ELLs in charter schools is different across the country and in flux in many states, so it is important for school leaders to constantly review policies to stay up to date.

Recruitment

Despite some improvements, charters continue to struggle especially with recruitment of ELLs into their schools (Winters, 2014), creating a predicament for school and community leaders. In order to promote more inclusive and welcoming environments that meet student and family needs, acknowledge their assets, and retain them within their schools, educational leaders need to become better informed regarding the populations they serve. Yet, research has shown that school leaders sometimes feel unprepared to address issues related to diversity and lack material and district-level supports to do so (Young, Madsen, & Young, 2010).

Culturally responsive approaches, including those that support ELLs, should not be engaged in sporadically, but should be embedded into the institutional culture of a school (Auerbach, 2009; DeMatthews, Edwards, & Rincones, 2016) and should be an integrated part of the organization's overall mission (Young, Madsen, & Young, 2010). Furthermore, educational leaders' perspective on community engagement can view "community needs as a 'bridge' to meeting school goals" (Auerbach, 2009, p. 16). Recognizing the language needs of the community, for example, a school can provide translation devices for all meeting-goers, and not only for the non-English proficient attendees (Capers, 2018), in order to encourage all to participate and to show that all perspectives and voices are valued.

In analyzing the success of ESCS, we caution that this case is fictional and presupposes optimal conditions for a charter school to serve immigrant families. ESCS benefited from a dedicated staff, a mission committed to diversity, and well-established community organizations with the resources to help ESCS. Too often, schools and educators may view immigrants through deficit perspectives and assume enrolling ELLs drains their resources rather than provides an opportunity. Although states such as New York should be applauded for their efforts to ensure charter schools fulfill their responsibility as public schools to serve all students, the reality is that most charter schools in New York underserve special populations. Although we would hope that school leaders are guided by ethics when recruiting students, all schools should be prepared for lawsuits by families and community organizations if they fail to provide ELLs and other immigrant groups with necessary and important resources.

DISCUSSION QUESTIONS

1. To what extent could Empire State Charter School further improve its approach to recruiting and retaining ELL students?
2. What actions can educational leaders take in order to ensure that the faculty and staff in the school are reflective of the community where the school is located?
3. If a school does not currently have community partnerships, how might an educational leader begin to develop relationships with local organizations? How can education leaders model ways for teachers to establish welcoming environments in their school buildings and assess whether or not their schools are positive spaces for the families and students served?
4. Considering your local context, how do you think that the ethical responsibility of educational leaders goes beyond legal compliance in terms of serving English Language Learners?
5. How do you define "community engagement"? Does the definition change in a school choice environment where students may come from distant sections of a district?

TEACHING ACTIVITIES

1. Work together to craft a strategy to recruit ELLs. As an added challenge, consider budgetary constraints.
2. Conduct research on local community organizations that support immigrants. Create a list for your context and contact them to see if they would be interested in collaborating with your school community.
3. Investigate Title VI. Summarize its provisions and the school leaders' responsibilities regarding compliance.

REFERENCES

Auerbach, S. (2009). Walking the walk: Portraits in leadership for family engagement in urban schools. *School Community Journal*, *19*(1), 9–31.

Buckley, J., & Sattin-Bajaj, C. (2011). Are ELL students underrepresented in charter schools? Demographic trends in New York City, 2006–2008. *Journal of School Choice*, *5*(1), 40–65.

Capers, N. (2018, October). Lift us up, don't push us out! Voices from the front lines of the educational justice movement. Panel discussion at book release. New York University, New York.

DeMatthews, D. E., Edwards Jr, D. B., & Rincones, R. (2016). Social justice leadership and family engagement: A successful case from Ciudad Juárez, Mexico. *Educational Administration Quarterly*, *52*(5), 754–792.

Green III, P. C., Baker, B. D., & Oluwole, J. O. (2013). Having it both ways: How charter schools try to obtain funding of public schools and the autonomy of private schools. *Emory LJ*, *63*, 303.

Lau v. Nichols, 414 U.S. 563 (1974).

National Charter School Resource Center. (2014). Legal guidelines for educating English learners in charter schools. Retrieved from: https://charterschoolcenter.ed.gov/sites/default/files/files/field_publication_attachment/NCSRC%20Legal%20Guidelines%20for%20Educating%20English%20Learners%20in%20Charter%20Schools_FINAL_0.pdf

New York State Education Department (n.d.). Regulations concerning English language learners/multilingual learners. Retrieved from www.nysed.gov/bilingual-ed/regulations-concerning-english-language-learnersmultilingual-learners

Office of English Language Acquisition (OELA). (2017). Fast Facts: English Learners and Charter Schools. Retrieved from https://ncela.ed.gov/files/fast_facts/05-19-2017/ELs_andCharterSchools_FastFacts.pdf

United States Department of Education (n.d.). Education and Title VI. Retrieved from https://www2.ed.gov/about/offices/list/ocr/docs/hq43e4.html.

United States Department of Education (n.d.) Programs for English language learners. Retrieved from https://www2.ed.gov/about/offices/list/ocr/ell/index.html

United States Department of Education (1970). DHEW memo regarding language children. Retrieved from https://www2.ed.gov/about/offices/list/ocr/docs/lau1970.html.

Winters, M. A. (2014). Why the gap? English language learners and New York City charter schools. Civic report number 93. New York: Manhattan Institute for Policy Research. Retrieved from https://files.eric.ed.gov/fulltext/ED564925.pdf

Young, B. L., Madsen, J., & Young, M. A. (2010). Implementing diversity plans: Principals' perception of their ability to address diversity in their schools. National Association of Secondary School Principals. *NASSP Bulletin*, *94*(2), 135–157. doi:10.1177/0192636510379901

Chapter 15

Negotiating Culturally Responsive Leadership in Remote Rural Settings

Maria Frankland, Andrea Mercado, and Catharine Biddle

CONTEXT

Waterview School District,[1] comprised of five towns, is located in a remote rural region of the northeastern United States. The local economy is based on resource extraction, with fishing and farming providing 37% of jobs in the region. Other major sources of employment, especially for im/migrant workers, include berry harvesting and the production of holiday wreaths. Im/migrant families typically arrive in Rivertown in July and register their children for school in early September. Migrant students move on to schools in other regions as the local fishing and agricultural work winds down for the winter.

The total population in this service area is approximately 4700. The Latinx (a gender-neutral term referring to those of Spanish-speaking and/or Latin-American heritage) population, the largest minority group of these five towns, more than doubled between 2000 and 2010 and now comprises 2.38% of the total population in this area, almost double the percentage for the state. The majority (39%) of Latinx families in the Waterview School District reside in Rivertown, total population approximately 1350.

The rapid influx of Latinx im/migrants is met with unease and suspicion by the non-Latinx residents, whose families, mostly White, have been rooted in the region for generations. The newcomers live in small enclaves on the west side of Rivertown and mostly associate with other Latinx families. The non-Latinx residents are happy to have inexpensive labor to support the agrarian economy as long as the im/migrants keep to themselves once the workday ends.

This fragile coexistence is breached when a new daycare center opens to provide services to im/migrant children. Constrained by federal regulations, the center refuses to accept local non-Latinx children whose parents toil in the fields alongside the im/migrant workers. The prohibition against citizens availing themselves of services funded by their own tax dollars is more than some Rivertown residents can bear, and several mothers organize protests against this perceived injustice. Amid the unrest, Estamos Juntos is established to support the growing Latinx community. The organization, which provides opportunities for intra-and inter-cultural community events, becomes a powerful advocate for members of the im/migrant community throughout the region.

CASE NARRATIVE

The Garcia Family

Miguel Garcia Ortiz and Teresa Lopez Padillo, Arturo and Gabi's parents, choose to settle in Rivertown on the recommendation of a cousin, who also suggests that they contact Estamos Juntos immediately upon their arrival. It is unusual for im/migrant families to arrive in Rivertown after Labor Day, so the unexpected appearance of Arturo, Gabi, and their parents at Schooner High School on an early-October morning caught school officials off guard. The monolingual Spanish-speaking family is accompanied by Yolanda Suárez Martinez, an advocate from Estamos Juntos who serves as an interpreter. Yolanda grew up attending events sponsored by Estamos Juntos. Now in her early twenties, Yolanda is proudly volunteering for the organization that provided her family with immeasurable support during their transition to life in Rivertown. Because their parents are migrant agricultural workers, Arturo and Gabi are classified as *migratory children* and their educational opportunities are subject to special protection under state and federal law (Theoharis & O'Toole, 2011; U.S. Department of Education, 2004).

With Yolanda interpreting, the Garcias explain to Principal Lisa Smith that both children had attended school in central Mexico until the previous March, when the family moved to the United States in search of employment. The Garcias are particularly excited to send their children to an American high school, and hope that Arturo and Gabi might one day attend college. For the Garcia family, Schooner High School is the gateway to the American dream.

Although it has been over five months since the children last attended school, Yolanda asks Ms. Smith to enroll Arturo in grade 11 and Gabi in grade 9 so that each may continue their schooling alongside their same-age peers. Ms. Smith agrees to register Arturo for a typical grade 11 schedule, but has concerns about Gabi's below-age-typical communication skills and behavior during the meeting. She soon learns Gabi has severe intellectual disabilities that require full-time, one-to-one paraprofessional (Ed Tech) support in the resource room. Mindful of the limited staff in both the EL and special education programs, Ms. Smith enrolls Gabi in grade 8 but denies the family's request for her to begin attending school with Arturo the following day. Instead, she promises to contact the family through the advocate as soon as appropriate personnel and services are in place. Understanding the local labor market, however, Ms. Smith knows that she cannot be sure when that will be.

Ms. Smith's Struggle

After the family's departure, Ms. Smith considers the enormity of the challenge before her. Like many rural school districts, Waterview struggles to meet the requirements of the Every Student Succeeds Act (Jimerson, 2005). It is especially challenging to find highly qualified teachers for special student populations, including English Learners and special education students. Already short-staffed in both programs, Ms. Smith now must find a Spanish-bilingual Ed Tech who is also qualified to work with special education students. Where would she find such a person? Her thoughts turn first to the im/migrant residents of Rivertown. The fishing and wreathing seasons are in full swing, and most members of the im/migrant communities are already working at least one job. Ms. Smith also realizes that the high school diploma requirement of the Ed Tech position immediately disqualifies at least half of the Spanish-speaking population of the region.

Ms. Smith also wonders where the district will find the funds to employ an additional Ed Tech. An out-of-district candidate is unlikely to relocate to this remote rural region without a significant financial incentive. There is no money in the budget for another staff member, and she hesitates to consider the response of the community to a request for emergency funds. All five towns would have to agree to the request, one of which approved the current budget by a razor-thin margin of two votes. Ms. Smith is aware of the legal requirement (American Immigration Council, 2016; Office of Migrant Education, 2017; United States Courts, 2018; U.S. Department of Education, 2018) to provide appropriate educational services for Gabi but worries about her ability to do so.

As Ms. Smith feared, her local search does not yield any qualified candidates. After the superintendent reluctantly agrees to add reimbursement of relocation expenses to the job offer, a qualified out-of-district candidate is identified and her candidacy is presented at an emergency meeting of the school board. A small but vocal cohort of community members attend the meeting to protest not only the addition of another Ed Tech but especially the reimbursement of her moving costs. Their commentary soon devolves to a critique of the resources devoted to special student populations, especially im/migrant students. The board chair calls the meeting back to order and the contract offer is approved by the board. The vocal cohort of community members storm out of the meeting and immediately post negative comments to social media. Soon more community members contact the principal and superintendent about this "waste" of taxpayer funds. Nevertheless, the Ed Tech is hired and relocated to the district at taxpayer expense. With the appropriate personnel in place, Gabi begins attending school in early November.

An Unexpected Request

On the last day of November, Ms. Smith finds herself sitting with the Garcias and Yolanda once again. Through Yolanda, the Garcias ask her to approve a 12-week absence for Arturo and Gabi. Ms. Smith stares across the room at Mr. and Mrs. Garcia incredulously. "You want to take Arturo and Gabi out of school for 12 weeks?" she repeats, unsure she has heard correctly. "But isn't that almost..." she pauses to do the math, "a third of the school year?" Yolanda nods in agreement. "And you don't see a problem with that?" Yolanda shakes her head *no*. "Well, I certainly do!"

Feeling her frustration rise, Ms. Smith takes a deep breath. She remembers something one of her graduate school professors said in an ethics class many years ago: *parents have the right to be the guiding voice in the lives of their children.* Ms. Smith had never really questioned this before, and has tried to respect the rights of parents throughout her career. This situation is different. In almost 40 years as an education professional, Ms. Smith has never been faced with a request that is so contrary to her fundamental beliefs about the importance of education and the role that schooling should play in the lives of children. Until this moment, she believed that her educational philosophy was congruent with that of the residents of the Waterview School District. Now, she begins to question whether she truly understands her community and how it has changed since she graduated from Schooner High School over 45 years ago.

After she recovers from her disbelief, Ms. Smith points out the extraordinary efforts that have recently been made to expedite the hiring of a qualified person to meet Gabi's needs. She also describes her concerns about Arturo's readiness for the SAT, which he is required to take in April. Ms. Smith explains that, because the state uses SAT scores as an accountability metric for all high schools, the interruption of Arturo's schooling would impact the school's accountability measures. She also explains that, because the junior class is so small, the absence of just two students would put the school at the minimum 95% participation rate required by both state and federal laws (ASCD, 2016; Every Student Succeeds Act, 2015). Further, knowing that EL students with limited or interrupted formal education (SLIFEs) have a higher dropout rate than monolingual English speakers (DeCapua, Smathers, & Tang, 2007, 2009), Ms. Smith worries aloud that Arturo might abandon his education altogether. If Arturo does not return to take the SAT with his classmates, the school's SAT participation metric will be negatively impacted.

Silently, Ms. Smith has another worry. Unbeknownst to most of the school community, Schooner High School has been notified by the state Department of Education (DOE) that it is at risk of being labelled a *school in need of improvement* (ASCD, 2016; Every Student Succeeds Act, 2015). The DOE will make a final determination based on the SAT scores of the current junior class. Ms. Smith has been warned by the Waterview superintendent that she, the assistant principal, and most of the Schooner High School teachers will be terminated if the school is sanctioned by the DOE. With these pressures weighing heavily upon her, Ms. Smith returns her attention to Yolanda and the Garcias. Taking a deep breath, Ms. Smith explains, uncertainly, "I just do not see how I can approve a three-month absence, especially for a member of the junior class."

Yolanda is taken aback by Ms. Smith's protests and her apparent lack of concern for the Garcia family and their cultural norms. Recognizing the presence of other staff and community members in the office, Yolanda raises her voice and loudly accuses Ms. Smith of discriminating against the Garcias. "You would not be protesting so loudly if a native Rivertown family was making this request! It is central to the family's culture to join them for the religious holidays, and you must understand how important being with family is to them."

Stung by these words, Ms. Smith carefully considers her response to Yolanda and the Garcias. What should she do?

TEACHING NOTES

Students with migratory families often experience limited or interrupted formal education (SLIFE) and are frequently designated as English Learners (ELs). In addition to having to readapt to new living and schooling environments, students are challenged with meeting local standards and metrics for academic achievement. When faced with schools that are underprepared for adequately supporting their English language acquisition while assisting their academic progress and meeting their socioemotional needs, SLIFEs are at an increased disadvantage to meet rigorous academic standards within the time limits required. Consequently, it is estimated that 70% of ELs that dropout of high school are SLIFEs (DeCapua, Smathers, & Tang, 2007, 2009).

Each of us has a set of personal values and beliefs that influence the decisions we make. These may occasionally conflict with professional norms and/or legal mandates. This case is an ethical dilemma because there is not a single right answer. A decision that privileges one perspective may harm another party, either directly or indirectly. Therefore, it is imperative that professionals approach moral dilemmas through the lens of an ethical decision-making model. Shapiro and Stefkovich (2016) suggest a Multiple Ethical Paradigms approach that incorporates the ethics of Justice, Critique, Care, and Profession.

The *Ethic of Justice* invites educational leaders to consider not only the rule of law but also issues of equity and fairness. The *Ethic of Critique*, based on critical theory (Noblit, 2005), requires an examination of inequities and power imbalances present not only within schools but also within society. Aligned with the principles of Social Justice Leadership (DeMatthews, Mungal, & Carroll, 2015; Theoharis & O'Toole, 2011), the aim of this paradigm is advocacy for all students, especially members of historically marginalized groups. The *Ethic of Care*, based on care theory (Noddings, 2005), invites consideration of social responsibility and the role of care and concern in the decision-making process. According to this paradigm, ethical leaders invite multiple voices, privilege relationships, and consider potential consequences when evaluating moral dilemmas. Finally, the *Ethic of Profession* reminds educational leaders of their obligation to follow the ethical standards of their professional organizations (Shapiro & Stefkovich, 2016). Ultimately, the education and best interests of the student must be at the center of all decisions.

DISCUSSION QUESTIONS

1. Recall that Ms. Smith is a lifelong resident of Rivertown. How might her reactions be influenced by 1) her personal values, beliefs, and biases, and 2) her relationships with community members? What is her ethical responsibility as a school leader?
2. Identify and discuss the points in the narrative when Ms. Smith could have applied an ethical decision-making model.

3. What assumptions might be made about the Garcias based on their decision to remove Arturo and Gabi from school for three months? How might your leadership decisions be influenced by such assumptions?
4. Discuss Arturo's potential extended absence as it pertains to the SAT. Consider the impact on (a) his postsecondary opportunities and (b) the school's annual performance metric. Which of these parameters did Ms. Smith privilege?
5. What district policies might not consider the parents' rights to be the guiding voice in the lives of their children? How might these policies be punitive as they were not designed for students like Arturo?

TEACHING ACTIVITIES

1. Use the Multiple Ethical Paradigms approach to consider:
   - Ms. Smith's refusal to allow Gabi to attend school until she has hired a Spanish-bilingual Ed Tech certified to work with special education students;
   - how Ms. Smith should respond to angry community members; and
   - whether Ms. Smith should sign the planned absence form.
2. Role-play potential scenarios from the perspectives of:
   - staff members who overheard the conversation between Ms. Smith and Yolanda;
   - school board members who learn that Ms. Smith has approved the Garcias' request;
   - community members who reluctantly agreed to fund the additional Ed Tech position; and
   - Mr. and Mrs. Garcia after just meeting with Mrs. Smith.

NOTE

1 This case is a fictionalized composite of actual persons and events. All names of persons, locations, organizations, and schools are pseudonyms.

REFERENCES

American Immigration Council. (2016). Public education for immigrant students: Understanding *Plyler v. Doe*. Retrieved from www.americanimmigrationcouncil.org/research/plyler-v-doe-public-education-immigrant-students

ASCD. (2016). ESSA and accountability: Frequently asked questions. Retrieved from www.ascd.org/ASCD/pdf/siteASCD/policy/ESSA-Accountability-FAQ_May112016.pdf

DeCapua, A., Smathers, W., & Tang, L. F. (2007). Schooling, interrupted. *Educational Leadership*, *64*(6), 40–46.

DeCapua, A., Smathers, W., & Tang, L. F. (2009). *Meeting the needs of students with limited or interrupted schooling: A guide for educators.* East Lansing, MI: University of Michigan Press.

DeMatthews, D. E., Mungal, A. S., & Carroll, P. A. (2015). Despite best intentions: A critical analysis of social justice leadership and decision making. *Administrative Issues Journal: Connecting Education, Practice, and Research*, *5*(2), 17–37. doi:10.5929/2015.5.2.4

Every Student Succeeds Act, one hundred fourteenth Congress (2015, January 6).

Jimerson, L. (2005). Placism in NCLB—how rural children are left behind. *Equity & Excellence in Education*, *38*(3), 211–219. doi:10.1080/10665680591002588

Noblit, G. (2005). Perspective 7: Critical theory. In J. L. Paul (Ed.), *Introduction to the philosophies of research and criticism in education and the social sciences* (pp. 76-79). Upper Saddle River, NJ: Pearson Education.

Noddings, N. (2005). Perspective 2: Pragmatism. In J. L. Paul (Ed.), *Introduction to the philosophies of research and criticism in education and the social sciences* (pp. 57-60). Upper Saddle River, NJ: Pearson Education.

Office of Migrant Education, U.S. Department of Education. (2017). Non-regulatory Guidance for the Title I, Part C Education of Migratory Children. Washington, DC. Retrieved from https://www2.ed.gov/policy/elsec/leg/esea02/pg8.html.

Shapiro, J. P., & Stefkovich, J. A. (2016). *Ethical leadership and decision making in education: Applying theoretical perspectives to complex dilemmas* (4th ed.). London: Routledge.

Theoharis, G., & O'Toole, J. (2011). Leading inclusive ELL: Social justice leadership for English language learners. *Educational Administration Quarterly*, *47*(4), 646–688. doi:10.1177/00131X11401616

United States Courts. (2018). Access to education—rule of law. Retrieved from www.uscourts.gov/educational-resources/educational-activities/access-education-rule-law

U.S. Department of Education. (2004). Laws and guidance/elementary and secondary education Part C—Education of migratory children. Washington, DC: U.S. Department of Education. Retrieved from https://www2.ed.gov/policy/elsec/leg/esea02/pg8.html

U.S. Department of Education. (2018). IDEA—Individuals with Disabilities Education Act. Retrieved from https://sites.ed.gov/idea/

Chapter 16

Distributed Leadership in Schools with "Emergent Bilingual Leadership Teams" for Collaborative Decision Making

Kate Menken and María Teresa (Maite) Sánchez

CONTEXT

The two case narratives presented in this chapter come from the City University of New York–New York State Initiative on Emergent Bilinguals[1] (CUNY–NYSIEB), a project involving 66 schools across the state. Each school participating in CUNY–NYSIEB formed an "Emergent Bilingual Leadership Team" (EBLT), a school-based distributed leadership group. Distributed leadership (also referred to as collaborative leadership) is when instead of there just being one person in charge who makes all the decisions, the leadership is shared amongst several people who are all involved in decision making. EBLTs include the school principal and other key administrators, bilingual teachers, English as a new language (ENL—also known as English as a second language or ESL) teachers, general education teachers, skill and content specialists, special education teachers, parents/families of emergent bilinguals, and/or students (about five people total). The schools that applied to participate in CUNY–NYSIEB all enrolled large numbers of emergent bilinguals and wanted to better serve this population of students. As part of their participation in the project, the schools committed to the following:

(1) *A multilingual ecology for the whole school* The language practices of all children and families are evident in the school's visual landscape, as well as in the interactions of all members of the school community.

(2) Bilingualism as a resource in education All of the languages spoken by emergent bilingual children are leveraged as a crucial instructional tool and, to the greatest extent possible, nurtured and developed. Translanguaging allows students to draw upon the full span of their language and social resources to make meaning, so translanguaging pedagogy is implemented.

The case narratives below are from the work of two CUNY–NYSIEB schools, where their EBLTs did the following:

- studied the schools' services to emergent bilinguals;
- created a plan to improve their instruction and programming aligned to CUNY–NYSIEB's principles;
- oversaw the implementation of the plan; and,
- developed their school's language policy vision.

These two narratives describe how EBLTs worked in each school and the changes they made over time to improve and transform the education of emergent bilinguals, offering examples that any school with emergent bilinguals could emulate.

CASE NARRATIVE 1: HILLSIDE ELEMENTARY'S EMERGENT BILINGUAL LEADERSHIP TEAM

Susan is the principal of Hillside Elementary, a K-5 school in a suburban area of New York serving approximately 300 students. The area in which Susan's school was located had received many families with Spanish as the home language but also families with a diverse array of other languages such as Mandarin, Russian, Arabic, French, and Hindi. Over the past five years, the percentage of emergent bilingual students increased from 8% to 30%. In the early grades (kindergarten and first), 50% of all students were emergent bilinguals. The school provided pull-out and push-in ENL[2] to emergent bilinguals.

Susan did not have a background in ENL or bilingual education, so she decided to participate in the CUNY–NYSIEB project to learn more about how to best meet the needs of the emergent bilinguals coming to her school. Once Susan joined the project, she convened an EBLT at Hillside Elementary that included herself, general education kindergarten and fifth-grade teachers, a reading support specialist, an ENL teacher, and the parent of an emergent bilingual student. This was the first time a group at Hillside Elementary had focused collectively on emergent bilinguals. The EBLT met at least monthly for 45 minutes per meeting and also met twice during the summer months for at least three hours per meeting.

The EBLT started the work of reflecting on their multilingual ecology by doing a walk-through of the school, when they noticed that all the signs in the school's entryway and hallways, including samples of student work, were only in English. The messaging that students who spoke languages other than English and their families implicitly received was: *In this school, we solely speak English.* The EBLT decided to make students' home languages more visible in the school. They first created a survey to learn which home languages their students spoke, and discovered at least 15 different languages. The EBLT identified short-term goals for creating a visual representation of all of the languages spoken by students and their families in the school, and presented their plan at a meeting with the entire school staff. The EBLT worked with teachers and community members to display the languages and countries of origin of the students and their families. For instance, a first-grade teacher and her students created flags of the countries where the families are from that were placed in the school entryway, and translated the school's motto into all of the languages of the school. The EBLT helped other teachers label the hallways and classrooms in the languages of their students and develop multilingual classroom libraries with texts available in students' languages. During the EBLT meetings, members discussed progress, readjusted their tasks and timelines, and identified next steps.

EBLT members also received professional development on incorporating students' home languages into instruction by CUNY–NYSIEB. The ENL, kindergarten, and fifth-grade teachers worked together to implement these practices into their classrooms and started working with other teachers in the school to share what they were learning. The kindergarten teacher started leading morning meetings with students in Spanish and Arabic (the languages of her bilingual students), with help from families who spoke those languages, which not only recognized students' home languages but also provided information to guide them during the day; in this way, the home language served symbolic as well as functional purposes. The ENL and fifth-grade teachers organized a study group exploring the *CUNY–NYSIEB Translanguaging Guide* (see Teaching Activities), to learn more about how to incorporate students' home languages in their classrooms, before moving onto other resources about bilingualism and language learning. Susan and all the EBLT members, as well as those teachers who worked closely with them, noticed a shift in their understandings of the importance of students' home languages. They presented their collaborative work during full-staff professional development several times per year and also presented to the superintendent and the board of education in their district.

At the end of the first year of work, EBLT members drafted a language policy for their school based on their vision for students' language learning. Their draft policy stated that they would "provide English instruction with opportunities and encouragement for students to communicate in home languages." The EBLT shared the language policy with other staff and then worked during the second year to receive input from others who had not been involved, making revisions as needed.

Over time, Susan recognized that teacher leadership had taken root in her building, and she turned over the leadership of the EBLT to the teachers. Although she attended all EBLT meetings, participated in the work, and ensured common time was scheduled for EBLT meetings, she stopped making any decisions that would impact emergent bilinguals at Hillside Elementary without first consulting the EBLT and allowing for such decisions to be made collaboratively. She also provided time during school-wide faculty meetings to share the work and ensured that the EBLT had the resources needed for members to accomplish the goals they set annually.

In summary, this case narrative shows how working in teams on an EBLT can enhance the education of emergent bilinguals, particularly in cases where the school principal—like Susan—does not have expertise in this area.

CASE NARRATIVE 2: POWERLINE HIGH SCHOOL'S EMERGENT BILINGUAL LEADERSHIP TEAM

Olivia is the principal of Powerline High School, which is located in an urban area of New York and serves about 450 students in 9th–12th grades. Approximately 60% of the school population is Latinx and 30% is Black, and 90% of the student body receives free or reduced-price meals. Emergent bilingual students comprise approximately 25% of the school population and are mostly from Spanish-speaking homes. Half of the school's emergent bilinguals are newcomers, having arrived in the U.S. within the past three years, and 23% of all emergent bilinguals are considered "students with interrupted formal education." At the start of their participation in CUNY–NYSIEB, the school provided push-in ENL classes and followed a co-teaching model in certain classes, such as history and science, where the ENL teacher co-taught with a subject area teacher. In addition, they had a ninth-grade self-contained ENL class for newcomers, all of whom spoke Spanish. Olivia decided to participate in CUNY–NYSIEB because the emergent bilinguals in her building were considered "low- performing" by New York State, so she wanted support to learn how best to serve these students.

When Olivia started working with CUNY–NYSIEB, she formed an EBLT that met monthly, comprised of an ENL teacher, a Spanish teacher, a Math teacher, a parent, and two student members. When it began, Powerline's EBLT was the school's first formal group to specifically focus on emergent bilingual students. During the first year, the teacher leaders of the EBLT decided to concentrate on strengthening the co-teaching of ENL and content-area teachers, by including students' home languages and integrating language and literacy teaching strategies into content-area instruction. For instance, members of the EBLT recorded classes and viewed them with the co-teachers to reflect on how they used oral and written language and how students' home languages were incorporated. Student EBLT members created a survey for their classmates about how their home languages and cultures were represented in the school and what more they would like to see. Based on the survey, the students began organizing multicultural events throughout the school year where they shared music, food, and other cultural traditions. Teachers developed multilingual classroom libraries with home language materials and also displayed student work in their home languages in classrooms and hallways.

Adriana was the parent leader on the EBLT, and she decided to form a parent group within the school's parent–teacher association where parents could openly discuss issues and concerns in their home languages, with interpreters available, free childcare provided, and meetings held at different times of the day to accommodate work schedules and obligations. When Adriana heard issues and concerns raised repeatedly by families that could not easily be resolved, she brought them to the EBLT for collaborative decision making. For example, one issue raised was the need for improved parent–teacher communication, with families seeking more opportunities to speak privately with their child's teachers in their home languages at times that worked for them. This led to the organization of several parent–teacher events with translators, as well as cultural celebrations.

By the end of their first year, as EBLT members reflected on their progress and planned the next year of work, they centered their discussion on the school's vision for emergent bilinguals and drafted a language policy for their school that emphasized "bilingualism, biliteracy, and students' linguistic and cultural identities." After numerous conversations about this vision involving all EBLT members and school staff, the EBLT determined that the school would better serve its newcomers through a Spanish–English bilingual education program. To open this new program, they applied for and were awarded funding from their school district, which included professional development for bilingual teachers. At the start of the new school year, the EBLT began the bilingual program in tenth grade, where most of the newcomers were, and in the following years expanded it to all grade levels. All EBLT members, including students, were involved in the hiring interviews of bilingual teachers. The school also started an after-school multicultural club with culturally and linguistically sustaining activities and events, chosen and designed by the student members, and the school began an internship program where bilingual students earned credit by becoming bilingual teaching assistants who provided home language support to newcomers in the co-teaching classes.

At Powerline High School, the EBLT took ownership of the improvement of services for emergent bilinguals and worked closely with teachers, families, and students to do so. From its inception, the EBLT met monthly, with meetings convened by Olivia, who remained extremely involved throughout but gave more and more decision-making power to the teachers, families, and students. This case narrative shows how teacher leadership, parent/family leadership, and student leadership were cultivated through the EBLT at Powerline High School, and how decision making pertaining to emergent bilinguals was shared by all EBLT members.

TEACHING NOTES

The EBLTs in the case narratives above are examples of what is called distributed leadership. Recent research argues the benefits of distributed leadership (also known as collaborative leadership) in schools serving emergent bilinguals (Ascenzi-Moreno et al., 2015; Brooks, Adams, & Morita-Mullaney, 2010; DeMatthews & Izquierdo, 2017; Hunt, 2011; Menken, 2017; Scanlan & López, 2012; Tupa & McFadden, 2009). Rather than concentrating leadership in one individual, such as the school principal, distributed leadership considers leadership interactive and shared among multiple official and unofficial leaders (Leithwood, Mascall, & Strauss, 2009). Teachers of emergent bilinguals, particularly those trained in bilingual education or ENL, often have the greatest expertise within their school about these students, and yet are marginalized within a school's leadership structures (Brooks et al., 2010). While school administrators still need to be knowledgeable about bilingualism and language learning, and remain engaged in all decision making for emergent bilinguals, distributed leadership brings educators with expertise in language learning, as well as students, families, and community members, into positions of leadership within a school. This way, any decisions about the education of emergent bilinguals can be made collaboratively with the necessary expertise.

Above we presented two case narratives where school leadership was distributed, as school administrators, a diverse representation of educators, families, and students worked together in Emergent Bilingual Leadership Teams. From these cases, we can see how the schools nurtured teacher leadership, family leadership, and student leadership. Specifically, the case of Hillside

Elementary, a school in a suburban area of New York with a linguistically diverse population, highlights the ability for distributed leadership to change a principal's practices. Meanwhile, the case of Powerline High School, located in an urban area of the state where the vast majority of the school's emergent bilinguals speak Spanish, points out how leadership can be distributed to students and families. We documented the efforts of each school's EBLT to improve pedagogy, practices, and programming for emergent bilinguals, grounded in a language policy they collectively envisioned. These cases show that when EBLTs focus on the education of emergent bilinguals, they can transform the education these students receive, and transform schools to be more embracing of students' home language practices, cultures, and identities.

DISCUSSION QUESTIONS

1. Describe "distributed leadership" (or "collaborative leadership") in your own words.
2. Why is distributed leadership important in schools serving emergent bilinguals?
3. In the cases provided, how does each school's Emergent Bilingual Leadership Team (EBLT) distribute school leadership and allow for collaborative decision making?
4. What sorts of barriers could prevent collaborative decision making within an EBLT, and how might those barriers be addressed?
5. List at least three actions taken by each school's EBLT described in the case narratives. Discuss how some of these might be implemented in your school or a school in your district/area.

TEACHING ACTIVITIES

The two activities below are from the *CUNY--NYSIEB Emergent Bilingual Leadership Team: Planning Resource Packet*, which includes these and many more activities for EBLTs that improve education for emergent bilingual students. The EBLT *Resource Packet*, used by both Hillside and Powerline, can be accessed for free online at: www.cuny-nysieb.org/wp-content/uploads/2016/05/CUNY-NYSIEB-EBLT-Resource-Package-2015-2016-09-17-15-Final.pdf

1. Complete "Item A: Emergent Bilingual Leadership Team (EBLT)" from the EBLT *Resource Packet* (pages 15–17). This activity helps schools form an EBLT.

2. Complete "Item B: Inventory of Language Education Resources" from the EBLT *Resource Packet* (pages 19–23). This activity offers a starting point for EBLTs to consider their school's environment and programming for emergent bilinguals.

NOTES

1 Emergent bilinguals are often referred to as "English language learners." We prefer García's (2009) term "emergent bilingual," which recognizes students' bilingualism and the ways they draw on their rich home language practices as they learn, and because the term places their bilingualism at the center of our understandings of their needs and strengths.

2 Pull-out ENL is when an ENL teacher removes emergent bilinguals from their general education classroom for ENL instruction, while push-in ENL is when an ENL teacher enters a general education classroom to offer ENL instruction within class.

REFERENCES

Ascenzi-Moreno, L., Hesson, S., & Menken, K. (2015). School leadership along the trajectory from monolingual to multilingual. *Language and Education*, *30*(3), 197–218.

Brooks, K., Adams, S., & Morita-Mullaney, T. (2010). Creating inclusive learning communities for ELL students: Transforming school principals' perspectives. *Theory into Practice*, *49*(2), 145–151.

DeMatthews, D., & Izquierdo, E. (2018). The importance of principals supporting dual language education: A social justice leadership framework. *Journal of Latinos and Education*, *17*(1), 53–70. doi:10.1080/15348431.2017.1282365

García, O. (2009). Emergent bilinguals and TESOL: What's in a name? *TESOL Quarterly*, *43*(2), 322–326.

Hunt, V. (2011). Learning from success stories: Leadership structures that support dual language programs over time in New York City. *International Journal of Bilingual Education and Bilingualism*, *14*(2), 187–206.

Leithwood, K., Mascall, B., & Strauss, T. (Eds.). (2009). *Distributed leadership according to the evidence*. New York: Routledge.

Menken, K. (2017). Leadership in dual language bilingual education. White Paper. Washington, DC: Center for Applied Linguistics.

Scanlan, M., & López, F. (2012). ¡Vamos! How school leaders promote equity and excellence for bilingual students. *Educational Administration Quarterly*, *48*(4), 583–625.

Tupa, M., & McFadden, L. (2009). Excellence is never an accident. *Phi Delta Kappan*, *90*, 554–556.

Chapter 17

Innovating Practices in New Immigrant Destinations

A University–School District Partnership Focused on Family Engagement

Rebecca Lowenhaupt, Jason DelPorto, and Yvonne Endara

CASE NARRATIVE

As the school year began, Assistant Principal Jason was feeling unsettled. Throughout his 13 years in the district, he and the principal at their middle school had taken pride in the tolerance and integration the town displayed as demographics shifted. A primarily working-class town of both long-term residents, including the well-established Armenian community, and more recent arrivals from Latin America and the Middle East, the school district served an increasingly diverse student population in terms of race, ethnicity, language, and religious affiliation. This diversity had long been a source of pride at the middle school, which was always looking for ways to highlight and embrace global perspectives.

But something felt different. Ever since the 2013 Boston Marathon bombing and the ensuing manhunt which took place in the town, tensions were more palpable. Disputes among students in the cafeteria and on the playground seemed tinged with bias. Students who wore hijabs to class felt more unsafe, and there were even some open expressions of explicit bias toward Muslim students. It felt as though relations among groups had deteriorated since the incident.

Immediately after the bombing, Jason had worked to facilitate conversations and cope with the trauma associated with the manhunt. Thinking more long term, Jason began to wonder if the tensions he felt had existed even before the incident, and if perhaps in fact the diversity work he and his team had promoted for so long might benefit from some more in-depth consideration.

At the district level, the superintendent and her team were also aware of these newly surfaced tensions. Disheartened by the recent uptick in incidents of bias, the district team was looking for ways to prioritize community involvement and inclusion. Despite previous efforts to promote tolerance and integration, districts and school administrators realized that various groups were inequitably involved in school activities.

At the same time, the new district coordinator for English Language Learners (ELLs), Yvonne, had brought up issues around access for families who did not speak English. She saw that the growing population of culturally and linguistically diverse families in the district were not getting all the support they needed, although there were many who were flourishing in the town. She also recognized some of the challenges of having such a small, heterogeneous group of immigrant families, given the distinct cultural backgrounds of many families. Her own background as a bilingual educator working with Spanish-speaking families was useful for reaching out directly to Spanish speakers in the district. But the recent arrival of many Brazilian families to the town, along with small but growing populations of Pushtu and Arabic speakers, presented a different set of challenges. Identifying local individuals to support an increase in the use of interpretation services, Yvonne had begun to encourage district leaders to consider new, innovative ways to develop capacity for more inclusive family engagement practices.

In the quiet Watertown neighborhood where he walked his dog, Jason had begun a conversation with his neighbor about these issues. An assistant professor at Boston College, Rebecca was interested in finding ways to learn more about how districts in low-incidence immigrant contexts created supports to encourage family engagement. As they discussed the situation in Watertown, they began to think about how they might collaborate. A small grant available through Boston College encouraged education faculty and local districts to work together on solving problems through research-based collaboration.

Together, Jason, Yvonne, and Rebecca approached the superintendent about applying for the grant and forming a partnership focused on increasing family engagement and building community among families in the district. With her approval, they established the partnership as a way to assert the district's commitment to these issues. This collaboration was built on the mutual commitment to find new ways to encourage active participation of all families in their school communities.

A Symbolic Move

Given community tensions, forging the partnership was in part a symbolic and strategic way for the district to assert its commitment to culturally and linguistically diverse families. By publicly announcing the formation of the partnership through a series of press releases, the superintendent tried to leverage the very existence of this collaboration for symbolic purposes even before any work was completed. By demonstrating the capacity of the district to partner with a recognized and admired institution on this issue, she hoped to highlight to both internal and external stakeholders the commitment to engage families more effectively. Even before any partnership activities were completed, the public support for the project both promoted the initiatives and signaled to the staff, families, and broader community that this issue was one all hoped to address. It also demonstrated that both the district and a local university were investing resources into resolving issues of inclusiveness and tolerance, thus naming an issue and promoting the search for solutions.

Articulating a Vision

Members of the partnership worked as a team to set out a plan. Each member of the core team came with distinct purposes for engaging in the project, but recognized that, working as a team, they could develop mutually beneficial activities and collaborate toward a common goal.

The team agreed on four guiding principles for effective family engagement practices that shaped their work and tried to keep these in mind as they decided what they wanted to do. The principles were as follows:

1. **Foster two-way communication:** Effective communication means that both parents and teachers initiate communication and share their knowledge. Too often, communication occurs when schools need to disseminate information to parents. The partnership seeks ways to facilitate two-way communication, so that families and schools can work together to support students in schools.
2. **Ensure access for all families:** All families should be informed of and involved in what is happening in the school regardless of their language, schedule, or access to technology.
3. **Strive for cultural responsiveness:** Teachers should be aware of the cultural norms of the families with whom they work. Understanding cultural and religious practices will help the teachers and schools plan more inclusive community activities.
4. **Prioritize teacher–family relationships:** Though they may not be the main point of contact, lead classroom teachers should be involved in communication with the family. Facilitating this relationship should be at the core of family engagement efforts, as schools ensure that

families have a relationship with and have the ability to initiate contact with teachers directly.

Gathering and Using Evidence

The first thing the partnership set out to do was provide some documentation about family engagement practices. Although public schools have become data-rich, with various forms of achievement, teacher quality, and demographic data readily available, most public schools do not gather evidence systematically about family engagement. While many people working in the district had a sense that there were issues in this regard, they did not have evidence to draw on as they made the case for change. The partnership focused on tackling this issue, building on the research resources from the university. During the first year of the partnership, the team conducted a needs assessment in an effort to understand and document current family engagement practices.

The team analyzed data to identify the racial and linguistic makeup of students in the district, then documented the makeup of families attending parent conferences for comparison. Similarly, the team also considered which families were active in the School Site Council and the Parent–Teacher Organization (PTO), revealing that immigrant families were not represented in these parent groups.

Through this needs assessment, the team learned that almost all families in the pre-K-8th grades attended parent–teacher conferences, especially during the fall. The middle school principal was surprised and pleased by this finding. He was sure the numbers would have been lower in previous years, but felt that implementing student-led conferences had boosted participation substantially there. (See Chapter 3 for more on student-led conferences.)

At the high school, engagement was extremely low, something the administrative team there was well aware of and working to address. The high school calendar included only one evening per year for parent–teacher conferences. Recognizing how insufficient this was, the principal had been advocating to incorporate additional evenings for parent–teacher conferences since she arrived in the district a few years earlier. Making the comparison between the low participation rates at the high school and other schools in the district, she brought the issue to district leaders. Her efforts, bolstered with evidence provided by the partnership, led to change, with three additional nights added to the calendar for the following year. The partnership also documented the impact of this change, showing participation increase substantially with the additional evenings.

Next, the team ran a series of focus groups to dig deeper and learn from various stakeholders. They began with district and school administrators, convening a series of focus groups with middle and high school administrators, coordinators and specialists, and elementary and preschool administrators. Additionally, teachers were asked to fill out a survey on their family engagement practices during the school year. Speaking with administrators and teachers surfaced some of the barriers to participation that they knew were keeping immigrant families from communicating with them and led to discussions about how to engage families more purposefully. The team also conducted a focus group with religious leaders in the community to gain a better understanding of the broader community.

Based on these conversations, the team also decided to host focus groups with families speaking languages other than English. Partners ran focus groups with Spanish, Portuguese, and Pushtu-speaking families, based on the size of those language groups in the district. For many of the families who attended, this was their first time being invited to share their views and perspectives with the district. All parents who attended received a Target gift card for participating. Many said they came because of the direct invitation in their own language and the presence of childcare at the meeting. They also said the gift card motivated them to attend.

While the focus groups with families provided more depth and detail for the needs assessment, more importantly they provided an opportunity to connect with families about their experiences. It became clear just how much families craved language-based groups where they could discuss school issues with others in their own languages. For example, the Pushtu speakers were able to talk together about their concerns related to food services. As observant Muslims, they worried that their children were exposed to restricted foods. In conversation with an administrator, they were able to set up a follow-up meeting with the director of food services, who was interested in addressing these issues. For the first time, families raised concerns about their experiences and had an opportunity to reflect on the school together and in their own languages with an administrator present.

Pulling together what they learned, the team created a report and presentation to share with district leaders and the school committee. Identifying a set of small-scale initiatives and with additional funds to support the partnership, the team embarked on a second year of work to address some of the issues raised during the needs assessment.

Manageable Initiatives

After the first year of documenting existing practices, the partnership identified a few small initiatives in an effort to seed change and develop capacity. The efforts were narrow in scope, and the research team documented the activities. The partnership identified multiple initiatives, one of which was the introduction of family liaisons in the middle school.

Of the initiatives, the liaison initiative was the most in depth and required the most support from the district. Because of the small incidence of multiple language groups, the district had not managed to set up specific supports for these groups. While some districts have a full-time staff member working as a liaison, this district was not able to set aside enough resources for each (or even one) of the language groups. Stemming from the lack of support and the recognition of the substantial cultural and linguistic barriers facing families who do not speak English, the initiative was an effort to think innovatively about bridging the divide between the school and these families.

Working together, Jason and Yvonne identified Portuguese, Pushtu, and Spanish-speaking liaisons who had worked as interpreters for the district in the past. Liaisons were paid stipends for approximately 20 hours of work over the course of the year. They were responsible for communicating with parents directly to answer questions, extend invitations to events, and help host kickoff meetings to improve families' access to school. Liaisons agreed that text messages provided the most efficient and comfortable method for direct communications, a format which presents some challenges in terms of documentation for legal purposes, logistics, and professional boundaries.

The liaison initiative, in its pilot year, had a number of positive impacts. Parents were excited about the opportunities for engagement, especially in the cases where liaisons had brought parent concerns to teachers and administrators without having to worry about linguistic barriers. This provided new instances of commitment from the school to work with families. Liaisons also conducted language-based meetings, which helped provide a space for parents to share their experiences and broader concerns within their community.

Despite the positive outcomes, it proved difficult to maintain the initiative. One of the liaisons took a full-time job in another district, and another liaison was unable to devote substantial time to the project once he started a new position. Although initially there was a commitment from the district to take on some of the cost, the district also lost momentum for initiating and managing a cadre of part-time non-traditional staff and were not sure how to continue to identify, train, and support the liaisons. Because they were navigating a tricky middle ground as community members and ad hoc workers, liaisons also found themselves in difficult positions, both ethically and practically. For example, often they were asked to both interpret meetings and advocate for families at the same time. They also worried that they had access to private information, and families were likely to reach out for support that did not relate to the school. These challenges raised a dilemma for the district. On the one hand, the small groups of families speaking multiple languages required an innovative, adaptable, and in some ways informal approach to providing support. On the other hand, this made it difficult to design a sustainable initiative.

TEACHING NOTES

Partnership work was primarily focused on helping a district with changing demographics identify small, high-leverage strategies for supporting the increasing cultural and linguistic diversity in terms of family engagement. Throughout the partnership, which developed organically over three years of collaboration, members sought to anchor their work in emerging literature and concepts from educational research.

Family Engagement Practices

Increasingly, policymakers and researchers have emphasized the need for schools to serve not only their students, but also the families who are key partners in their children's education (Cohen-Vogel, Goldring, & Smrekar, 2010). Relationships between home and school provide the continuity and connection that facilitate academic and socioemotional development (Epstein, 2011). Researchers have established positive outcomes associated with strong, trusting relationships between educators and families, including feelings of belonging, school safety, and educational attainment (Epstein & Sheldon, 2002).

In the context of immigration, education serves as an initial point of contact for families whose first extended interactions in a new context often occur at their children's school (Suárez-Orozco & Suárez-Orozco, 2001). Schools are gateways to other resources, such as social and health services, playing a key role in acculturation not only for students, but also for their families (Fennelly, 2008). As such, the ways in which schools build bridges to families through engagement practices can have particular significance in the lives of recent immigrants.

All students have multiple memberships in communities within and outside of school across various "spheres of influence" (Epstein, 2011). Educators connect these spheres through building relationships, incorporating families into the school, and reaching out into the community (Galindo & Pucino, 2012). By facilitating two-way communication, schools ensure that families can share their experiences, influence what happens in school, and learn from the perspectives educators have about their children (Swap, 1993). Although individual teachers often develop personal relationships which facilitate this communication (Hopkins, 2013), formal mechanisms of communication tend to emphasize pushing information out to families in one direction (Swap, 1993).

While there are many ways schools can leverage capacity within their schools to engage families more deeply, substantial barriers to engagement often make it difficult for educators and families to identify strategic systems to promote ongoing engagement (Lowenhaupt & Montgomery, 2018). Schools often struggle to bridge language barriers that keep parents who don't speak English from participating or reaching out directly to school staff (Good, Masewicz, & Vogel, 2010). English-speaking students often end up contributing to communication as interpreters themselves when their families need help with English (Dorner, Orellana, & Jiménez, 2008).

Even those schools that are able to ensure access for all families tend to struggle to identify mechanisms that support families' agency in their children's education (Lowenhaupt, 2014). Culturally appropriate family engagement practices seek to overcome barriers to participation, such as work schedules and lack of childcare, as well as decenter the school in a more equitable partnership (Christenson, 2004; Villenas, 2002). This is not easy work and requires strong relationships, ongoing effort, and increased capacity. Educators need support to rethink, innovate, and adapt the day-to-day practices within schools to reach a changing demographic of families. The partnership described in the case narrative aimed to do just that.

District–University Collaborations

In its design, the partnership drew on a growing body of research that provides guidance to educators seeking to collaborate with universities on areas of shared interest or concern (e.g., Coburn & Stein, 2010; Miller & Hafner, 2008). Given the importance of evidence-use for decision making and the increasing demands for administrative data, the value of partnering with others to gather evidence continues to grow.

It is becoming increasingly common for districts to seek external partners to support reform (Miller & Hafner, 2008). While there is a long tradition of public schools partnering with teacher training programs in universities, the emergence of new types of collaboration is relatively recent and offers a wide span of programmatic and research support for schools and districts (Coburn & Stein, 2010). Within a context of austerity, inter-institutional collaboration is one key mechanism for expanding resources beyond the limits of the public schools (Miller, Willis, & Scanlan, 2013).

While some of these collaborations have been positioned as transactional, where each institution receives a desired product or outcome, more relational forms of partnerships can provide shared opportunities for capacity building and ongoing growth (Coburn & Stein, 2010). The partnership described here sought mutually beneficial experiences that provided collaborative opportunities for integrated learning for both university and district stakeholders (Lowenhaupt & Montgomery, 2018). As a small core group, the team was able to engage in joint practices and pursue goals of interest to all. Throughout the collaboration, all aspects of the partnership were shared and conducted together. As such, the arrangement differed from other district-university partnerships that are set up as primarily transactional exchanges.

District–university partnerships also provide opportunities to focus on improving services for marginalized groups of students (Miller et al., 2013). Although these partnerships often address academic issues, several collaborations have extended beyond the classroom to address community issues (Warren, Hoong, Rubin, & Uy, 2009). The partnership described here was built with an explicit focus on tackling family engagement, steering clear of academic or classroom concerns and attending instead to relationships and communication within the community.

DISCUSSION QUESTIONS

1. Family engagement literature emphasizes the multiple spheres of influence youth navigate. What spheres might be especially relevant in the context of serving recent immigrants? How could educators in your context develop partnerships across these spheres of influence to serve students more effectively?
2. One area of growth the partnership identified was the need for two-way communication with recent immigrant groups. In the context of serving multiple different groups, this is challenging. What support or resources might help teachers do this more effectively?
3. The partnership also learned about multiple barriers to participation for families from recent immigrant groups. What strategies might districts use to minimize those barriers?

TEACHING ACTIVITIES

1. The needs assessment conducted by the partnership highlighted that many teachers were not comfortable engaging in outreach to immigrant families. They needed structure and tools for learning from families, along with the support of interpreters. Design a protocol and

set of questions for a focus group with parents. What kind of structure would you set up to support the event? How would you decide when and where to host the focus group? Who would you invite to participate? What questions would you ask?

2. One of the challenges facing districts with small groups of recent immigrants from many different places is a lack of resources to meet the needs of each distinct group. Building on the idea of partnering across institutions, consider your own context, or draw on the case study presented in this chapter. Thinking creatively about existing resources, develop a resources map identifying potential partners and resources. Which relevant institutions are in your community? Who within each institution might help form bridges? What barriers might hinder partnership? What kinds of support might these different partnerships offer? What mutually beneficial activities might provide additional resources?

REFERENCES

Christenson, S. L. (2004). The family–school partnership: An opportunity to promote the learning competence of all students. *School Psychology Review*, *33*, 83.

Coburn, C. E., & Stein, M. K. (2010). *Research and practice in education: Building alliances, bridging the divide*. New York: Rowman & Littlefield Publishers.

Cohen-Vogel, L., Goldring, E., & Smrekar, C. (2010). The influence of local conditions on social service partnerships, parent involvement, and community engagement in neighborhood schools. *American Journal of Education*, *117*, 51–78.

Dorner, L. M., Orellana, M. F., & Jiménez, R. (2008). "It's one of those things that you do to help the family:" Language brokering and the development of immigrant adolescents. *Journal of Adolescent Research*, *23*(5), 515–543.

Epstein, J. (2011). *School, family, and community partnerships: Preparing educators and improving schools* (2nd ed.). Boulder, CO: Westview Press.

Epstein, J. L., & Sheldon, S. B. (2002). Improving student behavior and school discipline with family and community involvement. *Education and Urban Society*, *35*, 4–26.

Fennelly, K. (2008). Prejudice toward immigrants in the Midwest. In D. Massey (Ed.), *New faces in new places: The changing geography of American immigration* (pp. 151–178). New York: Russell Sage Press.

Galindo, C., & Pucino, A. (2012). Family diversity and school–family relationships. In J. A. Banks (Ed.), *Encyclopedia of diversity in education* (pp. 885–889). Thousand Oaks, CA: Sage Publications.

Good, M. E., Masewicz, S., & Vogel, L. (2010). Latino English language learners: Bridging achievement and cultural gaps between schools and families. *Journal of Latinos and Education*, *9*, 321–339.

Hopkins, M. (2013). Building on our teaching assets: The unique pedagogical contributions of bilingual educators. *Bilingual Research Journal*, *36*, 350–370.

Lowenhaupt, R. (2014). School access and participation: Family engagement practices in the new Latino diaspora. *Education and Urban Society*, *46*(5), 522–547.

Lowenhaupt, R., & Montgomery, N. (2018). Family engagement practices as sites of possibility: Supporting immigrant families through a district–university partnership. *Theory into Practice*, 2, 99–108.

Miller, P. M., & Hafner, M. M. (2008). Moving toward dialogical collaboration: A critical examination of a university–school–community partnership. *Educational Administration Quarterly*, *44*, 66–110.

Miller, P., Wills, N., & Scanlan, M. (2013). Educational leadership on the social frontier developing Promise Neighborhoods in urban and tribal settings. *Educational Administration Quarterly*, *49*, 543–575.

Suárez-Orozco, C., & Suárez-Orozco, M. (2001). *Children of immigrants*. Cambridge, MA: Harvard University Press.

Swap, S. M. (1993). *Developing home–school partnerships: From concepts to practice*. New York: Teachers College Press.

Villenas, S. (2002). Reinventing educación in new Latino communities: Pedagogies of change and continuity in North Carolina. In S. Wortham, E. Murillo, & E. Hamann (Eds.), *Education in the new Latino diaspora: Policy and the politics of identity* (pp. 17–36). Westport, CT: Ablex Publishing.

Warren, M. R., Hoong, S., Rubin, C. H., & Uy, P. S. (2009). Beyond the bake sale: A community-based relational approach to parent engagement in schools. *Teachers College Record*, *111*, 2209–2254.

Chapter **18**

Mapping Just Borders of Distributed Leadership

Micropolitics of Engaging Undocumented Latinx Organizing in an Anti-immigrant Climate

Samantha M. Paredes Scribner, Erica Fernández, and Michael D. Corral

CONTEXT

This case is based on Latinx[1] immigrant parents' experiences over the course of several years. Readers will meet Lupe and Teresa, two undocumented Latinx mothers of elementary age students at an urban elementary school in the Midwest. Also playing a role in this case are Ms. Jackson (original school principal), Ms. Alexander (new school principal), Susan (grant personnel), Ellen (school-community liaison), and Juan (bilingual parent advocate). The characters in this case interacted over many incidents, in which competing priorities were negotiated in various ways. Below, we tell the story chronologically, through several vignettes of unfolding contests for legitimacy and *reconocimiento* within a complex organization. Each vignette poses its own questions for aspiring leaders. As a whole, questions of legitimation, micropolitics, ethics, and advocacy can be explored, pushing readers to articulate what counts as leadership in a school community, and how to negotiate conflict while encouraging self-empowerment among marginalized groups.

CASE NARRATIVE

Engaging Latinx Immigrant Parents at Jefferson Elementary

Ms. Jackson walked the halls of Jefferson Elementary, reflecting on the charge given to her by the superintendent. Jefferson was labeled a "failing school" and she was recruited to turn the school around. The school served approximately 570 students. Some 85% of its students qualified for free or reduced lunch; 60% of the students were Black, 29% Latinx, 3% Mixed Race, and 2% White. Additionally, 27% of the students were designated English Language Learners. According to state classifications, the district had assigned the school "Turnaround Status." This meant Ms. Jackson had the opportunity to make major changes in staffing (51% of the teachers were dismissed due to the Turnaround designation). Ms. Jackson knew this was a tall order, but as she moved through the halls, saw student work posted in the hallways, and heard teachers and children's voices (in English and Spanish) emanating from the classrooms, she was optimistic that, with the proper resources, they would see the necessary gains in student learning.

One of the major streams of funding at Jefferson Elementary was a full-service community school (FSCS) grant directed toward supporting "wrap-around services" for the families and students within the school. These resources funded personnel from the health and human service sectors to provide services to children and families—from food banks to healthcare and mental health services. These resources also prepared parent advocates to work with different populations of parents. Given the increasing number of immigrant Spanish-speaking families, a bilingual parent advocate was a major asset; the school had not quite caught up to serving this population with its own bilingual teaching and classified staff. While the FSCS grant would require more meetings and strategic planning, Ms. Jackson knew that, given the varying needs in the school community, it could help to mitigate some of the harmful effects of poverty on community living and student learning.

Study Circles

During the fall of 2014, thanks to the FSCS grant, parent advocates identified groups of parents at Jefferson to participate in "study circles"—meetings in which parents convened to learn about, discuss, and develop action around issues related to their roles as guardians. The bilingual parent advocate, Juan, was charged with convening a study circle with Latinx, Spanish-speaking parents. Because the parent advocates were funded by outside resources but were hosted at the school, Juan was truly able to serve as a boundary spanner between Latinx families and school officials.

The study groups began at the same time the state legislature passed an anti-immigration policy that impacted the lives of many of Jefferson's Latinx families. The anti-immigration legislation authorized law enforcement officials to question and arrest individuals based on their assumed immigration status. Government IDs previously provided to undocumented individuals became illegal, thus directly implicating the immigration status of those who were unable to legally obtain state IDs or state-issued driver's licenses. Counties across the state adopted the Secure Communities program, which allowed local and federal agencies to share files across jurisdictions (e.g., fingerprint files), making it easier for local law enforcement agencies to hold individuals based on their immigration status and for individuals picked up by police to get transferred to ICE detention.

Because much of the FSCS grant work was coordinated by the community liaison, Susan, Ms. Jackson was somewhat unfamiliar with the content of study circles. One fall morning, while doing classroom walk-throughs, Ms. Jackson decided to stop and ask Juan more about them. Ms. Jackson knew that Juan spent most mornings in the community room preparing for the arrival of parents who liked to stop by for coffee after dropping their kids off at school. Sure enough, Ms. Jackson entered the room, the aroma of coffee in the air, to find Juan hastily moving chairs around the large table at the center of the room. Amid the shuffling of chairs, Juan greeted the principal, "Buenos días, Ms. Jackson. How are you this morning? The coffee is almost done, would you like me to serve you a cup?" "Good morning, Juan. I'm good, thank you. No coffee for me, I already had three cups!" responded Ms. Jackson.

"Do you have a second to chat?" inquired Ms. Jackson. "Yes, of course," Juan responded. Ms. Jackson continued:

> For the past three Wednesday evenings, I've noticed parents coming in and out of the community room. Some stay. Some leave. Others bring their kids. I've also seen and smelled some delicious looking food. However, I don't know exactly why they are here or what you all are doing during your time together. I've heard something about study circles, but I'm not sure what that is or what you all are studying. Can you fill me in?

Juan responded:

> Oh! Of course, Ms. Jackson. So basically, study circles, they are usually done in like four to six sessions. But the purpose is to bring folks together to talk about a pressing issue that they are experiencing. The way that I have framed the purpose of the study circles is to focus on the topics of education and immigrant parents. Once the topic of the study circles has been decided and a group of people have been identified to participate, the group decides what rules will govern the collaborative space. The main thing is there must be a consensus on how to get along. Then, ideally, we bring parents together and start creating conversations about issues. And then we just kind of start talking.

Ms. Jackson interjected, "Talking about what? Immigration and schooling? How does that work?" Juan, careful with his response, not wanting to disclose everything that was discussed during the study circles, responded:

> We basically use these sessions to talk about the challenges that the parents experience within the school and broader community. We also discuss things that they would like to see done at the school that would help them as parents—help them with their children. Things come up, like miscommunication between the student, the school, and parents. For instance, ESL teachers don't always have enough time to translate for them which, they feel, results in a disconnection with the school.

Juan could tell that Ms. Jackson was surprised. Juan said:

> I don't know if you know this but we finished the study circles a month ago and since then parents have decided to create a parent group *Familias y Padres en la Comunidad* (Families and Parents in the Community, FPC). FPC meets every Wednesday evening to discuss issues that they are experiencing and talk about ways to address them. I know that the parents would love it if you could join us some Wednesday evening. I am sure they would love to talk with you.

Ms. Jackson, still processing what she heard, responded, "Thanks, Juan, for sharing the concerns. I thought we were doing a good job of meeting their needs. Let me check my calendar and I'll let you know if I can join a meeting."

Community School Grant Planning

A week or so later, Ms. Jackson was asked by the FSCS grant director to assemble a Community School Team to represent Jefferson Elementary at a grant planning retreat. Principal Jackson thought of the newly organized FPC parents as possible parent representatives, and remembered her promise to try to connect with them. In addition to the various representatives she was required to include, she decided to invite two of the mothers from the FPC (Lupe and Teresa) and Juan, so there would be a translator. This would be the first of several meetings out of which the school would begin to operationalize the implementation of the various wraparound services.

Three schools were represented, each sitting at its own large table: the principal, assistant principal, parent advocate, university grant partners, parent liaison and community liaisons, and several parents (one Black, one White, two Latinx). At one point in the meeting, the Jefferson table was engaging in an activity in which each party at the table shared a wish for the school. With Juan's help, Teresa began to describe an ideal situation where she and her fellow immigrant parents could come in to assist in classrooms, maybe sometimes read to students in Spanish or assist the teachers, without fear of being fingerprinted or being asked about their immigration status. She explained that immigrant parents, in the current climate, were fearful of the repercussions of current policies because of the stories of family separation and deportation of which they were already aware.

Ms. Jackson listened. She was a bit taken aback by these issues; they were so different than the ones the other two parents had shared. All she could say was, "Well, *that* is outside our authority. We cannot do anything about immigration issues."

Juan, translating to the parents, disguised his exasperation. And the parents were also confused. Lupe thought, "We know the principal cannot change the law. But they may be able to help families who are threatened and who want to help at the school..."

FPC Shutdown

As the year progressed, FPC mothers organized weekly meetings and cultural events. These actions were met with resistance from Ms. Jackson. On a Monday morning, in the community room, Juan, Lupe, and Teresa sat around the table and reflected on two specific conflicts between the FPC and Ms. Jackson. Frustrated, Juan said:

> Ms. Jackson knows that there is a meeting every Wednesday at night. She doesn't know what is going on in the meetings. The relationship has been, "Let them do what they need to do in the community room. As long as they don't go over 8:30 and they don't have kids running around in the hallway."

Teresa interjected, "We've invited her to come to the meetings but she hasn't come." Lupe continued, "It's true! Juan, didn't you personally invite her to our meeting?" Juan nodded, "I did. She said she would come. But I think she's very busy." "But why did she cancel our meetings last month and why didn't she allow us to put up a *Día de los Muertos* altar?" asked Lupe.

Juan replayed the events resulting in the cancellation of various FPC meetings and plans. One Wednesday evening, when the meeting was well underway, James, one of the evening custodians, came to the community room, and told the group that a child was running up and down the stairs and someone needed to go get her. Without hesitation, several parents and Juan ran to the stairwell and found the child (Marisela, a four-year-old who had wandered away from the gym). Juan returned Marisela to the gym and told the high school student volunteers to make sure no one left the gym area. Juan and the other parents returned to the meeting, thinking everything was settled.

The following morning, James reported the night's events to Ms. Jackson, who said she would look into the situation. Juan, having just arrived at the school, was putting down his backpack when Ms. Jackson greeted him. After exchanging pleasantries, Ms. Jackson informed Juan that she had heard about what had happened last night and right now all "parent" meetings were cancelled until further notice. Additionally, she told Juan she had been thinking about the Day of the Dead plans and, because it had religious connotations, parents were not going to be able to put up their display. Just as Juan was about to respond, Ms. Thomas, the school secretary, was on the walkie-talkie asking Ms. Jackson to report to the office for a matter requiring her immediate attention. Before exiting, Ms. Jackson told Juan she'd be available after school to talk more. Juan nodded and stood there for a few seconds in shock before continuing his morning routine.

Reminded of Lupe's question, Juan responded:

> I'm not sure why Ms. Jackson hasn't joined us. But I do think that the freedom we have had has been good because we can talk about anything. While nobody from the school has bothered to acknowledge our commitment to the community, you, and the other parents, have shown commitment by coming and wanting to learn how to be involved. So, it has its positives, which are really good, but the negatives are detrimental to celebrating your commitment, no? Unfortunately, right now it's kind of like we are in this hole doing our own thing and nobody is looking at it.

Lupe and Teresa somberly nodded in agreement.

A New Principal and New "Opportunity" for Legitimation

After three years, Ms. Jackson left Jefferson and a new principal, Ms. Alexander, began her tenure. In Ms. Alexander's first semester at Jefferson, the FSCS grant coordinator initiated an effort to create a parent–teacher association (PTA). One afternoon, before a FPC meeting, Ellen, the school–community liaison, invited FPC members to join the PTA. While advocating for the children was a common goal, FPC had distinguished itself as a parent-initiated, parent-organized, and parent-led group focusing on issues relevant to Spanish-speaking Latinx immigrant families, such as immigration-related concerns. The parents were flattered to be invited to participate, and eventually Teresa was named President and Lupe Vice President.

With FPC parents taking leadership roles in the PTA, school and grant personnel began to ask, "Why are there two parent groups in the school?" Susan, the director of the organization, wondered why FPC should continue if there was a newly established PTA at the school. At the initial PTA meeting—a meeting in which several FPC parents were in attendance—Susan openly questioned the rationale for maintaining two distinct parent groups, explaining that the groups were competing for already limited parent time. Teresa interrupted Susan and explained that the FPC served a different purpose, focusing on topics unique to Latinx immigrant parents.

Ms. Alexander interjected:

> Susan, I don't think you get it. The groups *are* different. The FPC is parent-developed and led; the PTA is staff-developed and led. FPC focuses on the needs and concerns of the group; PTA focuses on whatever the coordinator wants that month which doesn't always tie into what concerns the parents. FPC is more active in trying to gain more members. Meanwhile, the PTA, which is equally important, doesn't have a very active membership; there is no real recruitment. There is no buy-in; when you come to their meetings you don't know what you get from it. If you are not leaving feeling like you made a difference or this made a difference for you, then why would you come back the next time?

Ellen, who was also the PTA coordinator, was sitting in the back corner of the community room and gasped when she heard Ms. Alexander's comment.

While Ellen had been supportive of FPC, she too questioned the existence of two groups. "Ms. Alexander, with all due respect," Ellen interrupted, "the two groups are almost the same. The PTA has more infrastructures behind it and has more requirements behind it but they are the same people." Neither Ms. Alexander, Susan, or Ellen paused to ask the FPC parents what they thought the differences between the organizations were. Susan, trying to stay on agenda, finally paused the conversation. "It seems like we need to continue to talk about how we can converge both parent groups into one." Lupe, Teresa, and some of the other FPC members exchanged glances as if to say, "Can you believe this?!"

Immediately after the meeting, FPC members held an impromptu meeting in the school parking lot. Teresa, visibly upset, began:

> I don't get it. If this is what they want, that more parents be involved, why does it matter that we have two parent groups? I mean in the end, if *we* have a group like the PTA, but it's the FPC, it benefits them as well. The group doesn't just benefit us, it benefits them! We go back to the same thing, if the parents aren't doing well, neither are their kids. Why don't they get that?

Lupe interjects:

> Teresa's right. We have been a group for three years. We have been able to bring in parents to the school, to make other immigrant parents feel welcome. I mean look at everyone that is here. When we started there was just three of us. And today we have 15 parents, and this isn't even a FPC meeting!

Teresa exclaimed:

> Listen, everyone, tomorrow we have a FPC meeting, I think we need to all come and invite others so that we can come up with a plan of what to do next. This is our school too; they need to realize that we matter and that FPC matters!.

TEACHING NOTES

This case demonstrates how school leaders, teachers, and school–community advocates must navigate complex educational settings within which issues of racism, discrimination, immigration policies, Latinx communities, school turnaround, and parental engagement intersect. Central to this case is the issue of historically marginalized and minoritized groups who are often de-legitimized in their efforts to build strong communities and schools for their children. Yosso's (2005) work on community cultural wealth anchors the asset-based approach to negotiating issues raised in this example of parent engagement.

While it is defined differently across the literature, scholars agree parental engagement and communication between parents and school personnel can yield positive academic and social benefits (Epstein, 2001; Grolnick & Slowiaczek, 1994; Hoover-Dempsey, Ice, & Whitaker, 2009). One largely accepted method of parental engagement is known as "school-based engagement." When parents make the effort to be present and involved in their children's education, positive interactions can lead to positive academic and social outcomes for their children (Fredricks, Blumenfeld, & Paris, 2004; Grolnick & Slowiaczek, 1994; Hoover-Dempsey & Sandler, 1995). In the case of the Jefferson Elementary leadership (i.e., principals Jackson and Alexander, grant personnel, and school liaisons) and members of the FPC, the context of engagement cannot be considered outside the toxic political climate targeting Latinx parents and/or their families. When threats against immigrant parents intersect with threats of school closure, the parent–school relationship is made more tenuous.

Different groups of parents may need different types of support in order to confidently and securely engage with their children's schools. In this particular case, at times the concerns of Latinx immigrant parents were eclipsed by school and grant agendas. Given the challenges facing these parents, an active group of Latinx parents might have been welcomed rather than questioned, shut down or co-opted. The FPC work was an asset for their own children's academic needs, but just as importantly they were addressing the larger needs and concerns within their community.

Parent engagement is one way in which school/community leadership can be spread across a school community. If school leadership is distributed (Spillane, 2012), principals must recognize parents and community leaders as part of the school's leadership network. As such, the leadership task becomes negotiating influences across the school community for the benefit of student learning and well-being. In this case, the FSCS grant offered resources to support a broadening network of leaders and providers; however, the FPC parent group leadership was narrowly conceived by school personnel. If immigrant Latinx parents are to be included as community leaders, school leaders must be able to negotiate conflict and see these parents as knowledgeable about their needs and interests. In other words, the school leader is one of many community leaders (Khalifa, 2012). As such, they have to operate within and across many boundaries (or borders), negotiating conflict ethically and with cultural competence.

DISCUSSION QUESTIONS

1. How could Ms. Jackson leverage study circles to support immigrant parents in a way that honored them more fully?
2. Often community–school relations are the primary responsibility for a "boundary spanning" role such as a school–community liaison. According to organizational theory, these roles "bridge" or "span" the boundaries between organizations and/or their external environment. People in these roles should be skilled at navigating competing organizational goals and cultures. What are the pros and cons of having a boundary-spanning parent advocate lead parent learning at the school? What are the challenges?
3. Identify issues undocumented immigrants face in your area that intersect with the education of their children and their own engagement. Given the issues identified, what do school leaders need to know and do well to support these parents?
4. Consider both Ms. Jackson's and the parents' positions on the shutdown and the *Día de los Muertos* display. What are the values and concerns that are driving each position?

5. Given limited resources and many stakeholder demands, how might you, as a school leader, engage Latinx parents differently in this case?
6. PTA is a nationally recognized institution. FPC is a grass-roots organization representing interests of a specific group of parents at Jefferson Elementary. While PTA might "legitimize" the FPC parents with formal, recognizable structures and status, how does the FPC gain and hold legitimacy?
7. What is at stake for Latinx parents at Jefferson if they agree to merge the two organizations, FPC and PTA? How should school leaders negotiate competing purposes, values, and interests when trying to be supportive of marginalized parent groups?
8. Given the mission of the PTA, discuss the implications of the merger of FPC and PTA for the larger parent population at Jefferson.

NOTE

1 In an effort to be more gender inclusive, we use Latinx instead of gender exclusive terminology (i.e., Latino, Latino/a, or Latin@).

REFERENCES

Epstein, J. L. (2001). *School, family, and community partnerships: Preparing educators and improving schools*. Boulder, CO: Westview Press.

Fredricks, J. A., Blumenfeld, P. C., & Paris, A. H. (2004). School engagement: Potential of the concept, state of the evidence. *Review of Educational Research*, *74*, 59–109.

Grolnick, W. S., & Slowiaczek, M. L. (1994). Parents' involvement in children's schooling: A multidimensional conceptualization and motivational model. *Child Development*, *65*, 237–252.

Hoover-Dempsey, K. V., Ice, C. L., & Whitaker, M. C. (2009). We're way past reading together: Why and how parental involvement in adolescence makes sense. In N. E. Hill & R. K. Chao (Eds.), *Families, schools, and the adolescent* (pp. 19–36). New York: Teachers College Press.

Hoover-Dempsey, K., & Sandler, H. (1995). Parental involvement in children's education: Why does it make a difference? *Teachers College Record*, *97*, 310–331.

Khalifa, M. (2012). A re-new-ed paradigm in successful urban school leadership: Principal as community leader. *Educational Administration Quarterly*, *48*(3), 424–467.

Spillane, J. P. (2012). *Distributed leadership*. San Francisco, CA: John Wiley & Sons.

Yosso, T. (2005). Whose culture has capital? A critical race theory discussion of community cultural wealth. *Race Ethnicity and Education*, *8*(1), 69–91.

Chapter **19**

Developing Inclusive and Multilingual Family Literacy Events at Diverse Schools

Edwin Nii Bonney, Lisa M. Dorner, Lina Trigos-Carrillo, Kim H. Song, and Sujin Kim

CONTEXT

Over the past 30 years, there has been a proliferation of dual language immersion (DLI) schools in the United States (Boyle, August, Tabaku, Cole, & Simpson-Baird, 2015). Such schools teach at least 50% of academic content (e.g., math, science, literacy) *in and through* another language, with three traditional goals: to develop students' 1) biliteracy/bilingualism, 2) grade-level academic achievement, and 3) sociocultural competence/biculturalism. The majority of DLI schools, especially "two-way" programs, serve children from multilingual and im/migrant families, but challenges abound with equity, even though DLI programs are presumably designed to value diverse languages and cultures (Cervantes-Soon et al., 2017). This case describes one DLI school's attempt to engage multilingual, immigrant, and refugee families with greater equity through a *Multilingual Family Literacy Project.*

Riding the wave of new DLI schools across the country, the Spanish Immersion Elementary School (SIES, pseudonym) opened in a medium-sized Midwestern city in 2009. As a "one-way" or "foreign language" immersion program, SIES was originally designed to serve native English speakers to study and acquire proficiency in Spanish from kindergarten to fifth grade. However, the school attracted many native Spanish speakers as well as immigrants and refugees from a variety of countries, including Bosnia, Canada, Japan, Taiwan, Russia, and more. According to state-provided demographic categories, the current school population includes 55% African-American, 25% White, 15% Hispanic, and 5% other and multiracial students; 70% are eligible for free or reduced-price lunches. With such diversity, there clearly is not one dominant home language or language variety at SIES.

The Mexican-American principal of the school, Ana, has lived, schooled, and worked both within and outside the United States for over 25 years. She desires SIES to be a place where families' linguistic and cultural practices are included in the socialization and education of students. Walking into SIES, one immediately notices several welcoming and brightly colored posters in Spanish hanging in the lobby. Parents regularly hear conversations among teachers, students, and staff in Spanish, and they are greeted warmly by Bianca, the bilingual receptionist. The main hallway has a large world map showcasing the staff's home countries of Colombia, Honduras, Mexico, Peru, Puerto Rico, Spain, Venezuela, and the United States.

CASE NARRATIVE

SIES organizes a variety of family events for many reasons: to highlight the cultural and linguistic diversity of the student body, to encourage participation of parents in school activities, and for parents to engage with SIES educators. Family members from various backgrounds participate in these cultural events, especially when their children are performing or having a class party. However, native Spanish-speaking and immigrant parents are sometimes absent from literacy-themed events. Ana believes they may feel alienated or uncomfortable; she overhears rumors that immigrant Spanish-speaking families think such events are tailored toward native English speakers. Looking at previous literacy programs, Ana realizes such events were in English and skill-driven. Few focused on learning from parents or engaging their home traditions, as the cultural events do.

Ana, therefore, reaches out for support to plan SIES's next Literacy Day. Having developed a long-standing university–school partnership, Ana speaks first with Lisa (a local professor who has partnered with Ana for years), and Lisa reaches out to Kim, an expert in language education. Together, they develop a diverse team, including SIES's reading specialist and a teacher at SIES who's written her own bilingual storybook. Eventually, the group includes experts from many multilingual, racial, and ethnic backgrounds, including African-American, Chinese, Ghanaian, Korean, and Mexican.

The team meets three times. To meet Ana's goal for inclusive literacy-themed events, they create the *Multilingual Family Literacy Project*, which includes one major storytelling event for SIES's Literacy Day and a subsequent series of storybook workshops for a smaller number of participants. Because the team wants to privilege the Spanish language and highlight families' diversity, they resolve that their project will: 1) use Spanish as the primary language; 2) recruit at least one-third of participants from immigrant and multilingual families; and 3) encourage parents and children to learn from each other by sharing stories and using their diverse language and literacy practices. Although they will encourage participants to document family stories, they decide not to explicitly ask, "How did you migrate here?" Given the current anti-immigrant political context and negative discourses around legal status/documentation, the team recognizes that asking about family migration could feel threatening.

The team begins planning. First, they find a professional storyteller who can present a story in Spanish for elementary-aged students—not an easy task in this context, but accomplished by reaching out to local storytelling organizations. Second, through Kim's university, they secure resources for a luncheon and the first workshop, at which they aim to include 20 parents and their children. Third, the team drafts a two-sided letter in Spanish and English inviting parents to Literacy Day; it describes the storytelling event, lunch, and workshop; explains childcare and transportation; and asks families to "RSVP" and to mark their interest in future workshops. Classroom teachers collect the forms and return them to Ana.

In total, 38 parents express interest in joining the *Multilingual Family Literacy Project*. Two weeks before the first event, team members who speak Spanish and English use phone and email to contact all interested parents. Fifteen confirm their participation; nine parents are unreachable, and the remaining 14 cannot attend mainly because of work conflicts. Ana notices that most confirmed participants are African-American and White English-speaking mothers, although there is one mother from Taiwan, one father from Germany, and three of the mothers have Spanish-speaking spouses. Despite a lack of Spanish-speaking immigrants, the team presses forward, content that they have a diverse set of families otherwise.

SIES's Literacy Day starts with an informal lunch for 13 parents and their children, two supporting teachers, and six event organizers. One parent does not show up and the German father cannot convince his young daughter to attend. After lunch, the group joins the entire student body and teachers in the gymnasium for the professional storytelling in Spanish. The storyteller animates the children and gets the entire student body shouting out specific lines at certain points. His story is dramatized with multiple props, gestures, and repetitions such that monolingual English-speaking parents can understand it.

After the story ends, the 13 mothers and their children participate in a writing workshop. Here, team members discuss why families tell and share stories, how people learn from each other's personal and school literacies, and how families preserve their histories and practices through stories.

Then, an SIES teacher who recently published a children's storybook in Spanish and English explains how she developed her narrative, plot, and characters. She reveals that the book reflects her own childhood, and she encourages parents and children to create a story together using only words, only pictures, or both.

Afterward, parents and children are given markers, colorful paper, colored pencils, crayons, glue, pieces of cloth, and other craft materials. Tables have a list of questions to help parents and children brainstorm. While some children already have some ideas and ask their parents for help, other parents spend time remembering and sharing stories.

During the workshop, the team asks parents for feedback. The Taiwanese mother says, "In all my years at the school, I have never attended an event like this. I think there should be more events like this where parents and children can use their language practices in activities." However, she also adds that she felt intimidated: "I did not want to attend...When I saw the names of all the university people on the invitation, I thought this is too professional for me. I cannot do it." She explains she came because her fourth-grade daughter insisted. A White mother whose spouse is a native Spanish speaker confirms the same hesitation.

The organizers conclude the workshop by reminding participants that they don't have to complete their projects that day; they can attend subsequent workshops. Over the next three months, five pairs attend follow-up workshops. Although none of the families are Spanish-dominant im/migrants, they are multiethnic/racial/lingual; two fathers identify as Black and another as Hispanic. With support from the university, four families publish their books, and at the end of the school year they read them aloud in SIES classrooms. Children are especially excited to share their work, and many classmates express a desire to write their own story. Ana asks for copies for the school library.

TEACHING NOTES

Historically, family literacy programs were designed to improve the educational outcomes and the economic well-being of children from low-income, racially minoritized, and/or im/migrant families (Clymer, Toso, Grinder, & Sauder, 2017). These programs and their service providers emphasized training parents and teaching them new skills believed to be lacking, such as how to read and write in English. Such an approach, however, assumed that certain parents—especially non-English speaking ones—did not have *any* literacy capacity or practices to support their children's learning in the classroom. Service providers often ignored the fact that families have rich, multilingual, and diverse literacies within their homes and communities (Moll, 2015). In addition, traditional literacy programs often separated parents and children, "training" them separately and thus disconnecting them from each other and their *shared* family literacy interactions.

In contrast, educators who take a sociocultural perspective have a more expansive view. For them, literacy is not simply a skill set or the ability to read and write in English. Rather, literacy is a tool for learning and sharing ourselves with each other and the world (New London Group, 1996; Orellana, 1996; Street, 1995). Literacy includes social and cultural values (Mahiri, 2004), social practices that vary across contexts (Gee, 2010), different modes like print, digital, oral competencies (New London Group, 1996), and power structures in society (Street, 1995). Most times, people engage in richer literacy practices than they and others imagine. For example, grandparents share oral stories, children read in different languages and modes as they navigate their diverse communities (including online!), parents write and share traditional recipes, relatives write letters to demand action, mothers read about healthcare online and in print, and so on.

Family literacy programs that build upon the capacities and practices in which families already engage take an "Already Present" approach to literacy (Watson, 2018). In this tradition, projects flip the traditional script: parents train educators about their home and multilingual literacies. Moreover, children and parents work together, in order to share their different literacies and languages with each other. In turn, holding "Already Present" literacy and cultural events at school creates a sense of belonging for families and students (Vera et al., 2012).

Parents play an important role in the education of children by nurturing their growth and development, and by supporting their children's emerging multiliteracy practices. Rather than training parents to support their children's learning, family–school literacy events in multilingual and immigrant communities should draw from parents' already existing funds of knowledge, interests, and motivations. School leaders should create spaces for teachers, parents, and children to work together, spell, utter, write, draw, share, speak, invent, experiment, design, and create with language.

TEACHING ACTIVITIES

1. Discuss how Ana and her organizing team could improve their literacy event in terms of planning, recruitment, and project design. What worked and what would you do differently? (Consider using a table like the following to scaffold this activity.)

Table 19.1 *Designing and Improving Multilingual Family Literacy Events*

	What Worked	*Ideas for Improving*
Planning	SIES's organizing team included school leaders, community partners, and teachers from various racial, ethnic, and linguistic backgrounds. They discussed what questions they should *not* ask families.	Include a family member on the planning team. Ask families what kind of activity they would like to lead. Think broadly about what constitutes literacy.
Recruitment	SIES offered childcare, transportation, and lunch for Literacy Day. Invitations were sent home in Spanish and English, as letters, emails, and phone calls.	Ask a trusted educator to write and sign the invitation. Have children invite parents and other family members. Take care with translation, such as the word *alfabetización* in Spanish, which may suggest an event focused primarily on the acquisition of basic reading and writing skills.
Project Design	SIES designed a storytelling event that privileged the non-dominant language in the community: Spanish.	Connect bilingual storytelling events and workshops more directly to the curriculum. Consider offering family events as a regular part of classroom activities, e.g., inviting parents to regularly read in their home languages during "morning circle" time.

2. Read the *Toolkit for Educators: Reaching Out to Hispanic Parents of English Language Learners* developed by Colorín Colorado. Apply the toolkit's recommendations to the SIES case and make a one-page "tip sheet" on family engagement for a school that is working toward integration of newcomers and multilingual families. www.colorincolorado.org/sites/default/files/Colorin_Colorado_Toolkit_2012_0.pdf
3. Plan a multilingual family literacy project for a school in your context. Consider the immigration context, audiences, languages, recruitment, and importance of collaboration. Defend how you will take an "Already Present" approach.

4. Examine this list of questions Ana and her team provided to families to brainstorm for their storybook. What other ideas for brainstorming can you provide for families during a multilingual family literacy event?
   - What is the most important celebration in your culture or family?
   - What memories would you like to save in a book?
   - What are the things you enjoy in your community?
   - What story do you want your children to know?
   - Do you have a special family memory, celebration, or recipe that you hold dear?

REFERENCES

Boyle, A., August, D., Tabaku, L., Cole, S., & Simpson-Baird, A. (2015). *Dual language education programs: Current state policies and practices*. Washington, DC: U.S. Department of Education Office of English Language Acquisition.

Cervantes-Soon, C. G., Dorner, L. M., Palmer, D., Heiman, D., Schwerdtfeger, R., & Choi, J. (2017). Combating inequalities in two-way language immersion programs: Toward critical consciousness in bilingual education spaces. *Review of Research in Education*, *41*(1), 403–427.

Clymer, C., Toso, B. W., Grinder, E., & Sauder, R. P. (2017). *Changing the course of family literacy*. University Park, PA: Goodling Institute for Research in Family Literacy. Retrieved from https://ed.psu.edu/goodling-institute/policy/changing-the-course-of-family-literacy

Gee, J. P. (2010). A situated-sociocultural approach to literacy and technology. In E. A. Baker (Ed.), The new literacies: Multiple perspectives on research and practice (pp. 165–193). New York: Guilford.

Mahiri, J. (Ed.). (2004). *What they don't learn in school: Literacy in the lives of urban youth* (Vol. 2). New York: Peter Lang.

Moll, L. (2015). Tapping into the "hidden" home and community resources of students. *Kappa Delta Pi Record*, *51*(3), 114–117.

New London Group. (1996). A pedagogy of multiliteracies: Designing social futures. *Harvard Educational Review*, *66*(1), 60–92.

Orellana, M. F. (1996). Aquí vivimos! Voice of Central American and Mexican participants in a family literacy project. *Journal of Educational Issues of Language Minority Students*, *16*. Retrieved from www.ncela.gwu.edu/pubs/jeilms/vol16/jeilms1608.htm.

Street, B. V. (1995). *Social literacies: Critical approaches to literacy in development, ethnography, and education*. New York: Longman.

Vera, E, Israel, M., Coyle, L., Cross, J., Knight-Lynn, L., Moallem, I., Bartucci, G., & Goldberger, N. (2012). Exploring the educational involvement of parents of English learners. *School Community Journal*, 22(2), 183–202.

Watson, V. W. (2018). Building literate identities on what already exists. *English Journal*, *107*, 10–13.

Section II Resources

ORGANIZATIONS—REPOSITORIES OF RESEARCH AND POLICIES

Global Family Research Project: globalfrp.org/
U.S. Department of Education, Office of English Language Acquisition

- English Learner Toolkit: https://www2.ed.gov/about/offices/list/oela/english-learner-toolkit/index.html
- EL Family Toolkit (in multiple languages): https://ncela.ed.gov/family-toolkit

COMMUNITY PARTNERSHIPS AND IMMIGRANT SERVICES

Border Network for Human Rights: http://bnhr.org/
Missouri Immigrant and Refugee Advocates: www.mira-mo.org
Las Americas Immigrant Center: http://las-americas.org/
Texas RioGrande Legal Aid (serving Texas and surrounding states): www.trla.org

ILLUSTRATIONS—RESOURCES FOR LEARNING AND LESSONS

Toolkit for Educators: Reaching Out to Hispanic Parents of English Language Learners (Colorín Colorado): www.colorincolorado.org/sites/default/files/Colorin_Colorado_Toolkit_2012_0.pdf

Videos on the formation and implementation of Emergent Bilingual Leadership Teams (CUNY–NYSIEB): www.cuny-nysieb.org/translanguaging-resources/establishing-your-schools-emergent-bilingual-leadership-team/

Translanguaging: A CUNY–NYSIEB Guide for Educators: www.cuny-nysieb.org/wp-content/uploads/2016/04/Translanguaging-Guide-March-2013.pdf

Translanguaging in Curriculum and Instruction: A CUNY–NYSIEB Guide for Educators: www.cuny-nysieb.org/wp-content/uploads/2016/05/Translanguaging-Guide-Curr-Inst-Final-December-2014.pdf

SECTION III

DISTRICT LEADERSHIP

Chapter 20

The Importance of Enrollment and Graduation Planning for Adolescent Newcomer English Learners

Ryan Rumpf

CONTEXT

Alphaville School District is located in a growing suburban community on the outskirts of a large, metropolitan area in the Midwest. Residents are 82% White, 7% Black, 4% Hispanic, and a small number of other races and ethnicities. The school district serves approximately 14,500 students in grades kindergarten to 12. Alphaville has 30% of students receiving free or reduced lunch prices, 6% of students have an Individualized Education Plan (IEP), and less than 1% of students are identified as English Learners (ELs). Although the percentage is small, the district supports students from 16 foreign countries, with 11 languages other than English being spoken in the school.

Although there are four high schools serving students in grades 9–12, Alphaville offers English language development (ELD) classes at just one high school. Given the small percentage of ELs, the district employs one ELD teacher for grades 9–12 and buses high school age ELs to the ELD center school. All high school ELs receive one ELD class period on their schedule and are able to stay after school for tutoring that the ELD teacher offers on her own time and at her own expense.

CASE NARRATIVE

When Emmanuel walked into the high school to enroll, he was taking one of the final steps in his long journey to the United States. For years, he was pressured by local gangs to join their ranks in his home country of El Salvador. The fear that accompanied daily life affected not only Emmanuel, but also his family. They worried that he would end up as another statistic related to the gang violence that plagued the region. His mother had relocated to Alphaville when Emmanuel was 10 years old in the search for more lucrative work opportunities. Her frequent letters, filled with money earned in the U.S., gave him hope that one day, when the time was right, he too would be able to find a better, more peaceful, existence.

Emmanuel worked for his uncle doing odd jobs around the neighborhood and earning what little he could to help pay the bills. In mid-July, life in El Salvador worsened for Emmanuel after he witnessed a close friend of his beaten to death by a local gang member. The next day, he packed a bag with necessities for the long journey north. A month later, after paying a guide and navigating treacherous terrain filled with opportunistic thieves and murderous gang members, he made his way to Alphaville and his mother.

At 16 years old, he was eager to join the school; he hadn't attended classes in his home country of El Salvador since he was 12, but had a genuine interest in education. The prospect of meeting new friends, learning English, and becoming a part of an American community was exciting. Emmanuel knew that living and learning in the U.S. would lead to a more fruitful career than he ever would have had in El Salvador. He also knew that it would not be easy as he hadn't attended school in a few years.

In addition to his educational ambitions, he had other obligations to his family and roommates in Alphaville. His mother worked hard to provide for Emmanuel, but another person living in the house added expenses. He understood that he was expected to contribute to the financial well-being of the house and the people with whom he lived. Nevertheless, education was the priority, and Emmanuel was ready to begin his studies.

All students in Alphaville who wish to enroll after the enrollment period must complete the process at the local high school, rather than a centralized location that facilitates enrollment prior to the beginning of the school year. Emmanuel and his mother brought the necessary residency and immunization documents to the school to enroll. In the main office, the secretary handed the pair the enrollment packet filled with various forms to complete, in English. They enthusiastically grappled with the stack of enrollment forms, excited by the prospect of a quality education. Although his mother had been in the U.S. for six years, she struggled to understand many of the terms on the form. Completing the paperwork took Emmanuel and his mother over an hour as they consulted the English–Spanish translation app on their phones. When they were finished, they met with counselor Mrs. McMillan to finish the enrollment process and sign up for classes.

Emmanuel did not bring his transcripts with him to Alphaville. Mrs. McMillan had no experience of enrolling a student in this situation, so she called the building principal, Mr. Lawson, for guidance. Since they could not confirm his past educational history, the two decided to place Emmanuel as a ninth grader and enrolled him in the standard courses for his grade level. They knew he would likely qualify for the ELD program, but policy required them to notify the ELD department of his arrival and schedule testing at the earliest time available to the district's assessment team.

Emmanuel's first day of school was exciting, but intimidating. Mrs. McMillan arranged for a Spanish-speaking student to show Emmanuel around the school, especially where all of his classes were and when to be there. The two students shared many of the same classes; he was happy to meet his first friend. Emmanuel confidently walked into his first class, Algebra I, and took a seat next to his friend in the middle of the room. He couldn't understand much of what the teacher was saying. Moreover, the work they were doing looked much different than the math he did in El Salvador. He asked his friend for help when he had the chance, but even explanations in Spanish were incomprehensible. It was just so different.

Emmanuel made his way through the rest of the day. He enjoyed his time in Physical Education as the class worked out in the weight room. He sat through an English I class as the students analyzed a poem, and finished the day in American History. Although he was exhausted and understood little, he enjoyed his first day of school. He met a few new friends and was able to navigate the school, arriving at each destination on time. The next day, he had a new set of classes: Physical Science, Art, Computer Science, and Spanish. Halfway through his Physical Science class, a teacher, Mr. Ballow, came and pulled him out. He had to take the state-mandated English language proficiency screening assessment.

Mr. Ballow took Emmanuel to a small room and asked him to sit at the computer. He was nervous because he knew these tests were important and also anxious because he had little experience of working on a computer. Mr. Ballow gave him the standard introduction and some basic instructions, in English, then gave him headphones equipped with a microphone and started the test. All further instructions were given via the computer software, in English. Emmanuel struggled to complete the practice items, but when they were finished, he began the test. He hesitantly proceeded through the first section, the speaking test. The format and process were unfamiliar to him as he was tasked with providing spoken answers rather than selecting his answer choice from a list of options. He clicked on the specified tab to advance to the next question, but again struggled to understand what was being asked of him. When the first section came to an end, he felt as though he had failed the test. He didn't realize that there were three more sections.

During the second part, which tested listening comprehension, Emmanuel began to show signs of anxiety. Mr. Ballow noticed that he was becoming stressed, so he advanced through the remaining sections without Emmanuel answering. He knew he had failed.

When the test came to an end, the teacher took Emmanuel back to Physical Science. He felt demoralized. He tried to sit through the rest of Physical Science, but his anxiety became frustration as the class went on, in English. After two days, Emmanuel was ready to quit. He called his mother between classes to talk to her about his feelings toward school, explaining how he was just not smart enough to be there. She reassured him that he would catch on when he understood more English. Although he was not convinced he would be successful, he persevered through the rest of the day. He was able to follow along better in Art as he could mirror what other students were doing. His new friend was in his Computer Science class, and the Spanish teacher was able to help him, although he couldn't read or write well in his native language.

That afternoon, Emmanuel's mom received a call from the ELD department. They informed her that Emmanuel had been assessed and qualified for the district's ELD program. He would switch schools to attend Alphaville Central High, where he could take the ELD class. She was excited for Emmanuel because he would get an English class that would undoubtedly help him be successful in his other classes. The ELD teacher explained the process: he would go to Alphaville North and a bus would take him and other students in the ELD program to Alphaville Central. He would be enrolled in the same classes as he was in Alphaville North, but his English I class would be replaced with the ELD class. They also wanted to meet with Emmanuel and his mother to talk about graduation planning. She was excited to talk about graduation and the idea of watching her son earn a U.S. diploma. When Emmanuel returned from his second day of school, his mother was excited to tell him the news.

During dinner that night, Emmanuel's mother explained what the school had told her. He would be moving schools to join the district's ELD program at Alphaville Central. He knew it was because he had failed the test earlier that day. Emmanuel didn't want to change schools. He didn't want to go to Alphaville North High only for his small group of new friends to watch him go to another school. He was convinced that his new school was meant for students that were not smart enough to go to Alphaville North. His mother was surprised by his reaction, but assured him that this would be the better option. Emmanuel reluctantly agreed.

The next day, Emmanuel and his mother met with the Alphaville Central counselor, Mrs. Jones, and the high school principal, Mr. Smith. A translator was also in the room to assist the family with communication. They explained that, because he did not have transcripts, he would be able to graduate in four years when he was 20 years old. They also explained that if he did not graduate in four years, he would not be able to graduate because of his age. The pressure that Emmanuel had already felt about attending school was significantly compounded by this new discovery. He was not sure if he would be able to graduate in time. Accompanied by the district translator, Mrs. Jones showed Emmanuel and his mother around the new school. They showed him where all of his classes would be and introduced him to his ELD teacher, Mrs. Hake.

Emmanuel's first day at Alphaville Central was a surprise. The school was much more diverse, with students from many cultural and linguistic backgrounds. His ELD class comprised 16 students that all spoke English to some degree. Mrs. Hake spent time working with him one-on-one, but also worked with small groups of other students, leaving him to study individually much of the time. The other classes were just as difficult as what he had experienced at Alphaville North, except there were other Spanish-speaking students in the class that could help him follow along. He began staying after school for tutoring with Mrs. Hake and was gaining confidence. He was doing his best in each of his classes, but was not able to complete all of the work. Some of it was just too difficult for him to do in English. In most of his classes, he felt as though he understood what the teachers wanted him to learn, but the assignments and tests required more English than he was able to produce. Algebra I and Physical Science were different altogether. He felt lost the entire time as the concepts and format of the classes were simply incomprehensible for his English language proficiency level.

When Emmanuel received his grades for the first quarter, he was shocked. He failed every class except his ELD class and Art. He knew that he didn't do well on the tests and didn't turn in every homework assignment, but he did what he could to learn the material and complete the tasks. As he worked his way through the second quarter, he talked more with his teachers and tried to complete as much of the work as he could, but he continued to struggle on the tests and many of the assignments that required dense reading and detailed writing. When the first semester grades came in, he again failed nearly all of his courses. He showed his ELD teacher, who unsuccessfully advocated on his behalf. His teachers were expecting the same from him as they did from any other student. Accommodations and modifications were not provided as the grades would not accurately reflect the expectations of the course.

Around this time, Emmanuel decided that the tutoring was not helping him and stopped attending the sessions after school in favor of obtaining a job and contributing income to the household. He took a part-time job at the local factory that employed his mother and a few other friends. He earned the minimum wage, and worked for four hours after school each day and an eight-hour day on Saturday.

As the second semester began, Mrs. Jones set up a meeting with Emmanuel and his mother. With the assistance of a translator, she explained what happened when he failed a class. Since he failed most classes in the first semester, he would have to make up those credits or would not be able to graduate. She explained that he could complete an online class to recover the credits he had failed to earn in the first semester. Now, Emmanuel was attending school during the day, working part-time at the factory, and completing the online classes to recover his missed credits. This was not the experience Emmanuel had expected.

As he progressed through the second semester, he felt as though his command of English was growing. He could converse with native English-speaking students in the hallways and at lunch, but still struggled in many of his classes. His Physical Education class changed to a content-heavy Health class, but he moved into a small group in his ELD class as his English improved. As the second semester was nearing its end, the counselor once again called a meeting with Emmanuel and his mother. She explained, through a translator, that he had failed Math, Physical Science, and American History and would need to take summer classes to make up the credits. He still had much work to complete for the online credit recovery courses as well.

Over the summer, Emmanuel was able to work more hours and make more money for his family. He spent half-days in summer school completing the Algebra I and Physical Science credit recovery courses. He was encouraged when he was able to earn the credits. However, he was more motivated by the better quality of life he could afford as he worked more hours. He also turned 17 years old. When the next school year came, Emmanuel was once again placed in the district's ELD class. He also enrolled in English I, Geometry, Biology, World History, Art II, Spanish II, and Weightlifting. His English was improving and he gained some confidence in completing his work.

When the first quarter came to an end, Emmanuel saw a familiar sight on his grade card. He had failed Geometry, Biology, and World History. He grew angry and spoke candidly with his mother about his school work. Although his mother was disappointed as well, she understood the toll that this was taking on Emmanuel. He had tried and failed so much in his first year. They decided that his future was not going to be shaped by his education at Alphaville R-VII. When Emmanuel returned to school the next day, he walked directly into Mrs. Jones' room, respectfully laid his books on her desk, and told her that he would not be coming back to school.

TEACHING NOTES

In 1974, the *Lau v. Nichols* dispute, which focused on the availability of bilingual and ELD programs, was resolved in the United States Supreme Court with a unanimous decision in favor of the Lau family. The justices stated that placing English Learners in a class with the same facilities and curriculum does not guarantee equal treatment and puts students in an educational environment where they "are effectively foreclosed from any meaningful education" (*Lau v. Nichols*, 1974). More specific requirements for ELD programs came with the *Castañeda v. Pickard* case settled in the U.S. Circuit Court. The primary outcome of the case was the Castañeda Standard that, to this day, continues to mandate that language instruction educational programs for ELs be based on sound educational theory, implemented effectively with sufficient resources and personnel, and periodically evaluated for effectiveness (*Castañeda v. Pickard*, 1981).

Students such as Emmanuel present a formidable challenge for school districts. The number of students designated as ELs continues to grow, with ELs increasingly moving to states that are not traditionally immigrant destinations (Umansky et al., 2018). It is estimated that 10–20% of ELs are students with limited or interrupted formal education, also known as SLIFEs (Custodio & O'Loughlin, 2017). Teachers, administrators, and other school personnel tasked with enrolling, graduation planning, instruction, and assessment must be trained to address the unique needs of immigrant students, including SLIFE situations. However, the majority of states do not require formal education or professional development for teachers to work with this population (Education Commission of the States [ECS], 2018).

The effects of the various challenges faced by recently arrived immigrant students enrolling in high school can be seen in the achievement data and graduation rates. In a multistate study, Umansky and colleagues (2018) found achievement data in both Mathematics and English Language Arts remained in the lowest achievement level on state assessments, even after three years. Additionally, between 40 and 70% of ELs who arrived during their high school years did not graduate (Umansky et al., 2018). Clearly, more creative and proactive approaches are needed to provide an appropriate and equitable education for this severely at-risk population.

High school ELs, especially those with limited or interrupted formal education, face significant challenges. High school curricula generally expect students to be literate and to engage in critical thinking activities designed around content-area readings. One attribute of schools that are successful in meeting these unique needs is that the school is highly attuned to the students' needs and capacities (Santos et al., 2018). They understand their students and design support for the student both in school and at home. Successful schools offer a variety of course options such as sheltered content courses, English language development courses, and newcomer programs. They also have established policies allowing for creative solutions in meeting graduation requirements. Online courses, career and technical education programs, and individualized graduation plans allow students to earn credits, work toward their career goals, and fulfill their obligations to their families at the same time.

DISCUSSION QUESTIONS

1. What could the district have done during enrollment to ensure a smooth transition to the school?
2. What procedures impacted Emmanuel as he began taking classes? How could the district improve the EL identification and placement process to make Emmanuel more comfortable as he began classes?
3. Was the ELD class enough to support Emmanuel in all of his classes? What structures and processes could have ensured access to all assigned curricula?
4. When Emmanuel was withdrawing from school, what strategies could the district have used to dissuade Emmanuel from making the decision?
5. Imagine you are a school counselor developing a graduation plan for a student like Emmanuel. Using your state's or district's graduation planning tool, develop an individualized graduation plan that is academically appropriate, meets the state's graduation requirements, and prepares the student for success after high school.

REFERENCES

Castañeda v. Pickard 648 F.2d 989 (5th Cir. 1981).

Custodio, B., and O'Loughlin, J. (2017). *Students with interrupted formal education: Bridging where they are and what they need.* Thousand Oaks, CA: Corwin.

Education Commission of the States. (2018). What ELL training, if any, is required of general education classroom teachers? Retrieved May 31, 2018 from http://ecs.force.com/mbdata/mbquestNB2?rep=ELL1415.

Lau v. Nichols 414 US 563 (1974).

Santos, M., Castellon Palacios, M., Cheuk, T., Greene, R., Mercado-Garcia, D., Zerkel, L., Hakuta, K., & Skarin, R. (2018). *Preparing English learners for college and career: Lessons from successful high schools.* New York: Teachers College Press.

Umansky, I., Hopkins, M., Debach, D. B., Porter, L., Thompson, K., & Pompa, D. (2018.) *Understanding and supporting the educational needs of recently arrived immigrant English learners: Lessons for state and local education agencies.* Washington, DC: Council of Chief State School Officers.

Chapter 21

The Better Immigrant

Seeking Genuine Inclusivity of All Immigrant Youth

Trish Morita-Mullaney

CONTEXT

Sandy Elementary is home to the largest English Learner (EL) program in the Prospect School district in a large, Midwestern city, once deemed suburban. Children from all over the world attend Sandy. Most of the students are Hispanic and speak Spanish as their first language and have mid to higher levels of English proficiency. A newer and growing community of Burmese refugees recently arrived at Sandy; they have lower levels of English proficiency.

The newer EL student population comes from Myanmar (formerly called Burma) and speaks various languages including Chin, Burmese, and Karen. All of the Burmese students have low levels of English proficiency and are exempt from taking academic achievement tests in their first year of attending U.S. schools, consistent with allowable provisions within No Child Left Behind (2001) and the Every Student Succeeds Act (2015). As political refugees from Myanmar, the Burmese children come with legal status, related social services, and the enthusiastic support of the nearby church, which has a history of Christian evangelism in Myanmar.

The longer-term Hispanic EL student population is mostly U.S.-born, but their parents come from Mexico and Central America. Their levels of English proficiency are intermediate to high as they have mostly grown up in bilingual contexts, using English and Spanish interchangeably. A nearby Catholic church, Santa Maria, has long been involved with Hispanic families, starting as early as 1995, when it was the only location within the school district that had interpretation and social services. With the enhancement of social provisions within schools and other public services in the community available for U.S. children (but not their parents), Sandy teachers largely regard the Hispanic EL population as settled, integrated, and their needs not as dire.

The Mandatory EL Program Service Model

Students who are from the beginner (level 1) to advanced (level 4) standards of English are eligible for EL services. If they are less proficient, they receive more instructional time outside the classroom with an EL teacher or paraprofessional, which means they often miss key academic content within their grade level classroom. If they are more proficient in English, then their EL services are mostly facilitated within the classroom by the general education teacher and a limited amount of "push-in" time by EL staff. As such, the program model has Burmese children mostly being pulled out, whereas Hispanic children mostly receive EL services within the classroom.

Each student has an individual learning plan (ILP) that documents the frequency of EL service provision. These ILPs have a central focus on learning English; other non-linguistic elements of EL students' education are not included. Sandy Elementary is mostly concerned with advancing English proficiency, consistent with its primary focus on increasing academic achievement—two seemingly related constructs.

Sandy Elementary's general education and EL teachers and principal are highly stressed by the recent implementation of a state-mandated letter grade system of A–F that is formulated based on academic achievement, academic growth, and attendance. Currently, Sandy Elementary is a C school, and it is intent on maintaining or improving its C status, because being rated any lower would generate school sanctions. General education and EL teachers are reluctant to change any of the structural features of their EL model because of their perilous grade status.

The principal is concerned that this EL model unnecessarily segregates ELs by race, language, and immigration status. She is concerned that the EL model is only focused on the linguistic and academic features of students' education versus attending to housing patterns, poverty, race, and immigration status. This lingua-centric focus is creating different orientations toward Hispanic and Burmese students. Liz, the principal, overhears a general education teacher say, "The Burmese families value education and have church support and social services because they are refugees. They get extra tutoring after school at the church and their parents are learning English there. They do so much better than the other kids."

The principal knows the Burmese are conceived as the more cooperative and supported immigrants, in contrast to the less-supported and not equally cooperative Hispanic immigrants. Further, she is concerned that her faculty, who are all White women, have a similar lens that is constructing these racial ascriptions of the Burmese and Hispanic children.

CASE NARRATIVE

Liz, the principal, monolingual, female, and White, reaches out to Magdalena, the district EL director who is bilingual, female, and Hispanic, to discuss the 1) structural segregation in the EL program model; 2) a sole focus on English learning; and 3) the varying ascriptions of the Burmese and Hispanic students among her faculty. Liz feels the current EL program model reinforces English as the only aim, while simultaneously segregating children, reinforcing the idea of a better and worse immigrant. Liz shares her frustration with Magdalena.

Liz: My aim at improving ELs' English level and academic achievement has backfired. I thought it would really encourage teachers to see what they could do, but it's been at the expense of them paying attention to other actions and systems in the school that are separating the Burmese from the Latinos.

Magdalena: But, the teachers think it is going well?

Liz: We've always served kids by English level. We don't look at other factors and when teachers are in their grade-level teams, they only talk about English levels and academic test scores. Even the EL teacher.

Magdalena: So, language is safe. Talking about a students' race or immigration status is risky.

Liz: Yes! Language is a safe proxy.

After several long meetings, Liz and Magdalena determined that doing a professional development session with teachers would reveal how the current EL model and their related discourse propagated a hierarchy of the less than ideal (Hispanic) and excellent immigrant (Burmese). Magdalena had attended a workshop on culturally responsive teaching and critical race theory (CRT), and she felt this content would engage teachers in examining their own racial history, in contrast to their racially different ELs. As a Latina, she was empowered by her counter-storytelling and she was excited to share her experiences with an enthusiastic principal. Magdalena would share her counter-story of being a Latina EL and how such experiences made her transition to U.S.-English speaking school challenging. Magdalena's story contrasted with that of the U.S.-born White faculty. At a minimum, Liz hoped Magdalena's counter-story would foster empathy among faculty, leading toward a conversation about their segregated EL program. "It's about hearing stories from other perspectives. Teachers love stories!"

Professional Development Conundrum

Liz, the principal, told her teachers before summer recess that their full day of professional development would be devoted to discussing their EL program through a method called *counter-storytelling*, stories told in contrast to typical stories and stories that represent minoritized groups. Race, language, and immigration can be how these differences are illuminated. Liz and Magdalena both hoped the day would reveal the teachers' problematic perceptions around race without having to directly address the concerns about the different positionings of Burmese and Hispanic EL students.

Liz briefly introduced counter-storytelling and its purpose, asking if faculty had any experience with counter-storytelling based on her description. After a stiff silence, she introduced Magdalena. Magdalena shared her story of being a young EL in a local elementary school and how her first-grade teacher was unkind, and she spent a lot of time outside the classroom with an assistant. She recalled that her brown skin made her a quick target in public settings, so she learned to be as obscure as possible, sitting in the back of rooms and not volunteering in class to avoid ridicule. Magdalena concluded by connecting with the Hispanic EL students at Sandy: "They are doing their best. Sometimes, their parents aren't documented. They live in fear about being separated from their children. They also don't qualify for a lot of social services like their children may. This makes everything more difficult."

As Magdalena concluded, the faculty clapped and appeared to have taken in her counter-story, but many were uncertain of the immediate impact on their classrooms. Liz thanked Magdalena and invited faculty to talk at their tables about how racial and immigration differences are understood within their classrooms. Most faculty remarked about how well the children got along with each other across lines of race, language, and immigration status. Liz and Magdalena were disappointed with their congratulatory tone, hoping for a more in-depth examination of their EL program practices.

Despite the lack of depth, Liz and Magdalena proceeded with the next step in counter-storytelling. Teachers were invited to share their stories and experiences of race, language, and immigration. Each teacher was paired with a fellow teacher and they took turns sharing their experiences around these three areas. Liz and Magdalena were excited as they saw teachers become more engaged in the content, and the room was abuzz with rich dialogue. After each teacher had shared, Liz invited a pair of teachers, Mary and Diane, to come forward to share their stories with the entire group. Mary shared about her first Hispanic EL student from 1996 when she was a 27-year-old teacher. Mary detailed her shock as the newly arrived EL was negotiating a "huge language barrier." The child was teased, and racial slurs were both subtle and direct.

Diane's first experience with difference followed. She shared about the first refugee from Burma who entered her fourth-grade room with "zero English." She remembered never having to think about language before, and she quickly had to identify different methods for communication with her new Burmese EL as a 25-year-old teacher. Her fellow teachers in the room nodded as they agreed about the difficulties of managing such a language barrier.

When done, Liz thanked them and then used each story to reveal the different ways teachers discussed race, language, and immigration.

> Thanks for sharing your stories! As I was listening to Mary and Diane, I noticed that they talked about stories that were later in their lives. Twenty-seven and 25. For Magdalena, it was as young as five years old! Also, I noticed that Mary talked about race and language and Diane talked about language. Magdalena talked about race, language, and immigration. Magdalena spoke in first person, and Mary and Diane spoke in third person. So, I now turn to you. What do you think this means for you and your Hispanic and Burmese ELs in your classrooms? Talk to your tablemates.

There was a long silence and quizzical looks across the room. Diane shot up her hand and asked for clarification. "So, I'm not sure why we are doing this? I talked about language, because that was the issue that I had with my new Burmese EL. Not race or immigration, just language." Mary piped in, "Yea. I talked about race and language, because things were happening on the playground, and I don't know Spanish, so that was hard. Help me understand the point here?" Other teachers began to nod in agreement. They wanted clarity and purpose.

Liz and Magdalena returned to the purpose of counter-storytelling, but at this point the faculty was unconvinced. A teacher in the front of the room said, "I know this professional development was about our EL program, so what's the connection here?"

Liz and Magdalena looked at each other, and then Liz began to unload her deep concerns about the segregated EL program. She implored teachers to consider other factors besides language and to attend to non-linguistic features of their students' experiences, including race and immigration.

The EL teacher, Sara, spoke up, "But, we have to get our English scores up! The other stuff is nice to know, but not central to accomplishing EL progress and achievement. I take issue with making this about race and immigration."

At this point, most of the faculty was feeling judged, and Liz and Magdalena heard a teacher whisper, "Segregation? I'm not a racist. I love my kids."

It was noon time, so teachers were sent off on a lunch break, and Liz and Magdalena conferred and agreed it had not gone as planned. They resolved to speak more pragmatically in the afternoon about the EL model that was segregated, but they anticipated push-back from teachers.

TEACHING NOTES

This professional development event demonstrates that teachers are accustomed to content that looks pragmatically and concretely at instructional practices and structures to implement. Invoking the ethereal or the counter-storytelling method (Solorzano & Yosso, 2002) detracted from this practical focus. Further, the focus on non-linguistic factors including race and immigration (Hilburn & Fitchett, 2012) put faculty on the defensive, reinforcing a colorblind focus on English language learning (Bonilla-Silva, 2002; Morita-Mullaney, 2018; Welton, Diem, & Jellison Holme, 2015).

Lingua-centric Focus Forecloses on Other Identities and Experiences

The EL field's main focus is on students learning English and held within its mastery is supposed access, success, and credibility (Gutiérrez & Orellana, 2006; Hilburn, 2014; Morita-Mullaney, 2018; Sox, 2009). Morita-Mullaney (2018) found that EL district leaders foreground language over any other social variable as they are mostly positioned as linguistic mediators. Wiley (2007) critiques this lingua-centric purpose, demonstrating that ELs of color who master English are still persistently marginalized, even in schools. Sandy Elementary is a manifestation of this reality. Merely learning English also invokes an assimilationist stance, framing ELs as learning or not learning English (Valdés, 2001), ideals that educators can appropriate as the role of the EL program and the primary function within schools.

Racialization of the Preferred Immigrant

While Hispanic and Burmese children are both eligible for EL services and related supports within their general education classrooms, teachers began to show a preference toward the Burmese students, describing them as cooperative, hard-working, and idealized model minorities (Morita-Mullaney & Greene, 2015; Wong, Lai, Nagasawa, & Tieming, 1998) and coming with language support from outside the school via the church, thus showing enormous progress in English learning and academic achievement. In contrast, teachers positioned the historic Hispanic children as passive, less attentive to their work, with more limited support outside of school and thus showing limited progress in English learning and academic achievement. Chavez (2008) and Pérez Huber (2008) posit that Latinos are constructed as perpetually foreign and unassimilable.

Counter-storytelling without Schema Building

Liz and Magdalena's approach to counter-storytelling was indirect and created discomfort among the faculty, which foreclosed on sustained inquiry. Solorzano and Yosso (2002) state: "The counter-story is also a tool for exposing, analyzing, and challenging the majoritarian stories of racial privilege. Counter-stories can shatter complacency, challenge the dominant discourse on race, and further the struggle for racial reform" (p. 32). While altruistic in its intent, there was no stated rationale, putting teachers on the defensive and sending Liz and Magdalena quickly shifting toward a more direct and pragmatic approach.

Solorzano and Yosso (2002) argue that while counter-stories told by minoritized individuals counter deficit thinking and allow for differentiated and more additive orientations toward people of color, they are also a tool for people of color to claim their distinct identities. Dialogue within the field of CRT shows contrasting views on counter-storytelling and who the intended audience is. Is it for the minoritized to claim a space of resistance and healing? Or is it to be modeled for majority groups to disrupt negative attitudes toward people of color (Merriweather Hunn, Guy, & Mangliitz, 2006)?

Creating Critical Inquiry to Promote Connection and Discomfort

Fitchett and Salas (2010) propose a *scaffolding archetype* to understand and interpret how teachers are constructing their ascriptions of immigrant youth. There are three components to the Fitchett and Salas (2010) scaffolding archetype: 1) examination of U.S. immigration history to current day realities; 2) perspective-taking of the experiences of EL-immigrant families; and 3) well-scaffolded critical dialogue leading to critical self-reflection. The purpose of this scaffolding archetype is to draw educators into their local historical context to demonstrate how varying ascriptions of immigrant youth have been constructed over time and to foster sustained engagement in teachers' own introspection.

An examination of immigration history uncovers the rationale behind immigration statuses, shifting the focus from the cooperative or resistant immigrant toward policy, laws, and related structures. An overview of such complexities and situating it in the local will assist teachers in contextualizing the distinctions among their immigrant-EL communities. Perspective-taking is more fully conceptualized in relationship to families' immigration histories. Lastly, a well-scaffolded and critical dialogue is necessary to arrive at self-reflection. Critical dialogue is invariably uncomfortable, but if it is well-scaffolded, teachers stay within a zone of discomfort that facilitates their sustained engagement, deepening their understanding.

Morita-Mullaney and Stallings (2018) caution that beginning with critical self-reflection without a history that differs from their own is a recipe for shock value that may foreclose on sustained inquiry, as witnessed with Sandy Elementary. They recommend the methodical pacing from history to perspective-taking to critical self-reflection. They posit that discomfort is a given but, with rich historical knowledge that encourages understanding of the perspectives of their different EL students and families, persistent self-discovery can open up ideological spaces for transformation. Ultimately, this can inform the problematic construction of the children and the structure of the EL program.

DISCUSSION QUESTIONS

1. At the end of the professional development session, the principal and EL director coordinated on their next steps. Because Sandy faculty was so defensive, they reconsidered the relevancy of counter-storytelling. What would you suggest to Liz and Magdalena for the Sandy faculty?
2. The principal decided to start off with an assumed soft serve of *counter-storytelling*, not telling her faculty that she was disturbed by the "segregated" EL model. In what ways does this align with the Fitchett and Salas (2010) model of perspective-taking? How does it contrast?
3. In what ways could the Sandy administration and teachers involve faculty, EL families, and the local Burmese and Hispanic communities in the decision making around language program models? How could this be a part of the three-pronged approach of immigration history, perspective-taking, and critical dialogue?

TEACHING ACTIVITIES

1. Using the Fitchett and Salas (2010) scaffolding archetype and considering Sandy Elementary's current reality, plan a day of professional development for faculty. How would you facilitate activities related to 1) immigration history; 2) perspective-taking; and 3) critical dialogue?
2. Identify the discomfort that the faculty had during the counter-storytelling session. Discuss how you would negotiate educators' discomfort in your local setting.

REFERENCES

Bonilla-Silva, E. (2002). The linguistics of color blind racism: How to talk nasty about Blacks without sounding "racist". *Critical Sociology*, *28*(1–2), 41–64. doi:10.1177/08969205020280010501

Chavez, L. R. (2008). *The Latino threat: Constructing immigrants, citizens, and the nation*. Stanford, CA: Stanford University Press.

Every Student Succeeds Act, Pub. L. No. Public Law 114–95 (December 10, 2015).

Fitchett, P. G., & Salas, S. (2010). "You Lie—That's Not True": Immigration and preservice teacher education. *Action in Teacher Education*, *32*(4), 96–104. doi:10.1080/01626620.2010.549744

Gutiérrez, K. D., & Orellana, M. F. (2006). At last: The "problem" of English Learners: Constructing genres of difference. *Research in the Teaching of English*, *40*(4), 502–507.

Hilburn, J. (2014). Challenges facing immigrant students beyond the linguistic domain in a new gateway state. *Urban Review*, *46*, 654–680. doi:10.1007/s11256-014-0273-x

Hilburn, J., & Fitchett, P. G. (2012). The new gateway, an old paradox: Immigrants and involuntary Americans in North Carolina history textbooks. *Theory & Research in Social Education*, *40*(1), 35–65. doi:10.1080/00933104.2012.647976

Merriweather Hunn, L. R., Guy, T. C., & Mangliitz, E. (2006). Who can speak for whom? Using counter-storytelling to challenge racial hegemony. Paper presented at the Adult Education Research Conference, Minneapolis, MN.

Morita-Mullaney, T. (2018). The intersection of language and race among English learner (EL) leaders in desegregated urban midwest schools: A LangCrit narrative study. *Journal of Language, Identity & Education*, *17*(6), 371–387. doi:10.1080/15348458.2018.1494598

Morita-Mullaney, T., & Greene, M. C. S. (2015). Narratives of Asian/American Educators: A Case Study of Resistance and Rhetoric. In N. Hartlep (Ed.), *Modern Societal Implications of the Model Minority Stereotype* (pp. 292–323). Hershey, PA: IGI Global.

Morita-Mullaney, T., & Stallings, L. (2018). Serving Indiana's emergent bilingual immigrant (EBI) youth: A collective case study of EBI teacher educators. *The Teacher Educator*, *53*(3), 293–312. doi:10.1080/08878730.2018.1462422

No Child Left Behind, Pub. L. 107–110, 115 Stat. 1425 (2001).

Pérez Huber, L. (2008). Building critical race methodologies in educational research: A research note on critical race testimonio as method. *Florida International University Law Review*, *4*(1), 159–173.

Solorzano, D. G., & Yosso, T. J. (2002). Critical race methodology: Counter-storytelling as an analytical framework for education research. *Qualitative Inquiry*, *8*(23), 23–44. doi:10.1177/107780040200800103

Sox, A. K. (2009). Latino immigrant students in southern schools: What we know and still need to learn. *Theory into Practice*, *48*(4), 312–318. doi:10.1080/00405840903192912

Valdés, G. (2001). *Learning and not learning English: Latino students in American schools*. New York: Teachers College Press.

Welton, A. D., Diem, S., & Jellison Holme, J. (2015). Color conscious, cultural blindness: Suburban school districts and demographic change. *Education and Urban Society*, *47*(6), 695–722. doi:10.1177/0013124513510734

Wiley, T. (2007). Accessing language rights in education: A brief history of U.S. context. In O. Garcia & C. Baker (Eds.), *Bilingual education: An introductory reader* (pp. 89–109). Clevedon: Multilingual Matters.

Wong, P., Lai, C. F., Nagasawa, R., & Tieming, L. (1998). Asian Americans as a model minority: Self-perceptions and perceptions by other racial groups. *Sociological Perspectives*, *41*(1), 95–107. doi:10.2307/1389355

Chapter 22

How Leaders Learn About the Needs of Immigrant Students in a Turbulent Time

Sarah L. Hairston, Emily R. Crawford, and Warapark Maitreephun

CONTEXT

This case study takes place in Calhoun, a rural agricultural Midwestern community. Set amongst the vast working fields, the town center, which was once bustling but where many boarded-up windows are now visible, reflects a changing community. Chain restaurants and houses packed tightly next to one another proliferate from the town center. Calhoun's economy is largely based in agriculture, and it has large meat-processing plants nearby. Poverty in this traditionally middle-class community is a growing concern, but a new hospital keeps Calhoun from the economic demise that other rural communities surrounding it have experienced.

Due primarily to the meatpacking plants, Calhoun's population has undergone a big shift in the last two decades. Immigrants who hail largely, but not exclusively, from Mexico, El Salvador, and Guatemala have increasingly settled in Calhoun, doubling Calhoun's Latinx[1] population to 15%. Immigrants' levels of English proficiency and legal status vary: Over 10% of the population are native Spanish speakers; 94% identify as U.S. citizens. The immigrant community includes those who are newly arrived, first-generation, and second-generation. Throughout the town, ethnic restaurants, immigrant-owned stores, and places of worship reflect the demographic change.

Though Calhoun is still predominantly White and English-only speaking, the community generally welcomes Latinx immigrants. There is no notable history of conflict or political unrest stemming from immigration issues in the town. However, the election of a new U.S. president in 2016 has created uncertainty for Calhoun's immigrant population as well as a rise in discriminatory speech. Calhoun provides multiple resources intended to help newly arrived immigrants integrate into the community as well as resources for those local Latinx families and individuals struggling with issues of poverty. The majority of these resources are available through internal networks within the community, like church groups and social service organizations. Calhoun School District also collaborates with immigrant families and works to provide access to services.

The Calhoun School District includes an early childhood learning center, an alternative school, a career center, four elementary schools, one middle school, and one high school. The district serves roughly 2500 children with a classroom teacher to student ratio of 1:20 and a student to administrator ratio of 1:170. In the district over 60% of students are eligible for free or reduced-price lunch—a 20% increase in the last decade. The racial/ethnic composition of Calhoun's students closely mirrors the town's general population, with roughly 60% White, 20% Latinx, 10% Black, and the remaining identifying with two or more groups. Some 9% of students are English Learners (ELs). The school district aims to welcome families from all backgrounds, working from the principle of treating all kids equally. However, with a predominantly White, monolingual workforce, the district lacks the capacity and sometimes the information to meet the needs of the growing number of immigrant families and to help them overcome the many obstacles they may face. The ability to communicate with the district's Spanish speakers is important, but the few Spanish-speaking employees are spread thin. These employees become the primary "gatekeepers" of information for the district's immigrant families. Due to the mixed legal status of families, ranging from those who are U.S. citizens, to Deferred Action for Childhood Arrivals (DACA) recipients, to those who are undocumented, these gatekeepers must delicately balance communicating necessary information without divulging sensitive information.

CASE NARRATIVE

A nearby city newspaper, *The Tribune*, publishes a piece on immigration in rural America, and it focuses on the rising immigrant population in small agricultural towns across the state, including Calhoun. The article is harsh on the community's "forced assimilation instead of an expanding acceptance of diversity" of the town's immigrants. Furthermore, the article asserts the school district is failing to meet the needs related to changing student demographics. Calhoun's superintendent, Mrs. Davis, was interviewed for the piece and was quoted as saying: "The Calhoun School District feels we are well positioned to meet the needs of all of our students. We treat all of our students equally." The online comment section reveal both discriminatory views on immigration and community members coming to Calhoun's defense. Among the comments is one from Ms. Johnstone, the English as a Second Language educator at Calhoun High School, who indicts the district, saying: "The Calhoun School District has done NOTHING to address the needs of our Latino students. Well, that is, unless you call dumping students on a few individuals who speak Spanish as doing something."

The *Tribune* article, especially Ms. Johnstone's comment, shocks Superintendent Davis. With 22 years in school administration, Superintendent Davis is no stranger to discord—but this is her first year with Calhoun. Being new limits her experience and understanding of the Latinx immigrant and larger Calhoun community. Up to this point, Superintendent Davis has had no reason for concern about this population. Whether or not the news article is accurate, Superintendent Davis knows she needs a better understanding of the publicly aired perceptions. The superintendent has heard Ms. Johnstone does not always follow proper protocol but is considered knowledgeable about the Latinx population inside and outside the school setting. To better assess the situation, Superintendent Davis emails Ms. Johnstone and a long-term Latinx employee, Rosa Fernandez. Rosa is a paraprofessional at First Elementary who began volunteering with the district 15 years ago as a translator and interpreter. She is a respected community member with intimate knowledge of the Latinx community per her role with the district and as an active member within her church. Superintendent Davis' email asks Ms. Johnstone and Rosa to share concerns and what they perceive the district is not addressing in respect of immigrant students and families.

Ms. Johnstone writes a reply immediately to Superintendent Davis. In the reply, she details how Latinx families are struggling with the ebb and flow of immigration policies and directives. The email describes immigrant families separated by deportation, warns that several youths no longer have adult guardians present, and suggests that these children are potential prey for sex traffickers and gang involved in drug dealing. She emphasizes that emotional stress is taking a toll on student school attendance, academics, and well-being. Johnstone emails that these myriad concerns also heighten the stress and pressure placed on gatekeepers like the Spanish-speaking interpreters the district employs to assist families.

Before responding to Superintendent Davis' email, Rosa asks her principal, Principal Holtz, to discuss what she thinks is appropriate to share. Principal Holtz has been with the district nearly 30 years, with 15 as principal at First Elementary. The rising concerns of the Latinx population are at the forefront of Principal Holtz's mind, because she speaks frequently with Rosa and trusts her. Principal Holtz counts herself lucky to have Rosa Fernandez in her school; most schools do not have a Spanish-speaking person to assist families. Principal Holtz remembers the difficulty of navigating conversations and gathering information from Spanish-speaking families before Rosa came to First Elementary; Principal Holtz remembers feeling blind to Latinx families' differing circumstances. With Rosa's help, Principal Holtz feels now she can adequately address their concerns. To maintain trust among herself, Rosa, and the Latinx families, Principal Holtz has never felt it necessary to take concerns raised by Rosa beyond her building to share with other principals or the superintendent. Rosa's concern about how to respond to Superintendent Davis' email prompts Principal Holtz to go against her usual practice of keeping things "in house." She decides to check with her administrative peer, Principal Evans, Calhoun's high school principal, regarding the email sent to their employees. In the meantime, Principal Holtz asks Rosa to wait to respond to Superintendent Davis' email.

Principal Evans is a long-time resident of Calhoun, and he is also White and speaks only English. Principal Evans has been with the district for eight years, with five as high school principal. He grew up in Calhoun and prides himself on knowing the community. As soon as Principal Holtz begins to share about the email from Superintendent Davis, Principal Evans jumps in. "I know where this is coming from. Since the *Tribune* article, Ms. Johnstone has been on a mission to stir up problems that don't exist. She's spoken to me already, and I've told her to let it go, but she's insistent." Principal Holtz is surprised at her colleague's dismissiveness, saying, "But is there a problem? What I am hearing from our paraprofessional backs up Ms. Johnstone's claims." Principal Evans replies, "Absolutely not, or I would address the issue. Ms. Johnstone is putting me in an awkward position." Principal Holtz shares more details about Rosa's concerns:

> We have Latino children and families who are scared. There are immigration issues, money issues, and cultural issues that we just don't talk about at school, with families, or as a district. Rosa says we have children who are sad and worried. They miss school. Some of my teachers have said the same thing a few times.

Principal Evans replies, "I respect you as a colleague and friend, so if you say there is an issue, I trust you—but immigration issues aren't school issues." They table the matter, but in parting, Principal Holtz asks Principal Evans, "If you wouldn't mind, don't bring up Rosa. I want to keep her confidence."

A week later, Rosa and Ms. Johnstone email Superintendent Davis regarding their growing concerns around the immigrant students and families in Calhoun School District and receive a generic reply: "Thank you for following up. Our Latino families are important to our community. I will look further into this matter." Ms. Johnstone contacts Principal Evans again, raising the same concerns, saying, "We have to do something. Our responsibility doesn't end at the classroom." Principal Evans remains unconvinced there is an issue the schools should address, saying, "Ms. Johnstone, we are helping our families in need and are aware of growing poverty and immigration issues. That's why we started the Family Resource Center." Ms. Johnstone continues to push, cautioning that these students are susceptible to sex traffickers and gangs.

At the next principals' meeting, Superintendent Davis raises the subject. "It has been brought to my attention by a couple of people that our Latino families have growing immigration-related concerns we may be unaware of. Does this ring true for any of you?" Principal Evans glances at Holtz and responds, "We've had no specific incidents or complaints from families. The *Tribune* article created rumors. Latino families have needs, but they're not so different from other families'. Let's not react to a few loud voices." An elementary principal adds, "I don't have any issues with my Latino families; they support us educators. Anytime we have an issue, it takes a phone call home. If there is a concern with the Latinos, it is attendance. Latino students are more apt to be gone for extended periods of time." Others nod in general agreement.

Principal Holtz is quiet during this exchange. She wants to keep Rosa's trust but also help her colleagues understand what her information gatekeeper has shared. "The concerns are legitimate. I think we can afford to spend some time gathering information and finding ways to help our concerned Latino families." Everyone knows Principal Holtz does not cry wolf. "So, are you saying you know there is sex trafficking and gang issues among our Latino students?" questions Superintendent Davis. "No, I don't know of specific incidents, but information that has been shared with me regarding struggles our Latino community is facing may make certain kids susceptible," Principal Holtz responds. "I've been thinking about our conversation, Principal Holtz, and I just don't see it the same way," replies Principal Evans. Superintendent Davis, trying to keep her composure, says, "Principal Holtz, if there are issues I need to be made aware of, we should discuss it further." Principal Holtz responds:

> ICE[2] detained one of our fathers on a bus coming back from visiting family in Arizona. He was deported soon after. The mother doesn't work so she can take care of her youngest. They have since lost their home and are living with four other people in a two-bedroom house. The child from this family

> who attends our school has seemed anxious and depressed. The eldest son, Oscar—Principal Evans, you know Oscar—Ms. Johnstone says he hasn't been at school for the past two weeks.

Superintendent Davis, stunned, asks, "Are there other Latino students with prolonged school absences?" Troubled by her principals' reactions, contradicting reports, and a lack of critical information about their Latinx community members' well-being, Superintendent Davis decides to table the topic until a later time until she's had more time to think through the layers of the issues. She realizes her initial investigation into the topic was shortsighted. Further, building leaders in the district disagree on whether families have concerns about immigration policies and the extent of their responsibilities. She must figure out a new way to look at the issue without isolating both her Latinx population and critical gatekeepers, as well as develop better consciousness among her employees.

TEACHING NOTES

Research demonstrates that the sociopolitical climates in new immigrant destination regions like the South and Midwest may be particularly tricky for immigrant newcomers to navigate (Brezicha & Hopkins, 2016; Hamann & Harklau, 2015). Demographic change may occur rapidly in rural school communities, and communities may not have yet adequately developed the teaching and learning infrastructures needed to best support English Learners (Hopkins, Lowenhaupt, & Sweet, 2015). In consequence, leaders and teachers in communities less accustomed to welcoming immigrant newcomers may improvise educational responses (Hamann & Harklau, 2015). Further, educators may also be unsure whether and how to talk about issues stemming from a student's or family member's legal status, especially if there is no district policy or conversation about how to address such sensitive topics and what is appropriate (Crawford & Witherspoon Arnold, 2017).

Students and families who are vulnerable and scared do not openly reveal intimate information to schools (Murillo, 2017). Kam, Steuber Fazio and Mendez Murillo (2018) refer to the process of disclosure as "privacy management." Information, particularly if it is sensitive in nature like one's legal status, may be shared only with people who are highly trusted. This chapter uses the term "information gatekeepers" to signify people whom other individuals make privy to critical information. The concept of information gatekeeping is similar to but distinct from the concept researchers call "language brokering." Language brokers are those who act as bridges or social intermediaries for others, translating and interpreting across cultural and linguistic difference (Dorner, Faulstich-Orellana, & Jiménez, 2008). With information gatekeeping, brokering can occur, but information transferred may make the subject vulnerable in some capacity; there is risk, as the gatekeeper is in a position to choose whether and how to share information and the extent to which it gets shared with others. In this case, Rosa Fernandez was a key example of someone privy to knowledge of some school families' legal status and tried to determine what information to share with other school personnel without adversely affecting families.

In addition to information gatekeepers, school counselors and social workers can serve as additional, important trusted sources for immigrant students and families in difficult circumstances, for example connecting students and families to social or legal services and counseling support (Crawford & Valle, 2016). The U.S. Department of Education (2015) offers guidance and resources for school districts on how to work with undocumented youth. For further reading, scholar Aurora Chang (2018) provides helpful suggestions for educators on engaging with students who have concerns related to their legal status or the status of their family members.

DISCUSSION QUESTIONS

1. What do information channels look like in your district, community, or a typical school in your community? What are additional solutions to ensure information reaches all educational stakeholders in the district, including families whose first language may not be English?
2. Who are the information gatekeepers most knowledgeable about the concerns and needs of immigrant students and families in your district, community, or place of work?
3. What strategies can school leaders and community leaders use to build trust with information gatekeepers around sensitive topics like immigration status to safely ascertain information that may impact immigrant students' well-being in school?
4. How can leaders help ensure gatekeepers maintain the trust of families of mixed legal status?

TEACHING ACTIVITIES

1. Information Web and Bridging Information Gaps

Visually reconstruct the flow of communication regarding Calhoun School District's Latinx population. Include the perspectives of the narrative's major "players." Work individually or in groups to decide the following: 1) what information is passed along and to whom, 2) where information gets siloed and why, and 3) what information is needed or missing. Determine what are the key issues raised in the narrative. Answer these follow-up questions:

1. What would be helpful for the superintendent, principals, interpreters, counselors, social workers, and families to know? How can trusting relationships be built and strengthened among these different groups? Are there ways to relieve potential strain from information gatekeepers like Rosa?
2. What are similarities and differences in each player's response to the situation?
3. What circumstances may be shaping each person's perspective?
4. What strategies can leaders use to bring various players together to find *constructive* resolutions to some of the issues that need addressing?
5. How can district and other leaders better engage directly and sensitively with immigrant families?
6. What are creative solutions to reduce potential overreliance on key personnel like Rosa?

2. Issue Prioritization

Role-play one of the major characters in the narrative individually or in small groups. Use the following questions as potential prompts.

Use the following prompts, and identify the core issues Superintendent Davis should address:

- What issues are urgent or should be addressed quickly?
- What issues need longer-term consideration and planning?
- What kinds of strategic communications can help the superintendent better communicate information about immigrant students to district employees, from building leaders, to counselors, to teachers, to school resource officers?
- What alternative ways could be used to reach out to and address Rosa and Ms. Johnstone's concerns?
- What can the superintendent do to engage Principal Evans to enhance awareness and respond to potential issues occurring at the high school (e.g., Oscar's attendance, possible victimization of students by sex traffickers and drug dealers)?

Identify the core issues Principals Holtz and Principal Evans should address:

- What issues are urgent or should be addressed quickly?
- What issues need longer-term consideration and planning?
- If you were Principal Holtz or Evans, what kinds of information would be conveyed with gatekeepers, with other teachers and school personnel in school buildings, or with administrators at the district level? For what reasons?
- If you were Principal Evans, what steps could you take to develop cultural competency for yourself as a leader? If you were Principal Holz? With other educators in your building?
- Consider Principal Evans' working relationship with Ms. Johnstone. What steps can you take to find common ground and better work together to identify community members' needs?

NOTES

1 A gender neutral term referring to those of Spanish-speaking and/or Latin-American heritage.
2 Immigration and Customs Enforcement.

REFERENCES

Brezicha, K., & Hopkins, M. (2016). Shifting the zone of mediation in a suburban new immigrant destination: Community boundary spanners and school district policymaking. *Peabody Journal of Education*, *91*(3), 366–382.

Chang, A. (2018). *The struggles of identity, education, and agency in the lives of undocumented students: The burden of hyperdocumentation*. London: Palgrave Macmillan.

Crawford, E. R., & Valle, F. (2016). Educational justice for undocumented students: How school counselors encourage student persistence in schools. *Education Policy Analysis Archives*, *24*(81). Retrieved from http://epaa.asu.edu/ojs/article/view/2427

Crawford, E. R., & Witherspoon Arnold, N. (2017). "We don't talk about undocumented status…We talk about helping children": How school leaders shape the school climate for undocumented immigrants. *International Journal of Educational Leadership and Management*, *5*(2), 116–147.

Dorner, L. M., Faulstich-Orellana, M., & Jiménez, R. (2008). "It's one of those things that you do to help the family": Language brokering and the development of immigrant adolescents. *Journal of Adolescent Research*, *23*(5), 515–543.

Hamann, E. T., & Harklau, L. (2015). Revisiting education in the new Latino diaspora. In E. T. Hamann, S. Wortham, & E. G. Murillo, Jr. (Eds.), *Revisiting education in the new Latino diaspora* (pp. 3–25). Charlotte, NC: Information Age Publishing, Inc.

Hopkins, M., Lowenhaupt, R., & Sweet, T. M. (2015). Organizing English Learner instruction in new immigrant destinations: District infrastructure and subject-specific school practice. *American Educational Research Journal*, *25*(3), 408–439.

Kam, J. A., Steuber Fazio, K., & Mendez Murillo, R. (2018). Privacy rules for revealing one's undocumented status to nonfamily members: Exploring the perspectives of undocumented youth of Mexican origin. *Journal of Social and Personal Relationships*, 1–21. doi:10.1177/0265407518815980

Murillo, M. A. (2017). The art of the reveal: Undocumented high school students, institutional agents, and the disclosure of legal status. *High School Journal*, *100*(2), 88–108.

U.S. Department of Education. (2015). *Resource guide: Supporting undocumented youth*. Washington, DC: U.S. Department of Education.

Chapter 23

Organizing District-wide Change for Equity in a New Immigrant Destination

Megan Hopkins and Kristina Brezicha

CONTEXT

Superintendent Vista[1] has just begun her new position in Washington County School District (WCSD), a suburban K-12 district experiencing rapid demographic change in the southeastern United States. Washington County is located 100 miles from a major metropolitan area, Metro Center. Whereas Metro Center has long received immigrants from South and Central America and Southeast Asia, Washington County only began receiving immigrant newcomers in the last decade. In response to industry shifts and a declining local economy, Washington County community leaders worked in the late 1990s to attract new businesses to the area. These efforts brought a meatpacking plant, a national distribution center, and a clothing manufacturer to Washington County that generated thousands of blue-collar jobs. Drawn to these opportunities, and Washington County's affordable homes and well-regarded schools, more immigrants have steadily settled in the community.

Over the last ten years, Washington County's population increased from 30,000 to 45,000, and shifted from predominantly White to majority-minority, with the Latinx and Asian populations representing approximately 45% and 10% of the community, respectively. Although this growth revitalized Washington County's downtown area, with several Latinx- and Asian-run businesses and restaurants opening their doors, the mayor publicly blames newcomers for increasing crime rates and straining social services. This rhetoric has raised tensions between White community members and their immigrant neighbors. For example, one long-time resident lamented: "It's not the same anymore. It's horrible, it's all changed. These new people that came in, they're just not like us."

These tensions permeate WCSD, which has experienced a 900% increase in its Latinx population since 2000. The district has been slow to respond, and test scores are declining. Mirroring the community's response, WCSD leaders often attribute the district's low performance to newcomers; as one elementary principal notes: "The district has falling reading and math proficiency rates, and they blame the immigrants again. Immigrants are the scapegoats for everything that's going on in the community, from crime to district performance."

CASE NARRATIVE

Having heard this negative rhetoric, Superintendent Vista reviews data related to student assignment policies, educational programs, discipline, and teacher quality to better understand the district context.

Student Assignment Policies

The eight schools within city limits, including Washington County High School (WCHS), have experienced rapid growth and change over the last ten years, with as many as 25% of their students now identified as English Learners (ELs). In contrast, the five schools located in municipalities outside the city have experienced little to no change and continue to serve predominantly White students. In 2016, WCSD opened New Horizons, a STEM-focused magnet high school in one of these municipalities. In reviewing New Horizons' demographic data, Superintendent Vista sees that nearly all New Horizon students are White. Moreover, the school requires students to pass a rigorous entrance exam, and few non-White students have taken the test.

Educational Programs

Superintendent Vista finds that only 2% of students enrolled in the gifted and talented program are students of color and, of those, only a quarter are ELs. At WCHS, where Latinx and Asian students represent 55% and 12% of the student body, only 4% of students in Advanced Placement (AP) courses are Latinx, and 8% are Asian. On the other hand, 80% of students enrolled in WCHS's vocational program are Latinx. Furthermore, ELs tend to be enrolled in English-as-a-second-language (ESL) classes, basic math classes, and music and theatre electives, none of which meet college and career readiness standards or count toward graduation requirements. Moreover, no bilingual instructional approaches are offered at any school. Lastly, after examining participation in extracurricular activities, Superintendent Vista notes that White students comprise most participants. When she asks a school board member why newcomers rarely participate, his response is: "I brought that up a year ago [to the board]...And their response was, 'Well, they can't get to practice or they don't understand it.' "

School Discipline

Whereas Latinx and Asian students, as well as ELs, are underrepresented in accelerated programs, rigorous coursework, and extracurricular activities, Superintendent Vista learns that they are overrepresented in disciplinary incidents. For instance, while 30% of in-school suspensions last year were given to White students, 64% were given to Latinx students. Similarly, students receiving out-of-school suspensions were 59% Latinx, 34% White, and 7% Asian. Finally, eight of the ten students expelled last year were Latinx.

Teacher Quality

WCSD has had very low rates of teacher turnover in the last ten years. Nonetheless, the district currently employs only two Latinx teachers and one Asian teacher. Although the district serves 2,000 ELs, it employs only ten ESL teachers, who offer pull-out language support at the elementary level, and ESL courses at the middle and high school levels. Only four other teachers in the district hold ESL certificates.

After identifying these systemic inequities, Superintendent Vista holds a series of listening sessions. In discussions with principals, she notes the deficit language used to discuss immigrant newcomers. One principal described them as "bringing behavior problems," while another suggested that "education is not a priority in their lives." Many principals note that their buildings "feel like urban schools," due to "the nature of the population." Even an elementary principal who expresses a more positive attitude notes: "These poor babies come in knowing nothing and we have such a big job to do. How can we perform as well [on state achievement tests] as we did when our students came in speaking English?"

In listening sessions with teachers, Superintendent Vista learns that many teachers feel underprepared to work with newcomer students, especially those who speak little to no English. Many teachers express frustration at their inability to communicate with students' families, and say that many parents do not attend events that were previously well attended by White families, such as parent–teacher conferences. One teacher notes that, while some newcomers really want to learn and have parents who support them, others do not value education and never complete homework.

Many teachers find little use in district-mandated professional development, which, as a high school teacher states, consists of four half-days focusing on "diversity issues" but offers "nothing very helpful, no strategies or concrete ideas." An elementary teacher concurs, adding: "I don't have an ESL degree, so I feel like I'm set up to fail. None of the professional development days that we sit through give me anything I can use." Additionally, Superintendent Vista learns that teachers have little time to collaborate in grade-level or subject-area teams, which helps her understand why one principal argued: "Getting teachers to collaborate is like pulling teeth." When planning time is provided, teachers indicated that it "gets eaten up very quickly by security issues or situation drills."

Finally, to get a sense of the family experience, Superintendent Vista meets with a handful of parents and students from the middle and high school. In arranging the meeting, she has difficulty finding translators for the different languages spoken. During the conversation, one story strikes her as particularly poignant. An El Salvadorian mother describes how her son's teachers and the school paperwork referred to him as a "Level One." Not completely understanding the paperwork sent home in English, the mother thought Level One represented superior achievement. Only later did she learn that Level One referred to her son's low level of English proficiency, and that he had not advanced beyond Level One in his three years in WCSD.

The students with whom Superintendent Vista speaks indicate that they often do not feel treated fairly. One high schooler noted that discipline policies are inequitably enforced, saying that campus security guards do not make her feel safe because, "They have favorites. If they see two kids doing the same exact thing, they'll pick on one rather than the other." She continues that it is usually the White students who are not disciplined. While many students shared their dreams of becoming doctors, psychologists, or chefs, they are frequently enrolled in vocational programs that only tangentially align with their desired careers.

Superintendent Vista shares some of these stories with WCSD's Director of Curriculum and Instruction during an informal lunch meeting. Word of her concerns quickly spreads, and rumors circulate related to potential school sanctions and staffing changes. Superintendent Vista realizes these rumors have furthered a climate of distrust among her staff. She knows she needs to articulate her next steps soon, or she risks alienating the very people who voted to hire her.

TEACHING NOTES

Superintendent Vista's data analysis and information gathering activities are an important first step in a system-wide equity audit. Skrla and colleagues (2004) suggest that equity audits help unearth often-unidentified inequities in schools and districts. Given that few educational leaders have the time or bandwidth to engage in comprehensive data analyses, they recommend beginning with a manageable set of indicators derived from existing data that can reveal "levels of equity and inequity in specific, delimited areas of schooling" (Skrla, Scheurich, Garcia, & Nolly, 2004, p. 140). By providing evidence of systemic inequity in educational access and opportunity, these data can help confront prevailing beliefs that blame students of color, immigrants, ELs, or their families and communities for poor school or district performance.

Superintendent Vista focused her equity audit on three areas important for system-wide change: infrastructure, organizational culture, and instructional capability (Blumenfeld, Fishman, Krajcik, Marx, & Soloway, 2000). *Infrastructure* includes policy and management, such as funding and resource distributions, staffing, and program allocations. *Organizational culture* encompasses norms and routines that shape district and school culture. *Instructional capability* considers the knowledge and beliefs that influence educators' practices and their capacity to implement new curricula or strategies. Coherence across these areas is necessary to support system-wide change (Hopkins & Spillane, 2015) and to facilitate improvements in teacher quality and growth in English Learner achievement (Johnson, Bolshakova, & Waldron, 2016).

Across these three areas, Superintendent Vista gathered quantitative and qualitative data that allowed her to assess access and opportunity for immigrant newcomers in WCSD. Listening sessions with principals and teachers helped her understand the beliefs that undergird disparities in school assignment, program placement, and student discipline. These beliefs, which appear motivated by deficit thinking, are a potential equity trap that may hinder system-wide change if not directly addressed (McKenzie & Scheurich, 2004). Educators who engage in deficit thinking attribute students' lack of success to inherent deficits, such as linguistic or cultural inadequacies, challenging behavior, lack of motivation, and uncaring or absent families

(Valencia, 1997). These deficit-based perspectives shape teachers' practices and leaders' decision-making processes, leading to inequities at the classroom and school levels.

Current norms and infrastructures in WCSD appear only to have reinforced deficit views of immigrant newcomers. For instance, Superintendent Vista noted a culture of isolation among teachers, and a lack of trusting relationships. This culture, coupled with the absence of collaborative planning time and a dearth of relevant professional development, means that teachers have few, if any, occasions to problem-solve or learn from one another in ways that might challenge their beliefs or expectations (Spillane, Hopkins, & Sweet, 2017). The limited number of ESL instructional staff further suggests that content-area teachers have little exposure to language-related expertise (Hopkins, Lowenhaupt, & Sweet, 2015). Moreover, given that few resources have been allocated to translation services or the hiring of bilingual personnel, educators in WCSD have not had opportunities to interact with or learn from newcomer families, interactions that could begin to challenge prevailing deficit views and to shift teachers' approaches to parent engagement (Barajas-López & Ishimaru, 2016).

Although Superintendent Vista now understands how WCSD's infrastructure, organizational culture, and instructional capacity have allowed for, and even exacerbated, system-wide inequities, she has yet to engage others in the equity audit process. After initial data gathering, Skrla and colleagues (2004) suggest convening a group of stakeholders that includes educators and parents who are willing to engage in open, equity-focused dialogue. After findings from initial analyses are shared, the committee can discuss the disparities observed and possibly engage outside experts for additional analyses or advice. Once all perspectives are heard, the committee identifies possible solutions and assesses their viability. Ultimately, the goal is to implement the solutions identified, monitor results, and make necessary changes.

This process appears relatively straightforward, and the data in many ways speak for themselves. However, confronting the deficit thinking that underlies these data, and developing different beliefs about immigrants and students of color, is a complex and difficult task (Sleeter, 1996), especially given the anti-immigrant and racialized discourses that permeate our everyday lives (Ishimaru & Takahashi, 2017). Scholars suggest a range of strategies to address deficit thinking and to reframe district and school practices around an asset-based orientation, such as neighborhood walks and home visits (McKenzie & Scheurich, 2004; Moll, Amanti, Neff, & Gonzalez, 1992). Others support a more collaborative approach, where parents and teachers participate in joint inquiry around problems of practice, or cultural brokers facilitate transformation in community–school relationships (Ishimaru & Takahashi, 2017; Ishimaru et al., 2016). These strategies have yet to be taken up in WCSD and need to be considered to prevent the perpetuation of deficit thinking during the equity audit process.

DISCUSSION QUESTIONS

1. Superintendent Vista began her review by examining data related to student assignment policies, educational programs, discipline, and teacher quality to better understand the district context. What data stood out to you and why? What does this suggest about WCSD? What would your next steps be?
2. Superintendent Vista held a series of listening sessions with various stakeholders that gave her a variety of insights. What insights did stakeholders share that stood out or surprised you and why? What does this suggest about WCSD? What would your next steps be? Are there other stakeholders that Superintendent Vista should engage?
3. Consider Skrla and colleagues' advice to select a manageable set of indicators to use in conducting an equity audit. What quantitative and qualitative indicators would you select to assess a district's response to immigrant students? Remember to consider the three dimensions of infrastructure, organizational culture, and instructional capacity. Why did you select these indicators?

TEACHING ACTIVITIES

The following activities are designed to build on each other but can be completed independently depending on the time available.

1. Role-Playing Exercise

Below, we describe five profiles of Washington County stakeholders. Individuals can work in small groups to consider how each stakeholder would respond to the following question posed by Superintendent Vista: How should WCSD respond to the demographic changes in our district? After small group discussions, the groups should come together to share ideas.

Stakeholder 1: You have been principal at WCHS for 15 years. Prior to that, you were a beloved football coach and science teacher. You have good relationships with many community members and understand their concerns about declining school performance.

Stakeholder 2: You are the Director of Curriculum and Instruction, who previously worked as a third-grade teacher and instructional coach. You grew up in and attended school in WCSD. While you are happy to see your community coming back to life, you are concerned about the effects of population change in your neighborhood.

Stakeholder 3: You have taught civics and economics at WCHS for ten years and coach varsity soccer. You have good rapport with students, who often seek you out for guidance. You wonder about your ability to support ELs and are concerned that few immigrant students are enrolled in your AP course or participate on the soccer team.

Stakeholder 4: You are a Honduran parent to a high school sophomore and middle schooler. Having lived in Washington County for ten years, you helped form a community group supporting Latinx parents' engagement with WCSD and have positive relationships with many educators and immigrant families.

Stakeholder 4: You are a Mexican high school senior, and one of the few immigrant students on the varsity baseball team. You have many White and Latinx friends at WCHS. You plan to attend a local state university.

Stakeholder 5: You are a long-time school board member and business owner. Although you have complained about increases in crime and the prevalence of drugs in your community, you are not openly anti-immigrant as some of your hardest-working employees are immigrants.

2. Mapping System-wide Change

Using the data and information presented, small groups aligning to the above stakeholders should map each recommendation onto one or more areas identified as important for facilitating system-wide change: infrastructure, organizational culture, and instructional capacity. For example, in which area(s) would student assignment policies fall? What area(s) influence observed disparities in discipline? What area(s) are implicated in the district's lack of bilingual programs and instructional staff? Which area(s) need attention to address teachers' feelings of unpreparedness as well as parents' and students' concerns? After allowing sufficient time for small group discussion, construct a network diagram as a class to illustrate the relationships between these three areas and to identify areas for both immediate and long-term intervention.

3. Role-Play the Equity Audit Committee

Imagine that you are one of the above stakeholders. First, individually or in small groups, outline your questions and concerns as a member of the equity audit committee. Now, you (or one chosen member from your group) will role-play an equity audit committee meeting. Set up the class for a fishbowl conversation, with each group's spokesperson(s) seated around a table in the center of the room, and the remaining stakeholders facing them in a circle. With the activity leader assuming the role of Superintendent Vista, begin the role-play. Stop the conversation periodically to solicit feedback from the class related to potential leverage points and/or roadblocks in the conversation, and approaches for moving forward.

NOTE

1 All district, school, and individual names are pseudonyms.

REFERENCES

Barajas-López, F., & Ishimaru, A. M. (2016). "Darles el lugar": A place for nondominant family knowing in educational equity. *Urban Education*. Advance online publication. doi:10.1177/0042085916652179

Blumenfeld, P., Fishman, B. J., Krajcik, J., Marx, R. M., & Soloway, E. (2000). Creating usable innovations in systemic reform: Scaling up technology-embedded project-based science in urban schools. *Educational Psychologist*, *35*(3), 149–164.

Hopkins, M., Lowenhaupt, R., & Sweet, T. (2015). Organizing English learner instruction in new immigrant destinations: District infrastructure and subject-specific school practice. *American Educational Research Journal*, *52*(3), 408–439.

Hopkins, M., & Spillane, J. P. (2015). Conceptualizing relations between instructional guidance infrastructure (IGI) and teachers' beliefs: Regulative, normative, and cultural-cognitive considerations. *Journal of Educational Change*, *16*(4), 421–450.

Ishimaru, A. M., & Takahashi, S. (2017). Disrupting racialized institutional scripts: Toward parent–teacher transformative agency for educational justice. *Peabody Journal of Education*, *92*(3), 348–362.

Ishimaru, A. M., Torres, K. E., Salvador, J. E., Lott, II, J., Williams, D. M. C., & Tran, C. (2016). Reinforcing deficit, journeying toward equity: Cultural brokering in family engagement initiatives. *American Educational Research Journal*, *53*(4), 850–882.

Johnson, C. C., Bolshakova, V. L. J., & Waldron, T. (2016). When good intentions and reality meet: Large-scale reform of science teaching in urban schools with predominantly Latino ELL students. *Urban Education*, *51*(5), 476–513.

McKenzie, K. B., & Scheurich, J. J. (2004) Equity traps: A useful construct for preparing principals to lead schools that are successful with racially diverse students. *Educational Administration Quarterly*, *40*(5), 601–632.

Moll, L. C., Amanti, C., Neff, D., & Gonzalez, N. (1992). Funds of knowledge for teaching: Using a qualitative approach to connect homes and classrooms. *Theory into Practice*, *31*(2), 132–141.

Skrla, L., Scheurich, J. J., Garcia, J., & Nolly, G. (2004). Equity audits: A practical leadership tool for developing equitable and excellent schools. *Educational Administration Quarterly*, *40*(1), 133–161.

Sleeter, C. E. (1996). *Multicultural education as social activism*. Albany, NY: State University of New York Press.

Spillane, J. P., Hopkins, M., & Sweet, T. (2017). School system educational infrastructure and change at scale: Teacher peer interactions and their beliefs about mathematics instruction. *American Educational Research Journal*. Advance online publication. doi:10.3102/0002831217743928

Valencia, R. R. (1997). *The evolution of deficit thinking*. London: Falmer.

Chapter 24

Isolating or Inclusive?

Educating Refugee Youth in American Schools

Jill Koyama, Khristina H. Haddad, and Sarah Yacoub

CONTEXT

An estimated 1.2 million refugee students attend schools across the United States. Despite its anti-immigrant legislation and politics, and its English-only language policies in schools, Arizona is among the top ten states in resettling refugees, and several thousand refugee children attend Arizona's schools. On average, 900 refugees are resettled annually in Southern Arizona. Some 50% of those resettled are under the age of 24, and approximately 350 become students each year in the school district we call Desert Unified School District (DUSD).

During 2013–2016, the time frame in which we situate our case study, there were between 771 and 1104 refugee students enrolled in DUSD, a large district in Southern Arizona with approximately 48,000 students, 62% of whom were identified as "Hispanic." The refugee students came from 52 different countries, with the majority hailing from either Bhutan, Somalia, or Iraq. Of the 89 schools in the district, all but ten had at least one refugee student. Two district high schools had the greatest percentage of refugee students; 22% of the total refugee students attended one and 10% attended the other. In 2013, 38% of the total population of refugees had been attending a school in DUSD for three years or less. Most of the refugee students had experienced limited, interrupted formal education, or had even had no formal education prior to being enrolled in schools in Southern Arizona. All but a handful were enrolled in English Language Development (ELD) classes.

DUSD has a department, the Refugee Services Department, which aims to integrate refugee youth into schools and help with refugee families' transition to living in Southern Arizona. The department comprises a director, 10–11 full-time student-family mentors, and one part-time coordinator. Together, they provide a range of educational and social supports. The educational services, such as assistance with school registration, tutoring, and language support, are designed to counteract refugee youth's initial limited English language ability and intermittent schooling. Social supports include, but are not limited to, translating school information for parents, transporting family members to medical appointments, securing mental health services for youth, and providing programs in citizenship and adult ESL. The Refugee Services Department aims to bridge the voids created by disrupted family networks, poor mental and physical health services in resettlement camps, and ethnic-cultural neighborhood segregation.

The student-family mentors routinely work with refugee support organizations and resettlement agencies, although, as we highlight in our case study, the interactions are not without conflict and contestations. There are approximately 70 different agencies, organizations, and groups that offer services to refugees in the state. Some of these have international ties and receive federal funding, such as refugee resettlement agencies, and others are small, often temporary, such as church groups and school-sponsored initiatives. In this piece, we refer to the organizations with generic titles based on their main function to ensure confidentiality.

CASE NARRATIVE

At the beginning of a school year, Mr. Wright, the Assistant Superintendent of DUSD, with the support of the Superintendent, begins to share his vision of what he calls an "international school" for refugee students in the district. He offers the following reasons to support the creation of the separate school:

- Language services—including translation and refugee support services—could be concentrated in one school.
- Students would be able to more easily develop speech communities that would support their nascent English.
- Teachers, administrators, and staff could be chosen with the targeted newcomer population in mind—i.e., linguistic minorities and those trained in culturally responsive pedagogies.
- The school would be located in a neighborhood in which many of the refugee families are resettled, and thus the parents and families would have greater access to the schools.

The response to the international school proposal from teachers, administrators, and staff across DUSD is swift and disparate. Principals are split in their support. Some understandably want the refugee students who attend their schools to get more concentrated academic support and see the proposed international school as one potential way for the district to better meet the refugee students' needs. Others are less sure; a principal of a middle school, which nearly 40 refugee students attend, says she is suspicious that the international school is "more for the district than the kids." It "gets them out of the way," so to speak, she exclaims at a district-wide leadership meeting being led by Assistant Superintendent Mr. Wright.

In fact, having the refugee students and other migrant newcomers at one school would likely dramatically change how the district's schools with large numbers of refugees report their achievement data, and by extension are graded by the state and the federal government under current education legislation. As the refugee students have, in general, had interruptions in their previous formal schooling and are less proficient in English, they have been seen by some as dangerous to schools' scores and rankings. Congregating them in one school would, according to one assistant principal, "let other schools recover their scores in ELA [English Language Arts]."

Notably, Tamela Yamato, the director of the Refugee Services Department, and the family-student mentors with whom she works are adamantly opposed to the idea. They argue that the district is just trying to segregate the refugees so that they can't "bring down other schools' AYPs [Adequate Yearly Progress]," on which schools are graded and ranked. The director remarks that most principals and other school leaders are just not willing to "work with the refugees," and one mentor accuses principals and teachers of favoring Spanish-speaking students over refugee students. The mentors vow to discourage the refugee parents from supporting the new school. Tamela and the 11 mentors are very vocal about their opposition during two school board meetings in which the topic of creating an international school is discussed.

Even those who support the creation of an international school for refugees in DUSD worry that the refugees won't have enough interaction with other students, mostly native English speakers, and that they will not be socialized to American culture. One teacher expresses her mixed feelings: "I think it would be great for them to be together and have really focused teaching...but I do worry about their lack of, I guess, the challenges of integrating them here." She doesn't want them, she says, to live the rest of their lives in America in isolated refugee enclaves.

Yet several prominent community organizations, including one refugee resettlement agency, are strongly in favor of a school designated just for refugees and other recent arrivals. According to the director of the resettlement agency, "having the refugees all in one place will help us work more closely with the school...and provide better wraparound services, like counseling." Those in favor believe that they will be able to develop stronger collaborations with one school and hope that they can make the international school a safe and welcoming place for the refugees. The director of a large education program serving refugee youth is also in favor of starting an international school. She reasons that there, in one school, teachers can all be trained in "best practices for English Learners," and they can coordinate concentrated services for the students and their families. The students, she notes, will also just be more comfortable, more themselves, and can focus more on learning rather than fitting into the school.

Weighing the Perspectives

Armed with the opinions of the principals, teachers, counselors, community organizations, and staff of the Refugee Services Department, Mr. Wright weighs the options. He still very much believes that a separate international school for the refugees is the right decision, but he also has come to see the dangers of segregating the refugee students in one location. Reflecting especially on the perspectives of those working with refugees, he is conflicted. The staff of the Refugee Services Department are adamantly opposed, and he needs their support. They are, he knows, the link to the refugee parents and families, and without their support the school will likely not be approved. However, school principals overwhelmingly support the idea, and he needs to consider what is best for the entire district, which has been seen as failing for at least 15 years, long before he was hired the previous year.

After several months, toward the end of the school year, Mr. Wright turns to the resettlement agencies, which for the most part are at least interested in developing a detailed plan for an international school. He calls a meeting with the directors and main staff of the area's three resettlement agencies. The mentors and director of the Refugee Services Department learn of the meeting, although it was not publicized, and organize a series of meetings within the refugee communities. They hold these meetings in the apartment complexes where a majority of the refugees live and explain what they see as the dangers of the proposed international school to the refugee families. They ask them to sign a petition against the school and deliver the petition with 261 signatures to Mr. Wright.

Although not his intention, Mr. Wright feels that he has now caused a rift in the local refugee communities. He begins to get calls from the resettlement agencies saying that he must do something about the Refugee Services Department as the agencies work with its staff. Mr. Wright asks himself, "How did this get so out of hand?" When he speaks with the Superintendent, he is told to put the plan for the international school on hold and go out and "smooth things over with everyone." Mr. Wright still believes that the international school, or at least a targeted program housed in one school for refugees, is the right thing to do, but he turns his attention to "unruffling feathers." He starts by talking to the Refugee Services Department.

TEACHING NOTES

Scholarship on International and Newcomer Schools

According to Feinberg (2000), between 1980 and 2000, 110 newcomer programs for immigrant students were implemented. Of these, one-third were what are called "newcomer schools" or "international schools"—separate schools whose student populations are exclusively immigrant. Geographically, the newcomer schools are physically separated from other schools and they are frequently located in neighborhoods with high poverty, in which the newcomers live. Many of these schools reflect not only class, race, ethnic, and linguistic divisions, but also, more broadly, differences in power. Such schools have been shown (Feinberg, 2000; Garcia and Bartlett, 2007) to provide school districts with a way to adequately and compassionately attend to the education of "emergent bilingual" (García and Kleifgen, 2010) students, or those most often labeled "English Language Learners" (ELLs). They can offer respite from the marginalization and isolation often experienced by immigrant students in large comprehensive schools.

More specifically, a recent body of research directly addresses how international schools can create safe and effective learning environments through assets-based curriculum and culturally responsive pedagogy and leadership. Much of this research (Bajaj & Bartlett, 2017; Bajaj & Suresh, 2018; Bartlett, Mendenhall, & Ghaffar-Kucher, 2017; Mendenhall & Bartlett, 2018) draws much needed attention to how international schools in New York City and Oakland educate refugee youth and other newcomers. This scholarship calls for curricular, pedagogical, and assessment approaches that avoid tracking and segregating refugee students, and that also utilize the students' experiences and language as resources that can be integrated throughout the school day. Bajaj and Suresh (2018), for instance, demonstrate how Oakland International High School excelled at leveraging community collaborations, creating meaningful family engagement, and enacting flexible curriculum to meet the refugee students' and their families' needs. Mendenhall and Bartlett

(2018) also argue that refugee students benefit from a critical transnational curriculum and note that after-school and extracurricular programs provide important academic, language, and social supports to refugee youth. These schools are effective in meeting the students' needs in part because they use asset-based pedagogy and curriculum centered on heterogeneous student groups.

However, as we also know, newcomer schools are not created equally. The International Network for Public Schools, which includes 22 schools, mostly in New York and California, has an 82% graduation rate and serves as an exemplary model for newcomer schools (Bajaj and Bartlett, 2017). Others, such as one examined by Feinberg (2000) and called "Dreadful K-12," become a way to segregate emergent bilinguals without any additional language supports. Such sequestering serves to remove these students from the district's other schools, thus in theory limiting the lowering of test scores by refugees in other schools and allowing schools to retain their "high standards." It is also argued that such a school limits overcrowding in other schools, masking the underlying xenophobia and hostility toward immigrants held by some of the residents in the school district.

TEACHING ACTIVITIES

1. Role-Playing Exercises

Individually or in groups, choose a policy actor profile below and develop the case for or against the international school model from that actor's perspective.

Policy actor 1: You are a refugee middle-school student who needs to learn English quickly. You are eager to have concentrated English language instruction resources at a new international school.

Policy actor 2: As a refugee middle-school student who has lived in a camp for two years before coming to the United States, you favor joining an existing school in the hopes of making American friends and understanding more about life in a new place.

Policy actor 3: As a newly arrived refugee parent, you have benefited from social supports from a variety of agencies. Sometimes inadequate coordination creates unexpected challenges for you.

Policy actor 4: You are a member of the local refugee community and sensitive to the isolation experienced by your community. The decision about schools seems to you like a larger decision about the status of refugees in the U.S.

Policy actor 5: You are a teacher at an existing school in an underperforming district. Every year there are more students in your classroom who have special language learning needs.

Policy actor 6: You are a native English-speaking parent who is highly engaged in your child's education. You attend meetings of the parent–teacher association and are aware of the split in public opinions.

Policy actor 8: As Assistant Superintendent Wright, your vision of an international school is at the heart of the current disagreement.

Policy actor 9: As Tamela Yamato, Director of the Refugee Services Department, you need to facilitate the coordination of available services and are opposed to the international school.

2. Interactive Poster Presentation and Discussion

- Utilizing the policy actor perspective developed in Activity 1, create a visual representation of the perspective on a poster. Clearly mark the most important considerations from your perspective.
- Display all posters and encourage those representing other policy actors to comment in writing on the presented arguments.
- Review the comments and reconsider the original case. Present the revised cases to the group.
- Reveal your original preference and explain how your understanding of the situation and its possibilities has changed in the course of the exercise.

3. Examine Existing Fears and Articulate Desired Outcomes

- Individually, create a list of worst possible outcomes and biggest concerns for creating and not creating a separate school for refugees. List your concerns in a candid manner not meant for public presentation. Repeat this process, but this time create a list of best possible outcomes and minimal concerns.
- Have a facilitated discussion centered on the lists. At the conclusion of the discussion, return to your first personal list and reflect on your original fears and desires. Have some fears been resolved? Do some best possible outcomes seem more practical? Share your insights with your community.

4. Listening to the Voices of Refugee Students and Those Who Work with Them

Watch and discuss these videos in the context of Superintendent Wright's international school proposal:

- https://youtu.be/AWfykGrJkPQ
- https://youtu.be/rMGVJu_M-dc
- https://youtu.be/5TkBnQJpYFY
- https://youtu.be/k4QAewsaU4Y
- https://youtu.be/EXVwrTWXH7s

Issues to discuss:

1. Educating their children is a top priority for refugee families.
2. Accelerated language education is frequently the most urgent educational need.
3. Cultural difference makes understanding and being understood in a new place very difficult.
4. Refugee students and parents are unfamiliar with U.S. teachers and pedagogy, as well as U.S. school culture.
5. Both refugee students and parents may be hesitant or unable to speak in ways U.S. educators may expect.

5. Communicating, Coordinating, and Scheduling

After watching the videos in Activity 4, further examine the challenges refugee families face. In this exercise, identify, coordinate, and schedule the needs of refugee students and parents. Consider the following questions:

1. What do refugee students need?
2. What do refugee parents need?
3. How can priority be given to English language instruction?
4. Who will coordinate and oversee the efforts of volunteers and organizations?
5. Are translation services available?
6. How difficult is transportation?
7. Are there childcare needs that conflict with the schedule of school age children?
8. How will the family access the schedule?

9. What non-school events or needs might complicate the schedule?
10. What backup arrangements can be made for illnesses or emergencies?

Use a large whiteboard to create a Monday to Friday weekly schedule in which needs are coordinated with the school day and available services. The school day begins at 8:30 a.m. and ends at 2:30 p.m., after-school program optional.

- What are the challenges you see in the hypothetical schedule?
- How does this exercise inform your thoughts on the dilemma about the proposed international school?

REFERENCES

Bajaj, M., & Bartlett, L. (2017). Critical transnational curriculum for immigrant and refugee students. *Curriculum Inquiry*, *47*(1), 25–35.

Bajaj, M., & Suresh, S. (2018). The "warm embrace" of a newcomer school for immigrant and refugee youth. *Theory into Practice*, *57*(2), 91–98.

Bartlett, L., Mendenhall, M., & Ghaffar-Kucher, A. (2017). Culture in acculturation: Refugee youth's schooling experiences in international schools in New York City. *International Journal of Intercultural Relations*, *60*, 109–119.

Feinberg, R. C. (2000). Newcomer schools: Salvation or segregated oblivion for immigrant students? *Theory into Practice*, *39*(4), 220–227.

García, O., & Bartlett, L. (2007). A speech community model of bilingual education: Educating Latino newcomers in the USA. *International Journal of Bilingual Education and Bilingualism*, *10*(1), 1–25.

García, O., & Kleifgen, J. A. (2010). *Educating emergent bilinguals: Policies, programs, and practices for English language learners*. New York: Teachers College Press.

Lieberman, J. E., Nadelstern, E., & Berman, D. (1992). *After three years: A status report on the International High School at LaGuardia Community College*. Long Island City, NY: LaGuardia Community College.

Mendenhall, M., & Bartlett, L. (2018). Academic and extracurricular support for refugee students in the US: Lessons learned. *Theory into Practice*, *57*, 109–118.

Section III Resources

ORGANIZATIONS—REPOSITORIES OF RESEARCH AND POLICIES

Beloved Community, includes a new online Equity Audit tool: www.wearebeloved.org/

ILLUSTRATIONS—RESOURCES FOR LEARNING AND LESSONS

Atlanta Public Schools Equity Audit Report: www.atlantapublicschools.us/Page/41606

Succeeding with English language learners: Lessons Learned from the Great City Schools: www.wested.org/resources/succeeding-with-english-language-learners-lessons-learned-from-the-great-city-schools/

Index